D1259711

LINCOLN'S GADFLY, ADAM GUROWSKI

LINCOLN'S
GADFLY,
ADAM GUROWSKI

By LeRoy H. Fischer

UNIVERSITY OF OKLAHOMA PRESS : NORMAN

The publication of this book has been aided by a grant from
The Ford Foundation

973.7
F 529 L
124690

LIBRARY OF CONGRESS CATALOG CARD NUMBER: 64–20756

Copyright 1964 by the University of Oklahoma Press, Publishing Division
of the University. Composed and printed at Norman, Oklahoma, U.S.A., by
the University of Oklahoma Press. First edition.

In appreciation of my parents
DR. AND MRS. ANDREW LEROY FISCHER

PREFACE

In this book are recounted for the first time the Civil War actions and opinions of Count Adam Gurowski, the one man Lincoln recognized as a possible assassin. The controlling powers in Europe had once considered him one of the most dangerous and subversive influences on the Continent. His long experience as journalist, propagandist, and observer of public policy equipped him to turn in a masterly, if unconventional, performance as a self-appointed critic of the Lincoln administration. He did not need to use a keyhole for collecting information, because he knew everyone of political and military significance in wartime Washington. He simply walked in, sat at other men's desks, openly rummaged through their papers, and at other times extended unsolicited advice or impetuously broke into statesmen's conferences. He participated regularly in oral and written propaganda efforts to make or break the careers of political and military personalities. He frequently gave orders and warnings to Radical Republican leaders, and frequently his orders were obeyed and his warnings regarded.

Unlike most wartime Radicals holding elective office, Gurowski did not need to bow to expediency or compromise in working with the Lincoln Conservatives, nor did he hope for or receive personal benefits from his stated views. He could and did remain a man of firmly held political and military theories, the unflinching Puritan among the Radicals. He never yielded a principle even to his closest party associates, and no one of his fellows during the war held ground more firmly.

The Count's Civil War diaries and letters, on which this volume is based, contain an amazingly complete and lucid picture of the mind of a Radical Republican. His writings candidly divulge Radical methods

vii

and reveal the origins of their inspiration, ideas, and information perhaps more fully than any other source. He kept also the most faithful and complete record of their sentiments, and this record he wrote with remarkable color and precision in a language foreign to him. Gurowski was, moreover, unique among his political associates because of a European background combining a mixture of aristocracy, erudition, and revolution.

Although Gurowski was often erratic and sometimes self-contradictory (qualities shared by most Radical and Conservative Republicans), he delineated a clear community of interests and ambitions among Radicals. Broadly, what he said is of profound importance for an understanding of Northern wartime politics.

This does not purport to be a biographical study, although some elements of that approach are used. A full-length, scholarly book should be written on Gurowski's highly important propaganda and political activities in Poland and Russia; yet I survey the European years in two brief chapters. All chapters preliminary to the Civil War are used as background, designed to place Gurowski in perspective for his wartime actions and opinions. My purpose is to understand the Count as he revealed himself during the war years and to make pattern of the multitude of opinions on men and issues found in the jungle of his writings. It is not my function to pass moral judgment on the man, to praise or to condemn him. Since he knew how to write, I permit him, whenever possible, to plead his own case.

The general events of the war have been written again and again, and to present them once more would be superfluous. An effort is made to provide only the framework materials necessary to place Gurowski's wartime actions and opinions in their historical context.

The topical organization of the war chapters departs from the traditional compromise between the chronological and topical approaches. While topical design sacrifices a sense of chronological progression, it provides opportunity to concentrate in depth on important themes and to consider these more fully than would be possible with the compromise arrangement. A comprehensive treatment of each topic also clarifies the development of Gurowski's ideas and opinions.

Liberties are taken with some quotations. I dispense with initial and terminal ellipses, but I faithfully use this symbol to indicate omissions from the interior of sentences. I use "and" to replace the ampersand (&) consistently employed by Gurowski. His misspellings are retained, but are not followed by *"sic"* to note that these errors are original with him. I do not, in any instance, change the meaning of a quotation, and I make every effort to avoid quoting passages out of context.

My footnotes are intended to give sources for specific statements and quotations, and in a few cases to provide related information. They are not intended to offer a general bibliography of Civil War history. For this the reader is referred to the elaborate and critical bibliography in J. G. Randall and David Donald, *The Civil War and Reconstruction* (Second Edition, Boston, 1961), 703-76.

LeRoy H. Fischer

Oklahoma State University
Stillwater, Oklahoma
May 19, 1964

ACKNOWLEDGMENTS

M Y THANKS GO TO MANY for assistance in making possible the research and writing of this book. I owe a great debt to the late Professor J. G. Randall of the University of Illinois for invaluable counsel and for his matchless knowledge of the Civil War. His talented wife, Mrs. Ruth Painter Randall, critically read the entire manuscript and provided a great deal of encouragement.

For guidance in materials on Gurowski's European years, I appreciate the untiring help of Tadeusz Kozanecki of Warsaw, Poland; Irène Galezowska, archivist of the Polish Library of Paris; Professor Anthony S. Lis of the University of Oklahoma; Zbigniew J. Romanski of Detroit; and Miecislaus Haiman of Chicago, late custodian of the archives and museum of the Polish Roman Catholic Union of America. Officials of the national libraries of Poland and Russia made available photoprint copies of manuscripts and rare printed materials.

Many a choice Gurowski item for the prewar decade came from the vast manuscript resources of the Houghton Library of Harvard University, and for generous assistance there I am indebted to Miss Carolyn E. Jakeman. Nor will I forget the patience and consideration of Stephen T. Riley, librarian of the Massachusetts Historical Society, and his staff, as they searched out Gurowski letters in the Governor John A. Andrew Papers.

Unlimited assistance was also extended to me by Robert W. Hill, keeper of manuscripts of the New York Public Library; by Miss Dorothy C. Barck, librarian of the New York Historical Society; and by Clifford K. Shipton, librarian of the American Antiquarian Society.

For the student of Civil War history, Washington, D.C., of course, contains research collections of unparalleled importance. In the Library of Congress, Sergius Yakobson, chief of the Slavic and East European Division, came to my aid again and again, as did Henry J. Dubester, chief of the General Reference and Bibliography Division, and David C. Mearns, chief of the Manuscript Division, where Gurowski's Papers are housed. Many helped in the National Archives, but I recall particularly the untiring assistance of Thad Page. Because Gurowski lived in the capital city during the war, I was not long in searching out the Public Library of the District of Columbia, and in its Washingtoniana Division, Mrs. Edith Ray Saul and Miss C. Frances Wilson capably and willingly provided answers to a number of questions.

Other libraries and professional friends gave freely of their time in helping me search out Gurowski letters or solve difficult reference problems. My foremost debt is to Miss Edith L. Beckett, librarian of the Free Library of Calais, Maine, for carefully searching the James S. Pike Papers housed there, and to that institution's board of trustees for permission to use the Gurowski items located by Miss Beckett. Always coming to my assistance with an abiding interest in question after question was Miss Margaret A. Flint, assistant state historian of Illinois. Miss Sabina P. Logisz, assistant curator of the archives and museum of the Polish Roman Catholic Union of America, provided quantities of hard-to-locate information. Professor Glyndon G. Van Deusen and Miss Margaret Butterfield of the University of Rochester searched in my behalf the William H. Seward Papers in that institution's library. At Duke University, Mrs. Pauline C. Beers located a number of Gurowski letters in the William Pitt Fessenden Papers. I am indebted also for many favors to Thomas H. De Valcourt, curator of the Craigie House Library, to R. N. Williams II, director of the Historical Society of Pennsylvania, and to Professor C. Carroll Hollis of the University of North Carolina.

Through the kindness and interest of Laurence Gouverneur Hoes, Washington, D.C., I came to know much more about the personal life of the subject of this book. Mr. Hoes is a descendant of the family of Charles Eames, in whose home Gurowski lived during the war.

Over the years, Edmund L. Kowalczyk of Worcester, Massachusetts, consistently sent information on new Gurowski materials, and for these as well as for his continuing interest, I am most grateful. Ralph G. Newman of Chicago also contributed research clues and urged again and again the writing of this study.

Those who critically read the manuscript were unusually helpful, and for this time-consuming and highly important task I am grateful: the late Otto Eisenschiml, Chicago; Professor David Donald, Johns Hopkins University; Professor William E. Baringer, University of Florida; and Professor Holman Hamilton, University of Kentucky.

The Pennsylvania Commandery and the War Library and Museum, both of the Military Order of the Loyal Legion of the United States, have my unending gratitude for offering the $5,000 Literary Award for the best book-length manuscript on the Civil War. Naturally, I cannot thank enough the Loyal Legion's literary critics, whoever they were, for judging this study the winner. The hospitalities and courtesies extended by the Loyal Legion at Gettysburg were many, and I am particularly indebted to J. Truman Swing, executive director; James E. Heckel, chairman of the Literary Award Committee; William Buchanan Gold, Jr., commander of the Pennsylvania Commandery; and Brooke M. Lessig, president of the War Library and Museum.

My deepest appreciation is to my institution, Oklahoma State University, where this study was made possible. There a host of professional associates repeatedly demonstrated patience and forbearance. I appreciate especially the assistance of the Research Foundation, superbly geared to its purpose, and the University Library, with its competent staff and huge collection of Civil War materials. The College of Arts and Sciences also befriended this project, and my history colleagues helped and suffered far beyond the call of duty and friendship.

My wife, Martha, and our children, Barbara Ann, James LeRoy, and John Andrew, were most co-operative and thoughtful throughout the preparation of this book. How they put up with Gurowski for so long I will never understand, but I love them for it.

Despite all the assistance from those I have named and from others, this study has many faults. For all of these, for all errors of commission and omission, I alone am responsible.

LeRoy H. Fischer

CONTENTS

ILLUSTRATIONS

LINCOLN'S GADFLY, ADAM GUROWSKI

*Winner of the $5,000 Literary Award presented by the War Library
and Museum of the Military Order of the Loyal Legion of the United
States and the Pennsylvania Commandery of the Military Order of the
Loyal Legion of the United States at Gettysburg, Pennsylvania,
July 1, 1963.*

CHAPTER I

POLAND'S PATRIOT

I

Over at the White House, Lincoln called bodyguard Ward Hill Lamon into his office. The problem of assassination again troubled the President, and once more the same would-be murderer loomed in his thinking. "So far as my personal safety is concerned," Lincoln said, turning intently to Lamon, "Gurowski is the only man who has given me a serious thought of a personal nature. From the known disposition of this man, he is dangerous wherever he may be. I have sometimes thought he might try to take my life. It would be just like him to do such a thing."[1] Lincoln explained that when he met Gurowski at receptions, in small groups, or on the streets, he looked aloof and threatening and showed obvious disgust at his stories.

Lamon reviewed the Count's record for the worried President. Admittedly, there seemed cause for concern. Perhaps he had killed in his Polish revolutionary plottings. Why else had he received the death sentence? And why had he betrayed Poland to Russia, only to flee Russia some years later? Nobody in Washington knew, said Lamon. Probably there was something to the rumors that he had served Russia as a spy, and that money had been sent to him periodically from that country. The Russian legation liked the man, but would say no more. Always, the record revealed, he had opposed established government, and for months he had agitated relentlessly against the President and most of the cabinet.

Washington police had kept him under strict surveillance since the inauguration, but now, said Lamon, their concern was even greater. Lin-

---

[1] Quoted in Ward Hill Lamon, *Recollections of Abraham Lincoln, 1847–1865* (ed. by Dorothy Lamon Teillard), (Washington, 1911), 274.

coln moved restlessly in his great chair as he learned that Gurowski was known to carry a pocket pistol, and to have drawn it several times. The first revolver-pulling episode had occurred in the Washington bureau of the New York *Tribune* at the climax of an argument and had resulted in an order never to return. The next summer, he waved the weapon at a group of firemen to make them move more quickly in their work. A police officer arrested him and locked him in the station house. The magistrate fined him five dollars. Some months later, the conductor of a horse-drawn streetcar did not halt at the corner where the Count wished to get off. Out came the weapon and a command to stop the car. Again a police officer appeared, made the arrest, and some minutes later a judge levied a twenty-dollar fine. These stories were hardly reassuring, but Lamon ended by telling the President that security precautions would be strengthened.[2]

That same wet, spring afternoon, several blocks over on Pennsylvania Avenue, visiting free-lance journalist Robert Carter thought he saw a familiar figure approaching at his leisure. He soon recognized Gurowski, known to everybody in Washington. Carter had got acquainted with him a dozen years before up at Harvard, when they had spent literary evenings with Henry Wadsworth Longfellow, James Russell Lowell, Charles Sumner, and Edward Everett. The Count was still the same burly man of medium height, large round head, bulging forehead, graying hair, side whiskers, and a great paunch. The aristocratic air, semimilitary stride, and alternately jovial and scowling expression had not changed. The battered blue goggles, complete with side blinders, remained, as did the long, flowing, black cloak—Old World tailored— and a disreputable broad-brimmed felt hat of comical bell shape.

"Carter, my good fellow, I have been hoping to see you for months," Gurowski exclaimed happily, as he opened his arms. Carter greeted him warmly, turned around, and fell into step. After a minute, Carter asked, "What do you think of Lincoln?" Gurowski grew sullen, quiet,

---

[2] Tyler Dennett (ed.), *Lincoln and the Civil War in the Diaries and Letters of John Hay* (New York, 1939), 102 (October 18, 1863); Chicago *Journal*, August 5, 1864; W. D. O'Connor to Walt Whitman, August 13, 1864, in Horace Traubel, *With Walt Whitman in Camden* (3 vols., Boston, 1908–1914), III, 339–40; Boston *Post*, February 11, 1865. Unless otherwise indicated, all newspaper references are to daily editions.

then bellowed: "He is a beast!" Carter wanted more, but the Count refused to talk.

Reaching an intersection, they stepped from the walk into the ankle-deep mud of the street. "What about Seward," said Carter. Halfway across, the Count stopped, and went off like a rocket. "That damn man is shallow, insincere, ludicrously ignorant of his work, and a clever charlatan!" This time opinions rushed in torrents. Carter listened closely as the harangue against Seward mounted, but suddenly he noticed a large troop of cavalry approaching. He tugged at Gurowski's coat as he urged him to move. At last Carter could wait no longer, and headed for the other side of the street. Shouting soldiers, trampling and rearing horses finally aroused the Count, now encircled by cavalry. Above the din, he thundered a final word toward Carter: "Seward is an assish asinine ass!"[3]

2

Friends who knew Gurowski's extraordinary background were as astonished as Carter by his behavior, and they thought his past helped to explain him. His lineage, which he described "as old and high as that of any one in Europe," seemed to be much a part of him. He liked to tell the story of a forefather of the ninth century, a knight who had been taken prisoner while fighting the Moors in Spain. The Moorish king had offered his daughter's hand to any one who could beat her in a single chess game, provided the suitor agreed to execution if he lost. Others had met their doom, but Gurowski's ancestor won, blatantly refused to marry the princess, and still gained his release. He returned to eastern Silesia with a chessboard and princess painted on his shield, which became the family coat of arms.

Gentleman-farming, clerical orders, military service, and public office had attracted the family from the beginning. By the middle of the eighteenth century, Gurowski landholdings reached their zenith, while in public affairs the family had attained prominence and had shaped

---

[3] Based on Robert Carter, "Gurowski," *Atlantic Monthly,* Vol. XVIII (November, 1866), 628, 633; unidentified newspaper clipping in author's possession; Charles T. Congdon, *Reminiscences of a Journalist* (Boston, 1880), 237.

itself into two groups, conformists and radicals. In 1787, the Prussian king gave Adam's grandfather the rank of count to continue to all future descendants of both sexes. This honor came as a result of the early Gurowski's co-operation with Prussian authorities after that government had taken over the administration of the area containing his landholdings in the Partition of 1772, the initial dismemberment of Poland.

Adam's father, Władysław, while in charge of the household of the Prussian king, grew discontented with Prussian domination of western Poland. When Prussia, in the Partition of 1793, took over Great Poland, an area containing his father's landholdings, Władysław decided to join Tadeusz Kościuszko's insurrection. He made his way to Poland and to his aged father, who, although unsympathetic with the revolutionists, yielded to him. He immediately set about to equip at his own expense several hundred infantrymen and cavalrymen, but he himself served in the ranks. When the insurrection collapsed, he was briefly imprisoned, and his properties were in part confiscated by the Prussian government. In the meantime, his father-in-law, a prominent Prussian general, arranged for his wife to divorce him. Władysław then retreated to the remnants of his country estate near the old and beautiful city of Kalisz, Great Poland. Here he remarried and remained in the background, except to contribute generously to Napoleon's efforts to liberate Poland in the futile attempts of 1806, 1809, and 1812.

Cecilia was the only child of Władysław's first marriage. She grew up in the Prussian court with the royal children, including the future Friedrich William IV, king of Prussia, 1840–61, and Charlotte Louise (daughter of Friedrich William III), czarina of Russia, 1825–55. Cecilia married Brona Fredericks, who served on the household staff of Czar Nicholas I of Russia. According to her half-brother Adam, she kept "the highest position in society and at the court of Snt Petersbourg."

Władysław had six children, one daughter and five sons, by his second wife. Nicholas and Joseph became gentlemen-farmers on remnants of the family lands. Ignatius, who did nothing and lived off his wife, created an international sensation when he eloped with a Spanish Bourbon princess, Isabella Ferdinanda, cousin of the future Queen Isabella II of Spain. Mary Gurowski achieved some distinction by her mar-

6

riage to Count Berthold Mulin, official of the Prussian court and gentle-man-farmer. Bolesław, another son, chose revolution in the tradition of his father, as did Adam, eldest of the sons.[4]

3

Count Adam—Lincoln's Gadfly—first appeared at Russocice (Ruso-cici), near Kalisz, September 10, 1805, on his father's farm. Adam's early childhood was marred by a serious eye injury, resulting from a fall on a pocket knife. This forced him to wear dark glasses to keep out the irritating effects of the sun's rays and to cover the mutilation. Coached by his father to hate oppression, he became known for radical patriotic tendencies while still a schoolboy. The Grand Duke Constantine, the Russian viceroy of Poland and brother of Czars Alexander I and Nicho-las I, expelled him from classical preparatory schools in Warsaw and Kalisz in 1818 and 1819 for singing prohibited Polish patriotic songs and for wearing a Polish costume.[5] At the Congress of Vienna in 1815, the Kingdom of Poland had been created in the heart of prepartition Poland and placed under the control of Russia, with the czar as king of Poland. The estates of Gurowski's father were within this area. Thus when young Adam vented Polish nationalism, he opposed Russian authority rather than Prussian rule as did his father.

[4] Gurowski's manuscript autobiographical sketch, in author's possession; Marian Gouverneur, *As I Remember: Recollections of American Society During the Nineteenth Century* (New York, 1911), 249–50; Boston (weekly) *Museum*, May 24, 1851. The standard genealogical study of the Gurowski family is Kasper Niesiecki, *Herbarz Polski* (10 vols., Lipsk, 1839–46), IV, 334–35; X, 156–61. Supplementary genealogical material is in Samuel Orgelbrand, *Encyklopedja Powszechna Z Ilustracjami i Mapami* (16 vols., Warszawa, 1898–1904), VI, 427–28; and Stanisław F. Michalski (ed.), *Encyklopedja Powszechna Ultima Thule* (9 vols., Warszawa, 1930 to date), IV, 343.

[5] Julius Bing, "Life of Gurowski," 38½–39, MS, in Adam Gurowski Papers, Library of Congress; sketch of Gurowski written by him or under his supervision, in George Ripley and Charles A. Dana (eds.), *The New American Cyclopaedia: A Popular Diction-ary of General Knowledge* (16 vols., New York, 1858–63), VIII, 588; New York *Times*, May 6, 1866. Julius Bing was an obscure free-lance journalist of the American Civil War period. During the year before Gurowski's death he decided to write the Pole's biography. The Count consented and permitted the use of his papers. Bing worked rapidly, completed a rough manuscript draft, and then died. Gurowski's papers, together with Bing's manu-script biography, were returned to the Charles Eames family and later deposited in the Library of Congress.

The young Count's nationalism was the product of his environment. The French Revolution, with its implication of liberty for oppressed nationalities everywhere, contributed to Gurowski's resistance to established authority, as did his father's own hatred of those nations involved in the dismemberment of Poland. As Adam grew to manhood, the family economic situation worsened. Farming ceased to pay, debts on landed property increased, and oppressive agricultural taxes followed. The blame fell on Russia, who controlled the area. Hence during the tyrannical administration of Grand Duke Constantine from 1815 to 1830, Gurowski's nationalism led him to participate actively in the uprising of 1830.

Meantime he continued his education, this time outside Poland. In 1820, at the age of fifteen, he appeared in Berlin and for the next five years studied in several German universities. At the University of Berlin he sat under Georg Wilhelm Friedrich Hegel and acquired a taste for philosophy as well as appreciation of Hegel's dialectical method of thesis, antithesis, and synthesis. Even more important, he absorbed Hegel's concept of authoritarian government. He attended also the University of Heidelberg, where he spent two semesters as a student of philosophy in 1823–24. Here he studied jurisprudence under the noted scholar Anton Friedrich Thibaut, and history and classical philology under Friedrich Creuzer. He also spent some time as a student at the universities of Jena and Leipzig.[6]

Returning to Poland in 1825, Adam managed the family estate near Kalisz while conspiring against Russian authority. In 1827 he married Theresa Zbijewski, and two years later a daughter, Władysława, was born, followed the next year by a son, Melchior. Domestic happiness was short. Whatever connubial bliss the couple may have experienced was disturbed by periods of imprisonment for Adam resulting from his undercover revolutionary activity and from separation after the outbreak

[6] Gustav Toepke (comp.) and Paul Hintzelmann (ed.), *Die Matrikel der Universität Heidelberg* (7 vols., Heidelberg, 1886–1916), V, 251; *Verzeichnis der Sämmtlichen Studierenden auf der Universität Heidelberg im Sommersemester 1823* [Heidelberg, 1823], 23; *Verzeichnis der Sämmtlichen Studierenden auf der Universität Heidelberg in Wintersemester 1823–1824* [Heidelberg, 1823], 24; Bing, "Life of Gurowski," 40, 42; Washington *National Republican*, May 5, 1866.

of the 1830 insurrection. Early in 1832 his wife died, and the children were thereafter cared for by her parents.[7]

4

Gurowski's anti-Russian intrigue centered in the Patriotic Society, a semisecret organization he joined soon after returning to Poland. Czar Nicholas presently ordered the society destroyed, and it went underground, only intensifying its program. Opposition to Russian authority by the diet and other autonomous Polish governmental units encouraged Gurowski and his cohorts, as did the unrest due to unemployment and the high cost of living, especially in Warsaw. By early 1828, the fever of revolution spread to Warsaw University students, to soldiers in both the regular army and the Cadet School in Warsaw, and to Warsaw workmen. Loose, isolated conspiracies gave way by the close of the year to a coherent structure led by a group in the Cadet School.

A Grenadier Guards lieutenant, Piotr Wysocki, instructor in the Cadet School, organized a secret association among students and officers in December, 1828. Gurowski's brother, Joseph, joined early, soon followed by Adam. Both were of the radical faction, which planned complete independence through armed action beginning the following spring. The moderate wing, led by Wysocki, left direct action for a later period, after the association could be extended to high officials, particularly to former members of the Patriotic Society and the incumbent diet. In the meantime, the moderates planned to defend the constitution of the Kingdom routinely violated by Russia.[8]

Several months later, Grand Duke Constantine called Gurowski to the palace to give him a reprimand. Fearing assassination, Constantine had required that all Poles in his presence wear tightly buttoned coats and have their hands hanging stiffly by their sides. The weather being warm, the Count entered the audience room with his coat unbuttoned and his hands near his pockets. Constantine ran toward a door and

---

[7] Niesiecki, *Herbarz Polski*, X, 161; Bing, "Life of Gurowski," 47; Washington *National Republican*, May 5, 1866; New York *Times*, May 6, 1866.

[8] Wacław Tokarz, *Sprzysiężenie Wysockiego i Noc Listopadowa* (Kraków, 1925), 29; Maurycy Mochnacki, *Powstanie Narodu Polskiego, w r. 1830 i 1831* (Second Edition, 4 vols., Wrocław, 1850) II, 158.

shouted to him to stop and place himself in the prescribed position. Instead, Gurowski kept on coming and put his hands in his pockets, as if to draw a pistol. Guards rushed forward, seized him, and found no weapon. "If I had wished to kill your Highness," the Count coolly told the angry viceroy, "I would have done so long ago."[9]

Gurowski became a leading conspirator in the first violence planned, a plot to kidnap Nicholas I and his family during his coronation as king of Poland in May, 1829. Count Tytus Działyński, wealthy patron of letters, had suggested the idea to him. This act was to signal the revolution. The project appealed to Gurowski, who reasoned that for years of crime there would at last be a moment of punishment. Gurowski promised Działyński to "handle the royal family without ceremony." He hurried to tell the news to Wysocki and his cadet faction, who were already conspiring to begin their activities in March. Gurowski advised that the Wysocki program be combined with the coronation plot. The cadets willingly accepted Gurowski's advice, as did Wysocki. The time gained by postponing the March activities was to be used to further the spread of the plot. Działyński was highly pleased with Gurowski's report of the cadet's favorable reaction.

When initial enthusiasm died down, distrust and dissension developed. Wysocki insisted that key members of the diet be brought into the plot, in order to assure support of that body. Gurowski assisted in this effort. Then Wysocki promoted the idea that the diet take over the insurrectionary government. While this was being worked out with cadets and members of the diet, Działyński informed Gurowski that Gustaw Małachowski, one of the conspirators, could not be trusted. Gurowski rushed to tell Wysocki and an assembled group of revolutionists of Działyński's revelation. At this moment, Małachowski arrived with the plan approved by Działyński. Gurowski's assignment, which he had discussed with Małachowski, was to work among the Kalisz citizenry, in the vicinity of his birthplace, while fellow conspirators won support of other provinces of Poland and also Prussia and England. While Gurowski prepared to leave Warsaw on his Kalisz mission, Działyński appeared at the Count's house and talked of withdrawing "because our cause has

[9] Boston (weekly) *Museum,* May 24, 1851.

been betrayed—the plot has leaked out." Gurowski carried the news to Wysocki, and both agreed to continue their preparation for the revolution. Działyński, recovering from his apprehension, seemed disposed to carry out his part.

Gurowski went at once to Kalisz, worked among the people, and awaited further instructions from Działyński. When no word came, the young Count hurried to Warsaw and arrived three or four days before the scheduled coronation. He found Wysocki's association completely disorganized. The situation seemed even more discouraging, because members of the diet contacted about the conspiracy's plan unanimously disapproved the kidnapping. Małachowski himself began to advise against the scheme he had once supported. Gurowski now realized the hopelessness of the cause. He was depressed when he witnessed the peaceful crowning of Nicholas I as king of Poland in Warsaw cathedral, and saw Działyński dancing a polonaise with the Czarina at the coronation ball.[10]

5

Gurowski and his radical companions continued to work through the association for revolution and independence, although they were fed up with Wysocki's conservative leadership. The association grew slowly due to Wysocki's timid policy, but by September, 1830, a feverish excitement was in the air. News of the July revolution in Paris created a tenseness of expectation throughout Poland. In that same month the association sent Gurowski on a mission to Great Poland, the home of his father, where he was to win the support of the people for the approaching revolution.[11] Agents were sent by the association to all other Polish provinces. Membership and activity increased rapidly after the conspirators learned that the Polish army would be ordered to France by Russian authorities to assist in suppressing the revolution. Immediate action was imperative in the opinion of Gurowski and his fellow radicals, even though Wysocki wished to postpone the outbreak. Moreover, police

---

10 The coronation plot, as related here, is primarily from Mochnacki, to whom the details were known. *Powstanie Narodu Polskiego, w r. 1830 i 1831*, II, 158–64, 167; see also Artur Śliwiński, *Maurycy Mochnacki: Żywot i Dzieła* (Lwów, 1910), 114.

11 Tokarz, *Sprzysiężenie Wysockiego i Noc Listopadowa*, 60.

were on their track and making arrests. Then word came that Czar Nicholas had ordered an energetic suppression of the association and court-martial for its members. The extremists, with Gurowski concurring, hurriedly set the start of the revolution for the evening of November 29.[12]

The insurgents had unwisely failed to select a military commander in advance, and Gurowski spent most of the first night vainly searching out and advising generals.[13] Next morning a new element threatened to alter the entire revolt. The Administrative Council of the Kingdom of Poland disapproved the revolt and admitted new members known as appeasers. Rather than armed struggle against Russia, the council desired to use the revolutionary spirit to wring concessions from the Czar. General Józef Chłopicki, distinguished in the Napoleonic wars, was named commander of the Polish army. Two days later he proclaimed himself dictator until the convocation of the diet several weeks hence. Chłopicki opposed all revolutionary activity because he did not believe the insurrectionists could overcome Russian military power. He would work for mild concessions.

The revolutionists were not to be thwarted. On December 1 they organized a group which they called the Patriotic Society, with Gurowski a charter member. They demanded immediate hostilities with Russia and Polish independence. But General Chłopicki was an obstruction. The society brought several types of pressure on him, especially frequent harassing interviews, at least two of which Gurowski attended.[14] Gurowski also raged at Chłopicki through a column of the *Universal Daily:* "Not he who once acted and was significant, but he who today acts, comprehends and directs—should be sacred to us. Past glory is beautiful, but we believe only those who rose up with us and who gave us the guarantee and security of progress."[15] Gurowski and his fellow radicals

[12] The standard English treatments for the background of Gurowski's activities from 1815 to 1834 are W. F. Reddaway and others (eds.), *The Cambridge History of Poland: From Augustus II to Pilsudski, 1697–1935* (Cambridge, England, 1951), 275–323, and R. F. Leslie, *Polish Politics and the Revolution of November 1830* (London, 1956), 51–280.

[13] Tokarz, *Sprzysiężenie Wysockiego i Noc Listopadowa,* 192.

[14] Joachim Lelewel, *Pamiętnik z Roku 1830–31* (Warszawa, 1924), 56.

[15] Juljusz Stanisław Harbut, *Józef Chłopicki: w 100-letnią Rocznicę Powstania Listopadowego* (Warszawa, 1930), 136.

won their point with Chłopicki, who resigned in mid-January to join the insurrectionists, when he realized that Czar Nicholas would not compromise.

By this time, the ability, determination, resoluteness, and ambition of the young Count had impressed the members of the Patriotic Society, and from then on he played a major role in its activities. In the early dismal days of this organization, he labored long and unrelentingly to buoy up the flagging spirits of the members.[16] Together with the talented Maurycy Mochnacki, he established on January 5, 1831, *New Poland,* the newspaper voice of the society. Mochnacki, five years a newspaperman, had written the year before a brilliant book, *On the Polish Literature of the Nineteenth Century.* He gave fully of his ability and experience, while Gurowski contributed funds from his personal fortune and served on the editorial staff.[17] The Count, like Mochnacki, through the columns of *New Poland* and in the ranks of the society relentlessly attacked the diet of the revolutionary government for negligence and carelessness in conducting the insurrection. Gurowski's barbs were aimed especially at members who were hesitant about supporting a vigorous war policy. Armed with a saber and two pistols, one of the Count's victims sought him out in the *New Poland* print shop. Gurowski informed his visitor that he could defend himself armed with nothing more than a stick, and ordered him to leave. Like others to follow, the threatening adversary retreated before the Count's rage.[18]

Relentless castigation of the diet by Gurowski and Mochnacki brought unfavorable and intense reaction. Both young editors, fearing that the diet's displeasure might jeopardize the society, submitted their resignations, only to have them refused by a vote of forty-six to seven. On this cue Gurowski renewed his attack on the diet. He secretly planned a demonstration by the Patriotic Society to honor the memory of two revolutionaries. As arranged, an enthusiastic crowd assembled in the square opposite the diet building. Gurowski, dressed in a red cap with a white feather, mounted a monument and fulminated lengthily against

[16] Mochnacki, *Powstanie Narodu Polskiego, w r. 1830 i 1831,* IV, 233, 236.

[17] Śliwiński, *Maurycy Mochnacki,* 209, 214.

[18] *Ibid.,* 224; Lelewel, *Pamiętnik z Roku 1830–31,* 68, 76–77; Mochnacki, *Powstanie Narodu Polskiego, w r. 1830 i 1831,* IV, 233, 257, 258.

the vacillating policy of the diet, to a rhythm of applause.[19] Before the day was over, the diet mustered its courage and dethroned Nicholas as king of Poland.

During his weeks of ceaseless activity with the Patriotic Society, young Adam practiced what he preached. Appearing before a notary, he declared free those of his serfs willing to fight with the insurrectionists. To each of these he also gave twenty-four acres of land and a scythe for military combat. He was almost the only nobleman who tried to broaden the revolt in this way, for unlike others of his social and economic status, he had long believed in emancipation. Indeed, he had begun to agitate for it when he was ten years old.[20]

Restlessness and a sense of futility in his struggle to overcome the apathy of the diet led Gurowski to leave the Patriotic Society and its newspaper to join the Polish revolutionary army. Together with Mochnacki, he enlisted in Warsaw early in February, 1831, as a private in a regiment led by Józef Patelski.[21] At that moment a huge Russian force was crossing the Polish frontier to take Warsaw. Gurowski's military training was negligible, but almost immediately he found himself on the march to meet the approaching Russians. Then came heavy fighting for the Count in the Wawer and Grochów battles. On several occasions he "laid down the knapsack for a cushion, snow for a mattress and for a blanket."[22] But the rigors of military life did not appeal to him, and

[19] Śliwiński, *Maurycy Mochnacki*, 220, 227; Mochnacki, *Powstanie Narodu Polskiego, w r. 1830 i 1831*, IV, 238, 240.

[20] Śliwiński, *Maurycy Mochnacki*, 122, 215; Adam Gurowski, *Russia As It Is* (New York, 1854), 31; Adam Gurowski, *Diary: 1863—'64—'65* (Washington, 1866), 173 (April 13, 1864), cited hereafter as *Diary*, III; rough draft of a letter, Gurowski to Lincoln, no date, in Gurowski Papers. At the close of the uprising of 1863–64, Polish serfs were finally emancipated and allotted land for eventual ownership by Russia, although she had emancipated her own serfs in 1861. Gurowski rejoiced when the news of Polish emancipation reached him: "The aspirations of my whole life are finally fulfilled; they have become a fact. The Polish peasantry . . . is finally and emphatically emancipated . . . it receives land—that is, homesteads . . . . Half a century I spent not only in hope, but in working for it . . . . And now it is done, and whatever I suffered . . . is, at least in part, healed." *Diary*, III, 172–73 (April 13, 1864).

[21] Josef Patelski, *Wspomnienia Wojskowe Józefa Patelskiego z Lat 1823–1831* (Wilno, 1914), 116; Śliwiński, *Maurycy Mochnacki*, 244.

[22] Adam Gurowski, *Diary, from March 4, 1861, to November 12, 1862* (Boston,

realizing the inequality of the armed forces, he was again seized by a sense of futility. He deserted, a common procedure of the period and circumstances, went for a time into hiding, and then returned briefly to Warsaw's radical politics.[23]

6

The insurrectional National Government considered the Count a demagogue and a rabble-rouser. His activities since the outbreak of the rebellion, except for his military service, were all highly critical of individuals and bodies leading the stroke for independence. Their guidance, in his opinion, was ruining the revolution by ineptness and want of single purpose.

Not long after Gurowski had deserted the army, Małachowski, the National Government's minister of foreign affairs, sent him to Paris as a courier. The Count welcomed this assignment, for he had suggested to the foreign office that he be used for that purpose, and Małachowski snapped up this opportunity to rid Warsaw of a severe critic. The young agitator received three thousand Polish zloty in advance as payment for his courier services. He crossed Prussia armed with dispatches for the Polish mission in France and a letter of introduction from his radical friend, Joachim Lelewel, to the aged Marquis de Lafayette. Reaching Paris in April, Gurowski presented the dispatches to General Karol Kniaziewicz and Ludwik Plater, chiefs of the revolutionary mission, and immediately had them in an uproar. Kniaziewicz and Plater, conservatives and ardent supporters of the insurrectional Polish government, protested at once to Małachowski that Gurowski had been sent as a secret radical agent to check on mission activities. Małachowski denied this allegation and emphasized that Gurowski had no official status. The mission declared the Count to be a private person, but Kniaziewicz re-

1862), 272 (September 13, 1862), cited hereafter as *Diary,* I; rough draft of a letter, Gurowski to Lincoln, no date, in Gurowski Papers.

Until September 3, 1862, Gurowski regularly used the month alone to differentiate between his *Diary* entries. Thereafter, all entries were designated by the day of the month. Previous exceptions were the isolated passages of October 6, 1861, and July 4 and 10, 1862.

23 Śliwiński, *Maurycy Mochnacki,* 303; Lubomir Gadon, *Emigracya Polska: Pierwsze Lata po Upadku Powstania Listopadowego* (3 vols., Kraków, 1901–1902), I, 119.

mained convinced that Lelewel, leader of the opposition in Warsaw, had sent him to Paris to keep an eye on the mission.[24]

Kniaziewicz was correct. Gurowski had indeed come to Paris as an agent of the Warsaw radicals, though at the expense of the conservative government! Lelewel had told the Count to watch closely over the "reactions abroad to the ruinous operations of the government now in power."[25] In addition, Gurowski worked to expose and bring pressure against the conservative leadership. To this end he hobnobbed regularly with Lafayette, who was openly sympathetic to the radicals and their activity. The garrulous Count identified himself also with the French parliamentary opposition group and wrote long articles in their *Tribune, Globe,* and *Français,* in which he attacked the National Government and its Paris mission. Out of appreciation, the *Globe* editor once rescued him from police following his arrest for leading a street demonstration. Heinrich Heine, the well-known German poet and journalist, numbered among Gurowski's intimate Paris friends of liberal political principles.[26] Even to Brussels, Gurowski extended his influence by intriguing against Józef Załuski, who was serving in that city as a representative of the National Government.[27]

Several pamphlets, explaining the aims of the insurrection, and published in London by the Paris mission, were unacceptable to the Count, and he replied in French in *The Polish Cause from its True Point of View*. The pamphlets he criticized argued that decisions of the Congress of Vienna had caused the rebellion, but he maintained that the revolution had its origin in the First Partition of Poland (1772), because the actual question involved was independence from the partitioning powers. He concluded his essay by vilifying the Paris mission as unrepresentative of the Polish people and as usurper of their trust. By

[24] Gadon, *Emigracya Polska,* I, 119–20; Josef Dutkiewicz, *Francja a Polska w 1831 r.* (Lodz, 1950), 93–95.

[25] Gadon, *Emigracya Polska,* I, 120.

[26] Marie Joseph Paul Yves Roch Gilbert du Motier LaFayette, *Generał M. R. La-Fayette o Polsce: Listy, Mowy, Dokumenty* (Warszawa, 1934), 28; Allan Nevins and Milton Halsey Thomas (eds.), *The Diary of George Templeton Strong: The Turbulent Fifties, 1850–1859* (New York, 1952), 3 (January 5, 1850).

[27] Gadon, *Emigracya Polska,* I, 120, 170; Dutkiewicz, *Francja a Polska w 1831 r.,* 138.

grasping authority, he said, the mission paralyzed the spontaneous and sympathetic reaction of the French masses when the November Insurrection began.

A flood of refugees made their way to Paris with the fall of Warsaw in September, 1831, and the subsequent collapse of the insurrection. Gurowski greeted many a radical friend, such as Lelewel, but particularly close were Mochnacki and his own brother, Bolesław, both of whom had stayed with the army to the end. Almost immediately the philanthropic Central Franco-Polish Committee, sparked by Lafayette and assisted by Gurowski, realized it could not adequately care for the refugees. Consequently the Poles formed on November 6 the Provisional Committee of Emigrants at a meeting held in Lafayette's residence. Gurowski, Mochnacki, and twenty-four others attended. Trouble began immediately, for Bonawentura Niemojowski, a conservative and last president of the National Government, was elected chairman. A conservative majority, dedicated to a nonpolitical policy, had prevailed.

Thus the radicals considered the Provisional Committee a monstrosity. Gurowski and Mochnacki jumped to the attack. The Count published an appeal to the refugees demanding a new chairman and a new committee. At a subsequent meeting, Gurowski successfully argued with Niemojowski the matter of political participation. The Count contended that administrative and economic functions alone were inadequate. In the ensuing discussion, many became convinced that the body needed a thorough overhauling.[28]

7

Out of Gurowski's and Mochnacki's opposition to the Provisional Committee came the Permanent National Committee, a new quasi-governmental body of the Paris Poles in exile. Organized on December 15, the radical Lelewel served as chairman, Mochnacki as secretary, and Gurowski as a committee member. This was in reality the old Warsaw Patriotic Society reorganized and rededicated to a political program. There remained, however, a minority conservative element, which

[28] Gadon, *Emigracya Polska,* I, 122–24, 126–27; Śliwiński, *Maurycy Mochnacki,* 301, 303, 306–307.

caused some dissension but created no greater problems than the wranglings of the radicals themselves.[29]

Trouble, nevertheless, developed at once in the Permanent National Committee. Gurowski considered Lelewel and Mochnacki arbitrary and undemocratic as chairman and secretary. Openly critical, he offended Mochnacki, who had regarded him as the closest of friends. When Mochnacki went to Metz, France, to visit with an old newspaper associate and family friend of Warsaw days, he quietly left Paris without telling Gurowski or anyone else. The Count, as well as a number of other Polish *emigrés,* concluded that Mochnacki had deserted. The Gurowski group persuaded the committee to stop Mochnacki's monetary allowance and to remove his name from the list of foreign persons whose presence in Paris had been authorized. However, Mochnacki later returned to Paris, renewed his friendship with the Count, tapped him briefly for financial assistance, and utilized his political writings in his own literary efforts.[30]

Even outside the committee trouble had developed. In early January, 1832, General Józef Bem, a supporter of the insurrection's leadership, arrived in Paris hoping to convince the French government that a Polish legion ought to be formed in that country. The committee invited him to appear before it. He ignored the invitation and denounced the committee in strong language. The reaction of this body was swift. Gurowski and his brother Bolesław were among those who "demanded satisfaction" from the General. The Count personally excoriated Bem in an open letter. But the General held his ground, and Gurowski beat a retreat: "In view of the fact that the majority is convinced that the common good would suffer if I were to hurt the unfortunate personage, dedicated to the fatherland's cause, I request that my expressions and comments on the subject be regarded as irrelevant and inappropriate."[31]

[29] Gadon, *Emigracya Polska,* I, 127; Śliwiński, *Maurycy Mochnacki,* 312; Nikolaï Vasil'yevich Berg, *Zapiski N. V. Berga o Pol'skikh Zagovorakh i Vozstaniyakh 1831–1862 g* (Moskva, 1873), 13.

[30] Gadon, *Emigracya Polska,* II, 21; Śliwiński, *Maurycy Mochnacki,* 315–17, 329, 334, 354, 361.

[31] Gadon, *Emigracya Polska,* I, 17, 139–40; Michał Janik, "Prądy Panslawistyczne i Rusofilskie w Okresie Wielkiej Emigracji," *Pamiętnik Literacki,* Vol. XXXI (1934), 60.

Soon after his wrangle with Gurowski and the committee, Bem left Paris, unable to win over the French government to the idea of a Polish legion. The former leaders of the National Government, now that Gurowski seemed at bay, challenged him to a duel. Teodor Morawski, the last minister of foreign affairs, was their principal. Gurowski chose vicious Lepage dueling pistols at ten paces. Ordinarily neither contender would have survived the impact of the huge .62 caliber lead bullets, but fog, dampness, or a miracle caused the shots to misfire. According to the terms, the duelists could not shoot a second time.[32]

French authorities, as early as January, 1832, made efforts to move the Polish refugees to the provinces, much to the distaste of the committee. The French government took this action to relieve the housing and financial strain in Paris and to remove an element it considered inflammable to Parisian liberal groups. Under Gurowski's leadership on this issue, the committee quickly came to regard as traitors those who considered leaving Paris. He fulminated at them: "Polish interests demand that we all should remain in Paris. Let's do that which the Russian embassy fears, and we shall not need government charity. Poles in Paris are nightmares for the tsar, as even Hannibal was a nightmare for the Romans during his wanderings throughout Asia."[33]

Ill will and animosity without as well as within the committee had been caused in no small measure by Gurowski. A motion was made to expel him with the stated reason that he was responsible in part for a split in the ranks. But Lelewel and other radicals came to Gurowski's support and defeated the motion. Several weeks later another member of the committee changed a stand he had taken earlier on an issue before that body, because he had discovered that Gurowski agreed

[32] Gadon, *Emigracya Polska*, II, 17. Gurowski claimed that in Europe he fought more than thirty duels and served as second at about sixty others. "We Polish nobility, we fight generally with short half round Turkish swords," he explained. "It makes ugly gashes and I saw bowels come out . . . once." Gurowski to James Shepherd Pike, April 16, [1859 or 1860], in James Shepherd Pike Papers, Calais Free Library, Calais, Maine. A less accurate version of this letter is in James S. Pike, *First Blows of the Civil War: The Ten Years of Preliminary Conflict in the United States* (New York, 1879), 513. In a casual conversation, when asked how many men he had killed in duels, Gurowski replied in broken English, "Wonly . . . two!" Gouverneur, *As I Remember*, 248.

[33] Gadon, *Emigracya Polska*, I, 146.

with him. When questioned in the committee concerning his about-face, he explained that he did not want to be united in his opinions with Gurowski, because the Count had fled Warsaw in the face of danger. Gurowski, in the other end of the meeting hall, shouted "Liar!" Confusion prevailed; then Gurowski's brother Bolesław came to his defense. The altercation concluded with Bolesław's being challenged to a duel.

A few days later a provincial agent of the committee complained that he had made no progress because of Gurowski's wrangling. "The presence of one such rioter and rabble-rouser within the ranks," scolded another member of the committee, "is more damaging than a thousand visible enemies. I speak of Gurowski . . . throw him out of the Committee."[34] The problem came to a head at the meeting of March 16, 1832, when a motion was made to dissolve the committee and to create a new organization made up of individuals of identical democratic principles and ideals. The committee, immediately in an uproar, refused to allow discussion of the proposition. Then a small group led by Gurowski, including his brother, angrily stamped from the meeting hall amidst shouts of ridicule and sarcastic farewells.[35]

8

Next morning five of the radicals gathered in Gurowski's residence to launch a new organization, the Polish Democratic Society. According to its "Regulations," it was established "for the purpose of acting in the Polish national cause in the spirit of purely philosophical democratic principles." Further, all regular members were obligated "to dedicate all . . . political activity for the benefit of the Society. Therefore, each member should surrender all personal present and future . . . private interests and use them instead solely for the benefit of the Society." The group drew lots to establish the order for signing the membership roll, for the chairmanship would rotate to members as their names appeared on the roll. Gurowski saw to it that his brother Bolesław was one of the seventeen new members admitted at the next meeting. But Lelewel and Mochnacki refused to join, protesting that the organization carried democratic principles to an undesirable extreme. The Count also saw

[34] *Ibid.,* I, 146–47, II, 29. [35] *Ibid.,* I, 150.

to it that the republican newspapers of Paris favorably reported the birth of the society. Meanwhile, he labored tirelessly to extend its membership to soldiers and peasants, two groups conspicuously absent.[36]

Word drifted to Paris in the spring of 1832 that the Russian trials of leaders of the November Insurrection had ended. Amnesty had already been extended to the Polish masses. Gurowski's four brothers who had served with the army were included in the general amnesty, although Bolesław chose to remain in exile. The Count, however, was given special attention, listed among the most guilty, and excluded from amnesty. His estates were confiscated and assigned to two of his brothers, and he was sentenced to death. Fortunately for him, Russian extradition efforts were not recognized by France.[37]

The death penalty and confiscation intensified Gurowski's efforts for Polish nationalism. When a motion was made in the British parliament on April 18, 1832, attacking Russia for her disregard of Polish freedom, he was the first of the exiled Poles to reach London. He carried protests of the Democratic Society against all treaties from 1772 to 1815, which had contributed to the dismemberment of Poland. As a full-powered plenipotentiary of the society, he lobbied with parliament members to build active sympathy for the Polish cause. In the end, he found the recommendations of the French radicals and the full authority of acting in the name of the society of little value. Nothing occurred in parliament beyond the excoriation of the Czar and charges of timidity hurled at the British government. The Count was able to publish his protests and communications in only one London newspaper, the *Morning Herald*.[38]

[36] *Ibid.*, I, 151, II, 235–36, 242, 248, III, 188, 304–305, 328; Berg, *Zapiski N. V. Berga o Pol'skikh Zagovorakh i Vozstaniyakh 1831–1862 g*, 16; Władysław Mickiewicz, *Zywot Adama Mickiewicza* (4 vols., Poznań, 1890–1895), III, 428; Śliwiński, *Maurycy Mochnacki*, 340.

[37] Josef Bialynia Cholodecki, *Uczestnicy Powstania Listopadowego Wykluczeni z Amnestji Carskiej* (Lwow, 1930), 5; Gurowski's autobiographical sketch, in author's possession; Carter, "Gurowski," *Atlantic Monthly*, Vol. XVIII, 625; Niesiecki, *Herbarz Polski*, X, 161.

[38] Gadon, *Emigracya Polska*, II, 68–69, 238. The Polish question debate of April 18, 1832, is in *Hansard's Parliamentary Debates*, 3rd Series, Vol. XII, cc. 636–64; that of June 28, 1832, is in *ibid.*, XIII, cc. 1115–152; Gurowski's name was not mentioned in either debate.

Even Adam Mickiewicz, often acclaimed the greatest Polish poet, experienced the sting of Gurowski's barbs. Mickiewicz had long opposed Russian authority in Poland, and had experienced persecution at the Czar's hand. During the November Insurrection he traveled in Europe and did not join the emigrants in Paris until some months after the collapse of the revolution. By the time he arrived, his poetry on Poland's political plight had been widely applauded by both conservative and radical exiles. Both wings claimed him. When it became obvious that his sympathies were with the leadership of the insurrection, Gurowski and other radicals were determined to convert him, and, if this could not be accomplished, to disgrace him. The poet confided his view of the issue to a friend: "Here some dreadful criticisms are being readied against me in the French and German publications. I hear that Gurowski and others want to discredit me. They are to prove that I am crazy, in the expectation that the Poles will believe when they read such judgment of me in the foreign press and that the foreigners will be unable to prove or verify."[39]

The Count soon maligned the Polish verse writer in a French journal: "Mickiewicz's style is anointed with bitterness; in his fascinating metaphors flows bloody irony. His Christian humility masks his hatred. He avenges his sufferings, . . . but man charges the poet with lies. . . . [He] who would like to appear before the populace as a new Messiah . . . forgets to look for the reasons and causes of his misfortune in the will of God. He who wants to pass for a prophet must first prove that he was a martyr."[40] The friends of Mickiewicz rallied to his defense and vented their spleen on Gurowski. But the Count pressed the attack for nearly two years. He had determined to break the reputation of Mickiewicz and to destroy his image as the Moses of Poland. Gurowski's effort failed miserably, for Mickiewicz came to be acknowledged widely as the poetic spokesman of Poland's revolutionary and nationalistic spirit.[41]

[39] Mickiewicz to Stefan Garczynski, March 5, 1833, in Adam Mickiewicz, *Korespondencja Adama Mickiewicza* (2 vols., Paris, 1871–1872), I, 71–72.

[40] Mickiewicz, *Zywot Adama Mickiewicza*, II, 196.

[41] *Ibid.*, II, 195–97, III, 199–200.

Frustration came also to the Count as he sat in the councils of non-Polish radicals in Paris. In these circles he conspired with Louis Napoleon, the future French emperor, but then a republican, in planning revolts. He also advised Élénore Louis Godefroy Cavaignac, French journalist, politician, and leader in Parisian revolutionary intrigue from 1830 to 1834. Gurowski likewise wrote instructions for Giuseppe Mazzini, the Italian patriot living in exile in France and Switzerland following the 1830 uprisings, but working toward the liberation and unification of Italy under a republican form of government. The Count assisted him particularly in organizing a group of exiled Germans, Poles, and Italians for an ill-fated invasion of Savoy early in 1834.[42] In all these efforts, Gurowski experienced a growing sense of hopelessness.

Defeats came on every hand. In the Democratic Society, the Count was accused of negligence and carelessness in behalf of that organization's interests. He ceased to go to its meetings. He soon realized the gulf between his opinions and those of the society's membership. "The Paris group," he said, "has changed . . . . All this has bored me and demonstrated the impossibility of activity with such a scattered and motley crowd. The Society is changing into a rascal; national stupidity is taking the helm . . . . I have cried over this fatal stupidity imprisoning Poland everywhere. I see what is going on in Paris underminings and intrigues . . . . I am deeply convinced of the futility of my remaining with the Society. I shall continue merely to write. That is the only road, the only propaganda—I know no other. For it, an unmanageable Society is hardly necessary."[43] Even his attendance at the third anniversary celebration of the November Insurrection held at Lafayette's residence failed to reconcile him with his circle or to draw him to other Polish exiles.

Gurowski then established for his writings his own monthly journal, *Future,* edited by him and published in Paris. In the January issue of 1834, the only number to appear, he called for new blood to give

[42] *Diary,* I, 36 (April, 1861); L. E. Chittenden, *Personal Reminiscences, Including Lincoln and Others, 1840–1890* (New York, 1893), 320; Robert Waters, *Career and Conversation of John Swinton: Journalist, Orator, Economist* (Chicago, 1902), 15; Boston (weekly) *Museum,* June 28, 1851.

[43] Gadon, *Emigracya Polska,* II, 333–34, III, 59–60.

renewed life to Poland. This energy, said he, would come from the peasants, for democracy rested with this class and not with the Polish aristocracy. On other pages he criticized the society's members and activities. In reply, a member of the society moved to expel the Count. The motion failed, but almost a year from the day when Gurowski led in establishing the organization, he voluntarily withdrew.

Alone, and opposed now even to the radicals, he found the increasing conservatism that slowly engulfed the Parisian exiles equally frustrating. The radical wing had lost much of its leadership, and in ever-increasing numbers the emigrants accepted the conservative leader, Prince Adam Czartoryski, as virtually their king.[44] Inadequate direction, "the uttermost imbecility" in its leaders, had kept Poland from being victorious in 1831, Gurowski explained, and now the same thing stultified the Paris refugees in their efforts to keep alight the torch of Polish freedom.[45]

[44] *Ibid.,* III, 61, 286.
[45] Gurowski to Charles Sumner, April 23, 1861, in Charles Sumner Papers, Houghton Library, Harvard University.

CHAPTER II

RUSSIA'S KNIGHT-ERRANT

I

A SUSPICIOUS QUIET settled on Gurowski's propaganda activities following the first number of *Future*. Months passed before he published a startling announcement in the Augsburg *Gazette* on September 8, 1834: "I belonged to the opposition in Poland before 1830. I was persecuted. I participated in the revolution of November 29. I thought I was doing the right thing. Experience has convinced me otherwise. Today, with the same sincerity, I reverse my opinions—I cannot see any prosperity for the country of my birth. I am above all accusations which might be cast at me. Acting in this way, I have no hopes, whatever, of returning to Poland."[1]

Simultaneously the Count prepared a statement for the Petersburg *Weekly* (No. 95, 1834):

It is never too late to better oneself or to come closer to truth or to broaden one's knowledge. By shaking off the old and decaying ashes, one can broaden or at least clarify his convictions and opinions. One can acknowledge his country, which include all members of his original [Slavic] family. The strongest evidence of the political downfall of a nation is the lack of purpose to which all efforts can be directed, as well as a lack of faith in itself. Having failed to take advantage of an opportunity to unite eastern Europe, Poland became only a body without a soul—which through inactivity and decay interfered with the development of Slavism. The advantages accruing to Europe through the growth of Russia concern her more than her molded past.[2]

What happened to change Gurowski? He explained that during

[1] Janik, "Prądy Panslawistyczne i Rusofilskie w Okresie Wielkiej Emigracji," *Pamiętnik Literacki*, Vol. XXXI, 62.
[2] *Ibid.*, 63.

his years of study in Europe and particularly in Paris he had associated with people and ideas of many shades and hues. Time not spent with fellow Polish patriots he had used to observe and judge events, to ponder social problems and read history:

> A revolution in my mind was effected . . . . At that time not only political theoreticians, but new systems aiming to reform society in its foundations, as for example that of the St. Simonians, whose conceptions I studied and shared; all of them established as an axiom that society ought to be directed by a supreme will embodied in one individual, ruling or inspiring the rest . . . . The more my mind was overpowered by such ideas, the deeper I felt the curse of the existence of an exile, rootless on a foreign soil . . . . The devotion and interest felt for my ancient country became wholly superseded by my interests for the whole race, of which Poland was, after all, rather an insignificant offshoot . . . . By birth a Slavi, I looked around to see where was alive the powerful trunk of my race, and found that Russia alone represented it . . . . The study of, and devotion to the great truths revealed by Fourier, nay, his personal advice, influenced powerfully my decision. Whoever has read his works, knows how repeatedly Fourier points to Russia and even to a Czar, as the means of the speediest realization of the theory of association.[3]

The disaffected Count not only had imbibed deep of the socialistic doctrines of Henri Saint-Simon and Charles Fourier, but had turned into a leading proponent of Panslavism with Russia at the focus. Although he erroneously claimed to have originated the idea, he was actually one of the first Poles, if not the first, to promote vigorously through his writings and actions the point of view that Russia, rather than Poland, should lead the Slavic peoples. He explained: "Analyzing with conscientious scrutiny the causes of the political death of Poland, I lost the faith in any possibility of her resurrection. The destiny of the Slavic race, dawning now on the horizon, could not depend on one of its feeblest, withered and destroyed branches. Russia alone represented the Slavic vitality in the moving complications of Europe and the Western world. Among the various reasons of the destruction of Poland, the most deleterious was the utter want for centuries of any centralizing idea, of any

[3] Gurowski, *Russia As It Is*, ix–xii.

organized and directing power. Russia's growth was the result of the existence of such an influence."[4]

Gurowski's turnabout created a sensationally unfavorable reaction among Poles everywhere and won for him the lifelong scorn of his countrymen. He was variously characterized by Polish emigrants in France and throughout Europe as "stigmatized with eternal disgrace," as a "traitor by birth and deed," "a veritable scoundrel, crucified at the left of the Savior," an "abominable degenerate," the "bastard-count," "a perverse mind," and a "renegade."[5] From the time of the Count's disaffection to the present, derision and contempt accompany the mention of his name in historical studies of Poland published in that country. This same scorn is evident when his name appears in Polish publications in the United States. Rare was the Pole who wrote, "Gurowski is right in saying that our nation has fallen into decay, where it is so hard to find an honest man."[6] Polish immigrants to the United States ignored Gurowski so completely that his contacts with members of this group were negligible and unpleasant. Although the Count's apostasy was not the only example, his action was probably the most celebrated in the history of the Great Emigration because of the purpose and relentlessness of his subsequent action in Russia's interest.

2

A man without a country, Gurowski set out to implement his Panslavic convictions and to win the favor of Czar Nicholas. From the moment the Count declared Poland's national future to be hopeless and announced that he had deserted her, he published articles in the Paris press attacking Poland and glorifying Russia. In the meantime, he worked on a ninety-six-page pamphlet, written in French and titled *The Truth about Russia and the Revolts of the Polish Provinces.* Published in Paris in 1834, no more than a few weeks after he had deserted Poland, this essay explained his new position from the standpoint of

---

[4] *Ibid.,* ix–x; Gurowski's autobiographical sketch, in author's possession.

[5] Janik, "Prądy Panslawistyczne i Rusofilskie w Okresie Wielkiej Emigracji," *Pamiętnik Literacki,* Vol. XXXI, 69.

[6] Count S. R. Lanckoronski to John Tyssowski, September 14, 1855, in John Tyssowski Papers, Archives and Museum, Polish Roman Catholic Union of America, Chicago.

the past. History predestined, he contended, that either Poland or Russia should create an empire by uniting all Slavic nations, a life-and-death battle that had raged since the beginning of the sixteenth century. Annihilation of one by the other became thus a historical necessity, for the Slavs needed but one head, one fireside, and one purpose.

Poland could be likened to a man who had deserted his family, Gurowski explained. She had isolated herself from the Slavs and had refused to participate in the great events of Europe, withdrawing until her character had become shaped by constant intimidation. By borrowing from abroad politically and culturally, Poland had separated herself even farther from Slavic brotherhood, and her voice had become more and more unintelligible to Slavic ears.

Russia possessed in the meantime all that Poland lacked in statesmen, strength, action, and purpose, said the Count. While Poland lost territory, Russia grew like a giant—larger and larger—never tasting defeat. Foreigners settled in Poland's cities and thereby caused the Slav to merge his identity, but Russia remained virtually free of international elements.

Concluding his plea to Russian authorities, Gurowski viewed the relationship of Poland to Russia as that of province to state. He claimed Panslavia, under the direction of Russia, as his new fatherland. While Russia contained all the essential elements of prosperity necessary to Panslavia, she possessed its heart and soul as well.

The estranged Count kept his ear to the ground and waited. Unknown to him, Nicholas was not long in hearing of the pamphlet and in forming an opinion. "Gurowski's brochure is creating a great deal of commotion, but it is difficult to believe its brutality," wrote the Czar in St. Petersburg on January 11/23, 1835.[7] This element of doubt caused Nicholas to hesitate. But the Czar's silence made Gurowski more determined to win his confidence and trust.

The Count wrote two letters, one to a brother living in Poland, the other to Alexander Benkendorf, director of police in Russia. In the

---

[7] Quoted in Jan Kucharzewski, *Epoka Paskiewiczowska: Losy Oświaty* (Warszawa, 1914), 263. The Old Style calendar, used by Russia at that time, was twelve days behind the New Style.

former, Gurowski explained his new stand on the relationship of Poland and Russia and wrote of his hopes for Russia's friendship. Perhaps he appended a note requesting that the letter be sent to Benkendorf. In any case, it quickly reached his hands. In the letter addressed to the Director of Police, Gurowski wrote of Russia as leader of all Slavic peoples and of Poland's secondary position. Benkendorf turned both letters over to Nicholas. On the following day, the Czar wrote to Ivan Paskevich, the Russian governor of Poland: "His [Gurowski's] comment was exactly as if I were dictating to him my own confession. It is difficult to speak more justly and more effectively in defence of a good cause. Strange thing—what does this man want? Direct that a letter be sent to him indicating that, to prove his sincerity, he appear at the border and surrender himself to our mercy. We shall see whether he will do this. We shall try."[8]

3

When Gurowski appeared on the Polish frontier, Paskevich sent him temporarily to his former estate near the city of Kalisz. The Count soon obtained permission to travel to Warsaw, where he turned over to Paskevich a list of persons who, in his opinions, could harbor evil designs for a forthcoming meeting of European monarchs in Kalisz. He recommended also that the local peasantry be kept under surveillance. On the strength of the Count's advice, the Governor ordered an investigation and sent the chairman of the investigating committee to him to secure more firsthand information.[9]

Amnesty for Gurowski carried with it a civil service position of low rank, with a salary equal to that of a Russian lieutenant. His assignment was in Russia's capital city of St. Petersburg with the Ministry of Public Information and Education, and in this capacity he served as Panslavic advisor to the agency and to the Czar. He soon won the favor of Nicholas, but never his complete trust.[10]

[8] Nicholas I to Ivan Paskevich, May 19, 1835, in *ibid.*

[9] *Ibid.*, 263–64, 389.

[10] Gaden, *Emigracya Polska,* II, 26; Gurowski's autobiographical sketch, in author's possession.

During his years of employment and study in St. Petersburg, Gurowski wrote and delivered to the Russian government a number of memorials. These were aimed primarily at the Russification of Poland. In his recommendations on educational reform in Poland, presented to the Czar in 1839, the Count proposed first that the Russian language replace the Polish language in schools. Russian should be emphasized in the elementary schools because they were more widely attended. To ease the transition, the Slavonic language should be put to work in the interim. "Before too long," the Count insisted, "Polish will become a small and insignificant dialect, an idiom of the plainfolks. The Russian language, following the inevitable glorious destiny of the Russian nation, will engulf other dialects and will absorb the Polish language. The Russian language, in the near future, will become the only means of expression and communication in the tremendous areas of the Russian-Slavic Empire."

The Count suggested next that the time devoted to Latin be cut in half: "Good and loyal subjects are not created or formed by the speeches of Cicero or the paraphrases of Titus. I know from personal experience and observation of our youth with whom I have attended public schools to what extent we are turning the heads of the young with these examples."

Gurowski's third recommendation was that greater emphasis be given to history, which should not be taught without "serious deliberation," for "warped concepts of history frustrate all feelings and sentiments and create revolutionaries. Every fact and every word in history is either a useful truth or poison—depending on the skill of the one who leads the interpretation."

His fourth point called for an education system established on science, with mathematics, chemistry, and physics at the core: "Peace and order always favor discoveries, experiments and application of new things . . . .The exact sciences . . . teach us to comprehend that the authority of the monarchy stems from God, that without hierarchy existence is impossible."

Gurowski presented these recommendations to the Czar, believing that children and adolescents in Poland received during their education the worst and most false notions about their duties and obligations. Unmindful of the decisions of Providence, which in its intelligence decided the fate of the country, there is planted in these young minds as a singular and most important cult—the veneration of certain traditions of the past, traditions which are by no means august or venerable. This narrow circle of recollections, in itself, formed the entire catechism of the duties of a Pole. Naturally, it follows, therefore, that imbued with such hatred and ill will toward present conditions which are viewed as misfortunes, every Pole is always ready to disturb the present. Feeling insecure and weak, the Pole turns with faith and expectation to foreign and distant countries, rather than seek union with historic brethren. Such is the base of the patriotic education in Poland, which takes possession of the infant in the cradle, leads him through his youth to maturity, and leaves him an insecure individual, with poisoned mind and soul.[11]

The memorial produced significant reactions in governmental circles. It came as Count Sergey Uvarov, the Russian minister of public information and education, placed in effect in Poland his own educational reform program. The Uvarov Russification program was based on classical education, unlike Gurowski's system, which condemned that approach. In fact, the Count's recommendations seemed aimed at the heart of Uvarov's proposals. This placed the Minister of Education in the unpleasant situation of having his pet project and Gurowski's compared by the Czar, and humiliated him because the Count's proposals were more in line with the Czar's plans. But Uvarov boldly sent his criticism to Nicholas: "Commenting on the essence of Count Gurowski's memorial, I regard it a duty to mention that he deserves consideration in view of the good intentions of the author. By and large, though, he does not present anything worthwhile for the ministry to consider in the educational reform program in the Kingdom of Poland. The ruthless application of all ideas proposed by Gurowski would damage seriously the uniformity of the educational system in the Kingdom and the Empire and would unnecessarily impair the recently initiated educational program." The Czar pondered Gurowski's recommendations and Uvarov's criticisms and then wrote the Minister that he concurred

[11] Kucharzewski, *Epoka Paskiewiczowska,* 265–72.

in the main with the Count, especially in his proposal to cut the teaching of Latin. Uvarov revised Poland's educational program accordingly.[12]

4

Equally significant were Gurowski's propaganda publications in behalf of Russian Panslavism. Out of his reflective thinking and additional study came *Civilization and Russia,* a 232-page book published first in French at St. Petersburg in 1840 and in the following year in German at Leipzig, with a paper-bound edition also offered in Leipzig in 1848. His *Thoughts on the Future of the Poles,* a pamphlet of fifty pages, was published in French at Berlin in 1841 and in the following year in German at Leipzig. Another pamphlet was his thirty-nine-page *From My Book of Thoughts,* written in German and published in 1843 in Breslau.

Here followed the Count's break with Russian authorities, but he did not desert his Panslavic convictions. His books and pamphlets written during his remaining years in Europe lost none of their fervor for Russia's future. The capstone to his efforts came in his 316-page study, *Panslavism, its History, its True Elements: Religious, Social, Philosophical and Political,* published in French at Florence in 1848. This was the first volume of a projected two-volume work. In the second book, never completed, he promised to "undertake to prove in all its aspects, to what point it is contrary to the enlightened interests of Russia and Panslavism, to be involved with an army outside of its frontiers in old internal quarrels which would embrace the West. Such an aggressive war on her part would utterly weaken prosperity, would stop the admirable development already reached, would be in short disastrous for all interests and ruinous in men and money for the Empire."[13]

Without doubt, Gurowski contended, Russia held the secret of Slavic destiny, since she alone possessed the strength to bring union for that race. The great land of Panslavism must not be subdivided, but must remain immense and infinite like its fate. It must include all the various nationalities making up the Panslavic whole, all united

[12] *Ibid.,* 264–66, 268.

[13] Adam Gurowski, *Le Panslavism, son Histoire, ses Véritables Éléments: Religieux, Sociaux, Philosophiques et Politiques* (Florence, 1848), I, 315.

under the leadership of Russia, "in whose impenetrable and indistinguishable depths many solutions to the tasks of history and society conceal themselves. With this great wealth Russia represents the Slavic branch, and until everything that it is supposed to give to humanity has come to the light of day, not until then can any stopping of the growth of Russia be thought of."[14]

All elements, the Count maintained, pointed toward the continuing leadership of Russia. Even the individual Russian dominated foreign social life. In the drawing room he took possession of the most brilliant social gatherings. "The Russian appears everywhere with the assurance that the first step is his by right. And it is almost without his knowledge that he acts . . . as if something outside of him was pushing him to appear always as master, to doubt nothing." In realizing her destiny, Russia also possessed the necessary physical power. She alone dictated peace or war to surrounding nations. "Outer causes cannot determine the tipping of the scales. Russia decides as it has done for centuries . . . according to reasons and causes which are special and individual to it. This was the character of all its wars."[15]

Russia, the exiled Pole continued, needed the co-operation of all nations if its preordained growth and development were to continue without interruption. But she seemed universally misunderstood: "Human life would not suffice to refute all the errors and untruths which circulate about Russia's history, condition and political striving."[16]

Despite those nations that misunderstood Russia, despite those that stood in the way, Gurowski believed her destiny remained. She would continue to spread her civilization, for transportation and communication had also come to her assistance. The Orient as well as Western Europe would someday feel her impact. "The enormous social structure which the institutions of Russia have erected and which stretches itself more and more from Germany toward China . . . increases from time to time, . . . the last stone of that is far from being laid." "As a powerful

[14] *Ibid.*, 163, 262; Adam Gurowski, *Aus Meinem Gadankenbuche* (Breslau, 1843), 12.

[15] Gurowski, *Le Panslavism*, I, 256; Adam Gurowski, *Russland und die Civilisation* (Leipzig, 1841), 251–52.

[16] Adam Gurowski, *Eine Tour Durch Belgien im Jahre 1844: Aus dem Tagebuche* (Heidelberg, 1845), 144, 155.

state," he further predicted, "still widely removed from the attainment of the height destined for it, it can devote itself to no soft rest nor wish this for any price; for that means denying destiny to which providence drives it."[17]

Centralizing influence, the fundamental cohesive force that Poland never possessed, the Count thought, was inherent in Russia, and was being used in the best interests of Poland and all Slavic nations. The cultural achievement of individual Poles, he admitted, when compared with that of individual Russians, appeared to be greater, but this did not meet the deeper demands of a great civilization "because in the culture of the Poles since time immemorial everything has been individualized, single and thereby purposeless." Poles should now contribute their individual talents to the collective interests of the Russian empire, "to the destinies of which providence has irrevocably joined them."[18]

The youth of Poland, Gurowski recommended, excessive and encumbering in their native land, could well go to Russia with benefit accruing to both nations, by the blending and fusing of interests. The customs line between Poland and Russia ought also to be done away with to promote integration. For more than a decade the Count had recommended removing the line, and finally in 1850 it ceased to exist. With a separate customs system, he believed Poland drew no immediate advantage from her incorporation in the empire. The higher the degree of uniformity and intermingling in Russo-Polish economic, social, and political relations, the greater the benefit for both nations.[19]

The Count had abandoned Poland because he considered her political reconstruction impossible. Looking back on his decision, he saw no signs on the horizon to prove him in error, and during the Crimean War, he reaffirmed his judgment: "Poland is no longer a bloody phantom haunting nations and governments; it is a Chinese shadow, with which intriguers amuse fools."[20] His view remained the same in 1863 when

[17] Gurowski, *Le Panslavism*, I, 264; Gurowski, *Russland und die Civilisation*, 201, 252.

[18] Adam Gurowski, *Pensées sur l'Avenir des Polonais* (Berlin, 1841), 7, 37; Gurowski, *Aus Meinen Gedankenbuche*, 24.

[19] Gurowski, *Pensées sur l'Avenir des Polonais*, 41, 42; Gurowski, *Le Panslavism*, I, 290–91.

the Poles again struck for independence: "I do not share the hopes, I earnestly condemn the attempt, but I bleed internally for the victims, and ahead I see disasters, destruction, desolation among the poor peasantry, the true people with whom alone I am in mental communion."[21] He predicted that England's talk of assisting Poland would remain only talk until the insurrection collapsed, as had happened in 1831.[22]

5

Gurowski's personal situation in St. Petersburg continued to be anything but satisfying. Although his actions and propaganda writings spoke glowingly of Russia, rewards had not been forthcoming. No advancements came financially or in his position. He supported himself only through the generosity of his brothers Nicholas and Joseph, both of whom owned and operated portions of the family estate in Poland. His immediate superior, Uvarov, planned to unhorse him, for the Minister smarted at the preference the Czar had shown for the Count's educational program. Gurowski himself let it be known that he disliked Uvarov. Even the Count's half-sister, Cecelia, wife of a member of the household staff of Nicholas I, turned out to be an influential enemy.[23]

But the presence of his son, by then attending school in the capital city, and the favor of Czar Nicholas caused him to hold out longer than he should have. His purpose, not yet realized, to study Russia at first hand in its cultural, economic, and political aspects likewise caused him to hesitate. He finally applied for an extended leave to visit his brothers in the Kingdom. "I experienced," the Count said when explaining his departure, "that the good will of the most powerful aristocrat was not

[20] Adam Gurowski, *A Year of the War* (New York, 1855), 17; see also Gurowski, *Russia As It Is*, xiii.

[21] Gurowski to John A. Andrew, March 22, 1863, in John A. Andrew Papers, Massachusetts Historical Society, Boston. Much the same sentiment is in Gurowski to Horatio Woodman, June 22, [1863], in Massachusetts Historical Society, *Proceedings*, Vol. LVI (October, 1922–June, 1923), 238, and in Gurowski to Jan N. Janowski, October 25, 1863, in Jan N. Janowski Papers, Jagiellonian Library, Kraków, Poland.

[22] Adam Gurowski, *Diary, from November 18, 1862, to October 18, 1863* (New York, 1864), 204 (April 21, 1863), cited hereafter as *Diary*, II.

[23] Włodzimierz A. Francew, "Adam hr. Gurowski w Polsce w Latach 1841–1844; Przyczynek do Jego Zyciorysu," *Pamiętnik Literacki*, Vol. XXXIV (1937), 96; Gurowski's autobiographical sketch, in author's possession.

sufficient to shelter me against the intrigues of envious and unprincipled courtiers. Thus I was overwhelmed and blown up." He had, he believed, faced "the most inept and lowest persecution."[24]

Gurowski's retreat in early 1841 to his confiscated ancestral estate near Kalisz, now in the hands of his brother Nicholas, did not improve his status. Ostensibly he planned to return to St. Petersburg, and for that reason he was retained on the civil service rolls at the same low salary.[25] Again the financial support of his brothers was necessary. Meanwhile, he busied himself with propaganda publications for Russia and kept at his historical and political studies. He made an effort through the governor of Poland to obtain under the name of his brother Nicholas a government loan on his confiscated lands to salvage this property for his two children, particularly for his son. He also seriously considered obtaining from his brother "a little corner of land, where I shall be permitted to live for myself."[26]

But moral frustration commenced anew for Gurowski from the day he returned to his native soil. His brothers did not appreciate his presence. As participants in the November Insurrection, they did not understand or agree with his Russian collaboration. Sheltering a deserter of Polish nationalism doubtless brought ridicule, since their brother continued to be the recipient of considerable scorn and derision aimed at him by Polish patriots. The acid of hate ravaged the Count. He wrote to his friend, Governor Paskevich of Poland, about "the hostility so pronounced" that engulfed him, of a "position so precarious and so denounced," and of the "very powerful and implacable hates" he encountered.[27]

Gurowski soon decided to make a new start in St. Petersburg. Perhaps the Czar would give him another position, since employment in the Ministry of Public Information and Education would be untenable.

---

[24] Gurowski, *Le Panslavism,* I, 287n.; Gurowski's autobiographical sketch, in author's possession.

[25] Francew, "Adam hr. Gurowski w Polsce w Latach 1841–1844: Pryzyczynek do Jego Zyciorysu," *Pamiętnik Literacki,* Vol. XXXIV, 93.

[26] Gurowski to Ivan Paskevich, July 25/August 6, and November 12, 1841, in *ibid.,* 99–101.

[27] Gurowski to Paskevich, July 25/August 6, 1841, in *ibid.,* 99–100.

He explained his hope to Paskevich, and prefaced his request with a reference to his revolutionary past and his purpose for the future: "The only hope . . . as also the only wish, is to be able to acquire with time an honorable position,—in order that the results of a step of contrition, a step from the heart and conviction, that these results may not be marked by dishonor . . . in the eyes of the world." Then he warmed to his purpose:

> Intellectual and literary work requires resources of all kinds, impossible for an individual of limited means to procure for himself, resources that only a great city can offer. I have applied myself with all my strength to study . . . the good that Russia and her organization contains. The results of these studies of good faith were received with a magnanimous condescension by His Majesty the Emperor and by all the good men at Petersburg. To be able to continue in this route to which I have attached myself with fervor, encouraged by the reception mentioned above, I dare to hope that the sojourn at Saint Petersburg will be permitted to me, as the only place in all the Empire where I could be utilized according to my means.

Newspaper work in the capital city, Gurowski continued, would especially please him: "I could be used under the supreme breath of power to work . . . in the press . . . . Penetrated as I feel myself, with the thought of autocratic power, . . . I could be a useful instrument in its hands, becoming under its auspices and under its inspiration a writer . . . working for a newspaper of Saint Petersburg which would be an organization of the Government." However he viewed his present situation, St. Petersburg seemed the answer "for my isolation, the nearness of my son, the only link to the world, and the possibility of useful work . . . not in view of ambition but as the only place of refuge and rest."[28]

6

The call to work in St. Petersburg never came. The glorious future that he had expected as he turned his back on Poland did not materialize. Nicholas had extended amnesty, but little more. From the beginning Russian authorities, including the Czar, had not trusted him. To them

---

[28] Gurowski to Paskevich, no date, in *ibid.*, 101–102.

he was above all a leader of the November Insurrection. His conversion to Russian Panslavism seemed incredible, as the officials reviewed the amazing details of his participation in the insurrection collected at the time of his trial *in absentia*. When the chief of the Russian information bureau in Warsaw reported to Governor Paskevich that he planned to nominate Gurowski to a nonremunerative position on the public information council, he emphasized that the Count would remain under his close supervision and that only harmless assignments would be given to him.[29]

Gurowski's turbulent disposition also thwarted him. He could probably have held a high position in the Russian administration, despite his earlier revolutionary proclivities, if his nature had been winsome rather than quarrelsome. He himself admitted that his temperament gave him trouble in St. Petersburg and made many a powerful enemy in court circles.[30] It could have caused him no less trouble with his angry Polish neighbors and his immediate family.

Unwanted in Russia and Poland, the Count found his situation impossible. He likened it to slow death. Even the eyes of the Czar had impressed him as "two freezing icicles," the man himself "cold blooded," with forgiveness distilled "drop by drop," but never "wholly filling the cup or pardon." Moreover, his convictions about the role of the czaristic system in the Panslavic movement were changing. When he had entered government service at St. Petersburg, he was enraptured with Nicholas' Panslavic leadership, and "became conscientiously a believer in the lofty and providential calling of Czarism."[31] But Gurowski grew skeptical after close observation of the Russian government. His faith in Nicholas faded, and the whole czaristic system shattered before his hopes and aspirations. Although he still believed that Russia held the future of the Slavs, he maintained that her autocratic czaristic system did not provide the necessary leadership: "Still I strained my reason to hold

[29] *Ibid.,* 93–95.

[30] Julia Ward Howe, *Reminiscences, 1819–1899* (Boston, 1899), 227; Gurowski to Stuart, March 13, 1865, in Miscellaneous Manuscripts, Lincoln National Life Foundation, Fort Wayne, Indiana; "Nebulae," *Galaxy,* Vol. I (June 1, 1866), 269.

[31] Gurowski, *Russia As It Is,* xii, 45, 49, 50.

out, hoping for the best. One by one the scales fell from my eyes, and finally I violently broke the voluntary chain, retook the staff of the exile, and with it my liberty."[32]

Before he fled, the Count carefully contemplated his proposed action. The thought of leaving the scenes of his youth and the financial protection of his brothers plagued him. When he decided to go, he tenderly bade farewell to the home of his forefathers, for he realized that there would be no turning back. On a card written and left behind on the day of his flight, he assumed all responsibility for his action. This he did to protect his family. Then he wrote one letter, to the Czar himself, in which he explained that Nicholas and Russia should be indebted to him, for he had done them both some good.[33] He took with him a few personal belongings, including copies of his books and pamphlets. His small library remained, together with a mass of letters and manuscripts. Nothing in these, Russian police discovered, indicated disloyalty to the Czar. A growing despondency was all they could detect, other than an intense dislike for Uvarov. The police concluded also that the Count still liked Russia and considered her the pilot of Slavic destinies.[34]

When Gurowski crossed the Prussian border in April, 1844, his flight caused Russian authorities no small degree of amazement and consternation. Local officials requested extradition and set out to determine what his fate would be. The only offense he could be tried for was illegal crossing of a boundary, and this carried a slight penalty of three to twelve months imprisonment. On his return he would be arrested and brought to trial locally.[35]

---

[32] *Ibid.*, xii.

[33] Gurowski's autobiographical sketch, in author's possession; see also Waters, *Career and Conversation of John Swinton*, 15.

[34] Francew, "Adam hr. Gurowski w Polsce w Latach 1841–1844: Przyczynek do Jego Zyciorysu," *Pamiętnik Literacki*, Vol. XXXIV, 95–97, 102–105.

[35] *Ibid.*, 97–98. Years later Paskevich, while still governor of Poland, sent word to Gurowski in the United States by way of one of the Count's relatives in Poland that he could, if he desired, return to Russia with honor. Gurowski wrote Paskevich a violent refusal. Theodore Parker to Professor Eduard Desor, August 9, 1852, in Octavius Brooks Frothingham, *Theodore Parker: A Biography* (Boston, 1874), 322.

7

In Prussia, Gurowski had little peace, for Russia urgently and imperatively demanded his extradition. An existing convention between the two governments made this procedure legal. Count Adolph Heinrich von Arnim, the Prussian foreign minister, was willing to give up Gurowski, but King Friedrich William IV demurred, doubtlessly recalling his pleasant associations as a childhood playmate of the Count's half-sister Cecilia.[36] After several months, however, the Prussian government privately requested that Gurowski quietly leave the country in order that they might avoid the embarrassment of refusing to surrender him.[37]

Leaving Berlin, the Count made his way to Belgium, where he toured extensively and wrote a book containing his observations and impressions of that country.[38] During this time he was financed by his brother Ignatius, who lived off his wife, the Princess Isabella Ferdinanda of Spain. Gurowski made the most of the situation and settled down for a few months to a quiet life of luxury in the resort town of Spa, Belgium. Here he enjoyed mineral baths and made trips to visit Ignatius, a Brussels resident. But the calm did not last, for General Jan Nepomucen Umiński, prominent military leader of the November Insurrection living in exile at Spa, got word of his presence. The General publicly denounced the harried Count as traitor, thief, and scoundrel, and threatened to crack his skull with his cane if ever they met.[39]

Although the encounter did not materialize, the time had come to move again. The prospect seemed anything but pleasant, and Gurowski felt that a "hostile sharp wind drives continuously my lonesome barque into the ice cold regions of foreign lands out of the reach of those attached by blood or relations of friendship."[40] He removed himself briefly

36 Adam Gurowski, *The Turkish Question* (New York, 1854), 37; Carter, "Gurowski," *Atlantic Monthly*, Vol. XVIII, 626. The Count gratefully extended appreciation to Frederich William IV years later in a statement to the American press. Unidentified newspaper article, April 2, 1859, in Archives and Museum, Polish Roman Catholic Union of America.

37 Carter, "Gurowski," *Atlantic Monthly*, Vol. XVIII, 626.

38 Gurowski, *Eine Tour Durch Belgien im Jahre 1844: Aus dem Tagebuche.*

39 Janik, "Prądy Panslawistyczne i Rusofilskie w Okresie Wielkiez Emigracji," *Pamiętnik Literacki*, Vol. XXXI, 66.

to Heidelberg and to the scene of his student days. Then he was off again, this time to Switzerland and the resort town of Vevey on the Lake of Geneva. He busied himself with another lengthy travel book as he made his way about Switzerland, located a publisher at Lausanne, and dedicated the volume to his brother Nicholas. Doubtless the source of the Count's money at this time, Nicholas was nostalgically and affectionately told by him in the dedication that their "present separation could well be the last . . . . Down there, from the old manor of our father, you will love to follow and to know the impressions, the memories collected by a pilgrim thrust afar on foreign beaches."[41]

While in Switzerland, the Count wrote his brother Nicholas that he still believed in Russian Panslavism, even hinting that he still had faith in Czar Nicholas. During a recent stay at an abbey, he went on to say, he had requested prayers both for the Czar and for the entire royal family, as well as for the Gurowskis and their ancestors. Speaking with pride of his family background, he thought it "of some value to have behind oneself several centuries, a castle even if in ruins, and a name . . . . With such a heritage of the ages, I can act according to my convictions, as I am doing now."[42] Nicholas at last reciprocated and agreed to pay his wandering brother a small annual allowance from the income of his confiscated land, but these monies were seldom sent with regularity before or after the Count left Europe.[43]

In February, 1846, insurrection again flared in Poland. The Count, then in Munich, studied the uprising and published his opinions in a pamphlet. He stressed the hopelessness of the cause, pointing out that the peasants had been needlessly agitated to insurrection by radicals and emphasized once again his belief that the future of Poland lay with Russian Panslavism.[44] While in Munich, he formed a close and intimate

[40] Gurowski, *Eine Tour Durch Belgien im Jahre 1844: Aus dem Tagebuche,* 339.

[41] Adam Gurowski, *Impressions et Souvenirs: Promenade en Suisse en 1845* (Lausanne, 1846), 3–4.

[42] Quoted in Francew, "Adam hr. Gurowski w Polsce w Latach 1841–1844: Przyczynek do Jego Zyciorysu," *Pamiętnik Literacki,* Vol. XXXIV, 98.

[43] Carter, "Gurowski," *Atlantic Monthly,* Vol. XVIII, 626; Howe, *Reminiscences, 1819–1899,* 220.

[44] Adam Gurowski, *Die Letzten Ereignisse in den Drei Theilen des Alten Polens* (Munich, 1846).

friendship with the German writer Joseph von Görres, professor of history at the University of Munich and long an opponent of German reactionism.[45]

Italy beckoned, and Gurowski spent more than two years there in study, travel, and at various resorts. He passed through the Sardinian states and made his headquarters in Naples, all the while under police surveillance because of his political past. The cultural remains of ancient Rome appealed to his interests, and while in the city, he had several audiences with Pope Pius IX. The Count busied himself with what he hoped would be his life's contribution to knowledge, a multiple-volume study of Panslavism. In January, 1848, while living in the famous old abbey of Monte Cassino, he completed the first tome and dedicated it to the Panslavs, whom he described as "my friends and my enemies." A Florence printer brought out the book, entirely financed by Gurowski.[46]

When plans were well along on volume two, word reached the Count from Switzerland that the University of Bern needed a lecturer in political economy. He applied for the job because he was living in Italy, torn by political revolt, from which Switzerland offered a secure refuge. He also desired to be near his only daughter, who had married and was residing in Switzerland. The Bern post commenced in mid-October, 1848, the year most of Europe exploded in revolution. During the winter semester at the university, he lectured on current political economy. In the spring semester he treated both political economy and its history in his lectures. He thought himself in his element at the university and evidently enjoyed his academic work. The administrative authorities were not pleased, and when the term ended in the middle of August, 1849, the contract was not renewed.[47]

[45] Nevins and Thomas (eds.), *The Diary of George Templeton Strong: The Turbulent Fifties, 1850–1859,* 3 (January 5, 1850).

[46] Boston (weekly) *Museum,* May 31, June 14, 1851; Police Records, in State Archives, Turin, Italy; Gurowski, *Le Panslavism,* I.

[47] Patent for Gurowski's professorship at the University of Bern, in Gurowski Papers; Richard Feller, *Die Universität Bern, 1834–1934: Dargestellt im Auftrag der Unterrichtsdirektion des Kantons Bern und des Senats der Universität Bern* (Bern, 1935), 166; *Verzeichnis der Vorlesungen vom 15. Oktober 1848 bis 1. April 1849 an der Hochschule*

8

Again a wandering exile, Gurowski pondered his situation and decided to abandon the Old World. In a farewell letter in the Frankfort *Gazette,* he explained that he felt "obliged to seek asylum on America's humane soil . . . since justice is not to be expected on this planet . . . . Persecutors . . . have robbed me of all that is dear to man on earth."[48] The Count had a final visit with his daughter, but there could be no leave-taking of his son, then an officer in the Russian navy.[49]

Gurowski's decision was undoubtedly influenced by the unsuccessful outcome of the Continental revolutionary movements of 1848–49 as well as by his personal inability to adjust to the position at Bern. Although not a participant, he nevertheless sympathized with the revolutionary cause, having lost faith in autocracy. In a sense he shared the disappointments and frustrations of those who engineered, fought, and lost the revolutions, although he believed that rebellion had no place in Poland. Intellectually he belonged to the insurrections, which included radicalism, republicanism, a philosophy of progress, a cosmopolitanism that crossed national boundaries, and a program of national reforms. The defeat and despair that engulfed and prompted thousands of Europeans, especially Germans, to come to America in the wake of the revolutions also motivated his decision. Mere opportunism did not bring him. But like the Forty-eighters, he found new hope and bright prospects in his decision to leave Europe and the scenes of his frustrated past. When he first glimpsed the shores of America at New York City in November, 1849, he was probably the best educated and most interesting of the small group of Poles who had emigrated to the United States in the wake of the recent revolutions.[50]

Bern [Bern, 1848], 3; *Verzeichnis der Vorlesungen vom 8. April 1849 bis 15. August 1849 an der Hochschule Bern* [Bern, 1849], 3.

[48] Frankfort *Gazette,* October 8, 1849, in Bing, "Life of Gurowski," 148.

[49] Gurowski's autobiographical sketch, in author's possession; Boston (weekly) *Museum,* May 25, 1851; Carter, "Gurowski," *Atlantic Monthly,* Vol. XVIII, 626.

[50] Carl Wittke, *Refugees of Revolution: The German Forty-Eighters in America* (Philadelphia, 1952), 43–44, 79, 81.

CHAPTER III

NEW WORLD APPRENTICE

I

ON ARRIVAL IN AMERICA, Gurowski momentarily reflected on his status: "Now I am an exile, in search of reason, freedom, and true Democracy—obliged to begin a new life—a life of care, obliged to carve my way by the labor of the head or of the hands—may be to clear woods and carry the spade or the plough."[1] In the new land the aspirations of his youth were reinvigorated, and freedom, he mused, was his to use for the first time. Proud of his adopted country, he immediately applied for citizenship.[2]

For a while he lived a leisurely life in New York City with funds from his confiscated estate. He circulated freely in social and intellectual circles, where the aristocratic attorney George Templeton Strong found him an unusual foreigner in black moustache and blue glasses, "about the most entertaining man going ... despite the difficulties of his jargon of French and German and villainous English." Strong was impressed by his wide circle of distinguished acquaintants and labeled him "a man of catholic and comprehensive taste." Gurowski visited frequently in the home of Therese Robinson, where George Bancroft, William Cullen Bryant, and James Bayard Taylor gathered. Mrs. Robinson, in the limelight with her novel *Heloise,* thought Gurowski "interesting, highly intelligent, ... a man of a vast deal of information," and a superb conversationalist. The Count soon journeyed to Cooperstown, New York, to call on novelist James Fenimore Cooper, whom he had known in

[1] Gurowski's autobiographical sketch, in author's possession.

[2] Gurowski, *Russia As It Is,* xiii; Gurowski, *The Turkish Question,* 3; Gurowski, *A Year of the War,* title page; Gurowski to Abraham Lincoln, March 12, 1861, and January 21, 1863, in Robert Todd Lincoln Collection of the Papers of Abraham Lincoln, Library of Congress.

Paris. The visit must have been cordial and heated for, like the Count, Cooper was an aristocrat, preferred republics to monarchies, and enjoyed controversy.[3]

2

Harvard's intellectual atmosphere and the literary coterie which made Boston and the college famous soon attracted Gurowski. He went to Massachusetts in June, 1850, with the expectation of joining the Harvard faculty, and took up residence in Cambridge in a house near the college library.

After six months of hopeless effort, the Count received an invitation from Edward Everett, formerly governor of Massachusetts, minister to Great Britain, and more recently president of Harvard, to give in his home a series of six public lectures on Roman civil law. A printed announcement of the lectures sketched their content and gave as reference famous Harvard scholars. Although twenty or thirty persons, mostly students from Harvard Law School, attended the lectures, they were not a success. The Count handled the subject matter ably, but the topic itself was a handicap, for not even those interested in law found it impelling or vital. More of a hindrance was the lecturer's imperfect pronunciation and his odd mannerisms. His plentiful supply of English words had been learned almost wholly from books, and his accent overbore his points. His diction was made still harder to follow by his habitual use of German and French idioms.[4]

Gurowski could not live happily unless he was embroiled in a controversy, and the opportunity to engage in one soon presented itself. In another effort to obtain employment at Harvard, he attacked Francis Bowen, editor of the *North American Review* and nominee for the McLean professorship of history. Bowen had taken the unpopular stand of

[3] Nevins and Thomas (eds.), *The Diary of George Templeton Strong: The Turbulent Fifties, 1850–1859*, 2–3 (January 5, 1850); Therese Robinson to Julia Ward Howe, New York, April 27, 1850, in Gurowski Papers; James Fenimore Cooper (ed.), *Correspondence of James Fenimore-Cooper* (2 vols., New Haven, 1922), II, 640.

[4] Carter, "Gurowski," *Atlantic Monthly*, Vol. XVIII, 626–27; printed announcement of the lectures, in Gurowski Papers; Edward Lillie Pierce, *Memoir and Letters of Charles Sumner* (4 vols., London, 1878–93), IV, 128; Diary of Edward Everett, January 21, 1851, in Edward Everett Papers, Massachusetts Historical Society, Boston.

opposing the cause of Hungary and Louis Kossuth in their fight for independence from Austria. The editor, despite widespread criticism, maintained his ground and returned the fire in a scholarly article citing an array of authorities.[5]

Then Gurowski, with public opinion on his side, closed in for the kill through a carefully prepared open letter to the editor of the Boston *Transcript*. The crusty Count contended that Bowen's authorities were anti-Hungarian and unreliable. He explained that official Hungarian sources threw a different light on the revolution than did noted contemporary historians dealing with the subject. Then he clinched his argument:

> But, happily for the honor of what is loftiest in human nature, the views and sentiments cherished by the North American Review, are not those of the American people at large; not those of its most eminent men. Truth and justice have found once more a high-spirited avenger. The letter of the Honorable Daniel Webster . . . rendering justice to the tendencies of the Hungarian revolution and to its great and immortal chief, Kossuth; and speaking officially in the name of the American government, and of this great people, greater morally, even than materially, —takes just the opposite views . . . to those maintained, with such tenacity, by the editor of the North American Review.[6]

"Gurowski," Everett wrote in his diary, "engages in the crusade against Bowen with the insane wish to bring his name before the public as a candidate for the Historical Professorship." The Count won publicity but not the appointment. He and others, however, who opposed Bowen on his Hungarian stand prevented the *Review* editor from being elected to the McLean professorship.[7]

Some months later the Gurowski-Bowen feud threatened to take

[5] [Francis Bowen], "The Rebellion of the Slavonic, Wallachian, and German Hungarians Against the Magyars," *North American Review*, Vol. LXXII (January, 1851), 205–49; an earlier article by Bowen advancing the same thesis is "The War of Races in Hungary," *North American Review*, Vol. LXX (January, 1850), 78–136.

[6] Boston *Transcript*, January 4, 1851.

[7] Diary of Everett, January 4 and March 19, 1851, in Everett Papers; Ernest S. Bates, "Francis Bowen," in Allan Johnson and others (eds.), *Dictionary of American Biography* (22 vols., New York, 1928–58), II, 503; Samuel Eliot Morison, *Three Centuries of Harvard* (Cambridge, 1936), 290–93.

on a different aspect. On this occasion the Count appeared at the door of the reading room of Harvard's Lyceum Hall, wrapped in a huge German-made cloak with vest of bright red flannel. His head covering was a high, bell-shaped, broad-brimmed hat hung with a sky-blue veil to keep the sunshine from his eyes. On his nose sat the inevitable huge blue glasses equipped with side blinds.

He greeted journalist Robert Carter, vigorous opponent of Bowen on the Hungarian issue, and struck up a conversation on the problem. After Gurowski released several long volleys in loud but bad English, much to the dismay of nearby readers, a Bowen supporter, Professor Theophilus Parsons of the Harvard Law School, joined the conversation and disagreed with Gurowski's opinions. The Count flared up in a rage and finally challenged the Professor to settle the controversy with pistols or swords. The indignant Professor declined, and Gurowski, puzzled at a gentleman's refusal, made a quick withdrawal, asking Carter to explain the Professor's behavior.[8]

Following this incident, Carter often visited Gurowski in his lodgings. The Count littered his well-furnished second-floor sitting room and bedroom with papers, books, clothing, and other items. A visit with the voluble and argumentative European, according to Carter, was an unusual and sometimes astonishing experience. On one occasion the pair discussed a point of medieval history on which Carter knew very little, but took a positive stand for the purpose of fathoming Gurowski's knowledge. The argument raged for hours; when Carter left, the question still remained unsettled. Early the following afternoon he called again, and when he knocked, the Count shouted, "Come in," and retreated into his bedroom. Exposing only his head until he saw that the caller was Carter, he returned to the sitting room, "absolutely in a state of nature. He had not even his spectacles on. In his hand he held a pair of drawers, which he had apparently been about to assume when I arrived," Carter noted. "Shaking this garment vehemently with one hand, while with the other he gave me a cigar, he broke out at once in a

---

[8] Carter, "Gurowski," *Atlantic Monthly,* Vol. XVIII, 628–29. A slightly different version of the duel challenge is in an unidentified newspaper clipping dated "Boston, Thursday, July 11," in Gurowski Papers.

torrent of argument on the topic of the preceding day. I made no reply; but at the first pause suggested that he had better dress himself. To this he paid no attention, but stamped around the room, continuing his argument with his usual vehemence and volubility."

Half an hour later someone knocked. Gurowski bellowed, "Come in!" A woman-servant opened the door, but instantly withdrew; Carter turned the key and again implored the Count to dress. He kept on with his argument, still clutching his drawers. Soon another rattled on the door. "It is Desor," said the Count, "I know his knock; let him in." Eduard Desor, a Swiss geologist and zoologist who lived nearby, had also been involved in a dispute with Gurowski, who immediately took it up. Desor did not care to argue, and soon walked out. Gurowski returned to his medieval argument, but Carter warned that he too would depart unless he dressed himself. The Count unwillingly agreed and entered his bedroom. Periodically, however, he would pop out to argue a fresh point that had come to mind. Three hours later the Count was partly clothed. Announcement of dinner closed the discussion, and he hastily finished dressing.[9]

3

Gurowski's favored Harvard haunt was the college library, and during his residence in Cambridge he frequently used it. He was a familiar sight to many a professor and student as he studied Roman law in preparation for his lectures and as the first step toward a book on the subject. He also read in English history and philosophy, but stayed clear of New World literature, believing it nonexistent, until near the end of his Cambridge residence, when he busied himself with Nathaniel Hawthorne's *Scarlet Letter*.[10]

Of those in the Harvard community who understood and endured Gurowski, the most faithful was Henry Wadsworth Longfellow, professor of modern languages. The poet himself, like the Count, had studied at the University of Heidelberg, knew much of European life

[9] Carter, "Gurowski," *Atlantic Monthly,* Vol. XVIII, 630.
[10] Harvard College Library list of books used by Gurowski, in Harvard University Archives, Cambridge, Massachusetts.

and customs, and admired republican government. Gurowski came often to Longfellow's dwelling, the Craigie House, along with other unusual and distinguished Europeans and Americans. There he always found warm fellowship and encouragement. The friendship commenced one summer evening on a street, where Longfellow met him strolling "in a slouched straw hat, loose sack and trousers, . . . white buckskin shoes tied with white strings . . . and a pair of blue spectacles with sidelights," and asked him home to smoke a cigar on the porch.[11]

Then the Count received invitations to dine at the Longfellow table. On one occasion he appeared for lunch, and to the dismay of his indulgent host, "stayed all the afternoon, and to tea,—and did not go away till eleven at night! We all feel as if a huge garden-roller had gone over us." Next morning before sunrise, when Longfellow was breakfasting by candlelight, the Count called and left a note at the door. "Luckily," Longfellow confessed, "he did not demand admission." As if to make himself more disagreeable, Gurowski called two mornings later, before the poet was dressed, and asked whether his note had been received. "The aspect of things," thought Longfellow, "grows serious. These early hours are precious. If they too are invaded, what will become of me?"

Nevertheless, Longfellow had to see much of the Count during the months ahead, when teaching duties rested a heavy hand on the poet's lyre. Gurowski gave little or no consideration to Longfellow's need for time, and, with other cigar-smoking friends, often turned his study into a village tavern over talk of politics and the corruption of European society, much to the poet's annoyance. The Count usually led the discussions "like an old rake who has lost all faith in virtue."[12] On such occasions Gurowski associated with Cornelius Conway Felton, professor of Greek at Harvard; James Russell Lowell, the antislavery poet; and Charles Sumner, sometime lecturer in the Harvard Law School and now on the threshold of a career in the United States Senate. Theodore

[11] Samuel Longfellow (ed.), *Life of Henry Wadsworth Longfellow: With Extracts from his Journals and Correspondence* (3 vols., Boston, 1891), II, 183–84 (journal, July 1, 1850).

[12] *Ibid.*, 196–97 (journal, December 15, 16, and 18, 1850), 201 (journal, January 26, 1851).

Parker, noted Unitarian clergyman, whose abolitionism and extensive library Gurowski admired more than his sermons, often joined the group.[13]

The favor with which Boston and Cambridge had received Gurowski into its elite circles soon evaporated. His eccentric temper and manner, his rough and unsparing criticism of men and events alienated one friend after another. The Count's dogmatic radicalism was leveled without qualification at slavery and its Northern supporters at the moment when Massachusetts was in the midst of a conservative pro-slavery reaction over its support of the Fugitive Slave Law of 1850. He could not be silenced; he would not be put down. In the heart of the area where many considered Daniel Webster's word law, Gurowski declared in rebellious phrases that he could read and interpret the Constitution as well as Webster: "I say that the Fugitive Slave Law is unconstitutional,—is an outrage and an imposition of which you will soon be ashamed. It is a disgrace to humanity and to your republicanism and Mr. Webster should be hung for advocating it. He is a humbug or an ass, an ass if he believes such an infamous law to be constitutional; and if he does not believe it, he is a humbug and a scoundrel for advocating it." Beacon Street and Harvard's intellectuals were amazed at such outbursts.[14]

The small sum of money Gurowski had brought from Europe dwindled rapidly. With no immediate prospect of another remittance from his brother Nicholas, he had to look for gainful employment by early spring, 1851. The kindly Longfellow offered him money, but Gurowski declined with "great delicacy of feeling." He explained to the poet that in accepting financial help he would have "lost all ease in . . . relations with you, and this has more than price, more than the incon-

[13] *Ibid.*, 188 (journal, August 23, 1850), 202 (journal, February 9, 1851), 204 (journal, March 16, 1851); Longfellow's manuscript journal (March 29, April 12, May 4 and 6, 1851), in Henry Wadsworth Longfellow Papers, Craigie House, Cambridge, Massachusetts; Adam Gurowski, *America and Europe* (New York, 1857), 307–308.

[14] Carter, "Gurowski," *Atlantic Monthly*, Vol. XVIII, 627–28; Gurowski's anti-slavery actions and opinions are treated at length in Chapter XI; Diary of Everett, February 8, 1851, in Everett Papers.

venience of moving the earth." On the following morning the stormy petrel met Edward Everett on the street and pointed out that he did not eat a warm dinner as often as once a week because he could not afford the expense.[15]

Unknown to his friends, Gurowski found work as laborer in the horticultural gardens of Charles M. Hovey, originator of the first large strawberry in the United States. Several days after the beginning of his employment, Carter called at Gurowski's apartment about dark, as the Count returned from work, fatigued, dirty, and with blistered hands. When Carter and other friends told him that manual employment was unsuited to his blood and education, he replied proudly that labor could never degrade a Gurowski.[16]

Carter and Longfellow thought it time to intervene. They arranged with the editor of the Boston *Museum,* a flourishing weekly literary journal, to have Gurowski write an article on European life in each issue for a fee of ten dollars. The editors of the Boston *Transcript* considered the *Museum* fortunate to obtain the services of a writer "so well informed" on Europe's political and social problems, and the *Museum* itself lauded the Count as unusually competent for the task, since he could write on issues and conditions which were as sealed books to others. The articles were on random topics and appeared under the general title of "Sketches of Europe." Carter revised the garbled English of the exile's essays and kept him at the task for two months.[17]

[15] Longfellow's manuscript journal, March 29, 1851, in Longfellow Papers; Longfellow (ed.), *Life of Henry Wadsworth Longfellow,* II, 205 (journal, March 31, 1851); Gurowski to Longfellow, Monday morning [March 31, 1851], in Longfellow Papers; Diary of Everett, April 1, 1851, in Everett Papers.

[16] Carter, "Gurowski," *Atlantic Monthly,* Vol. XVIII, 630–31; "Nebulae," *Galaxy,* Vol. I, 269; Howe, *Reminiscences, 1819–1899,* 220.

[17] Longfellow (ed.), *Life of Henry Wadsworth Longfellow,* II, 205 (journal, April 3, 1851); Boston *Transcript,* quoted in Boston (weekly) *Museum,* May 3, 1851; *ibid.,* May 10, 1851; Carter, "Gurowski," *Atlantic Monthly,* Vol. XVIII, 631. Gurowski's articles in the Boston *Museum* were titled "Russia—The Peasantry," April 26, 1851; "The Princess Christian di Belgiojoso," May 3, 1851; "Affairs of Germany," May 10, 1851; "The Courts of Europe and their Everyday Life," May 17, 1851; "Naples," May 31, 1851; "French Journalism," June 7, 1851; "Pope Pius IX," June 14, 1851; "Joseph Mazzini," June 28, 1851.

4

Then the Count went to the resort town of Newport, Rhode Island, to pamper his poor health and to associate with Americans of the upper social stratum, who, he believed, regarded a summer's visit to Newport as the crowning event of their civilization. Here he became a favorite of humanitarian Samuel Gridley Howe and his wife, Julia Ward Howe, and spent much time with the couple at their Cliff House. Long a champion of handicapped peoples and individuals, Howe had served as surgeon and soldier in the Greek War for Independence, had assisted Polish refugees in Prussia on the collapse of the November Insurrection, and currently operated in Boston the Perkins Institution for the Blind. The Count's independence of spirit, his antislavery convictions, and probably his injured eye, apart from the common denominators in their background, won Howe's affection and sympathy. Mrs. Howe, soon to achieve distinction as author and reformer, agreed with Gurowski's abolitionist conviction, admired his literary ability, and understood his eccentricities. Gurowski later considered her an able author earmarked by both a philosophical and poetic spirit.[18] The Count also whiled away congenial hours in the company of Charles Sumner and other Boston friends on vacation, but a Newport resident concluded he could not avoid the man even in his own home and on one occasion took refuge in the loft of his barn and drew the ladder up after him.[19]

At Newport, however, a berth on the Harvard faculty seemed to Gurowski more elusive than ever. Depressed and ill with dysentery and gout, he called on Longfellow, Felton, and Everett to use their influence in securing a social studies teaching position in the Smithsonian Institution at Washington, since it was "out of the question of finding something like an intellectual occupation . . . at Cambridge, Boston, or Massachusetts." In the past Everett had talked casually with the Count about teaching in the Smithsonian, and now he was called on to send

[18] Carter, "Gurowski," *Atlantic Monthly,* Vol. XVIII, 631; Boston (weekly) *Museum,* June 28, 1851; Howe, *Reminiscences, 1819–1899,* 221; Gurowski, *America and Europe,* 389.

[19] Longfellow's manuscript journal, July 6, 1851, in Longfellow Papers; Howe, *Reminiscences, 1819–1899,* 222.

a letter of recommendation to Joseph Henry, the director. Gurowski hoped he would be called on to teach a course on primitive races, a popular theme. Perhaps, the Count added, "the course which shamed me in Boston would be good in Washington."[20]

Gurowski's three musketeers took the matter up immediately, although with little enthusiasm. Everett said that he would write to Henry if Longfellow and Felton would pass on the Count's English and mannerisms. The recommendations to Henry were then made, but brought a flat refusal; the reason, as Gurowski was told, was Henry's haughty independence of all except his governmental superiors. In the meantime the Count had received professional offers from Georgetown University, Washington, D.C., and Holy Cross College, Worcester, Massachusetts, both operated by Jesuits. These opportunities were repugnant to Gurowski because of the Catholic affiliation of the two schools, and in despair he pleaded with Longfellow: "My dear Excelsior, poet with generous heart, think a little for me and find a way out, an expedient, because everything is so black in my soul, my heart, and my intelligence that I do not dare to dwell on it."[21]

Returning to Cambridge, Gurowski received little encouragement from close friends of previous times, and even Longfellow probably suggested a return to Europe. The usual invitations to dine and visit came no more. The Count's thoughts turned to earlier months, when he had sat at the festive board of Felton, whose hospitality and love of good food was almost Homeric, or when he had passed pleasant hours at the home of Everett, or better still, those incomparable afternoons and evenings at Longfellow's, where all his world seemed to gather. He also missed Lowell and the warmth of his home, for the poet was traveling in Europe. Even Carter proved elusive. No alternative appeared other than taking permanent leave of Cambridge, perhaps even of the United States.[22]

[20] Gurowski to Longfellow, October 6, 1851, in Longfellow Papers.

[21] Everett to Felton, October 8, 1851, in Everett Papers; Gurowski to Longfellow, October 21, 1851, in Longfellow Papers.

[22] Longfellow's manuscript journal, October 24 and November 20, 1851, in Longfellow Papers; Gurowski, *America and Europe*, 377; Everett's Diary, February 8 and

To avoid the emotional strain of face-to-face good-byes with Felton and Longfellow, Gurowski wrote each a lengthy farewell letter. He expressed lavish appreciation for their many kindnesses, and concluded by explaining that, if he "ever desired heartily to be able to cast anchor, to penetrate into the soil, to establish myself for life, it was here in the midst of a people and civilization which everything taken into consideration is the best that I have found."[23]

Years later, during the Civil War, the Count would laud Massachusetts and all New England for furnishing sizable numbers of volunteers, both rich and poor, for the Union armies. Men and women of that region and especially of Massachusetts, he maintained, followed in the wake of the federal armies to help provide for the Negro refugees and poor whites, to establish schools for both races, and in general to reorganize society.[24] New England was to him the brains, heart, and conscience of the nation, and was made up of laborious, intelligent, hardworking, and daring common people: "When I say New England, I think of New Englanders, who with their brains and with their hearts touch everything, embrace and understand everything, shape and mould everything, who organize, create townships, cities, communities, and republics. . . . New England is the goal of humanity."[25]

Harvard and its graduates also interested the Count. When historian Jared Sparks resigned the presidency in 1853, Gurowski was angered that James Walker and not Felton succeeded to the post, since the Count had for some time featured his friend in that position, which in 1860 finally became his. The Harvard graduate of the 1850's and the 1860's did not impress Gurowski as a man qualified to meet the needs of his environment. Emphasis on classical education produced conceit, dried

---

May 25, 1851, in Everett Papers; Gurowski to James Russell Lowell, July 8, 1851, in James Russell Lowell Papers, Houghton Library, Harvard University.

[23] Gurowski to Longfellow, [dated by Longfellow, November 27, 1851], in Longfellow Papers. Much the same statement appears in Gurowski's letter to Felton. [November 27, 1851], in Cornelius Conway Felton Papers, Houghton Library, Harvard University.

[24] *Diary*, II, 280–81 (July 22, 1863), 327 (September 19, 1863), III, 379–80 (October 23, 1864).

[25] *Diary*, III, 332–33 (September 4, 1864); see also Gurowski, *America and Europe,* 297–98, and Gurowski to Andrew, November 5, 1863, in Andrew Papers.

up hearts and minds, and left the student with superficial information. Never, Gurowski continued, had he "met with such misproducts of sham learning and of sham civilization." Harvard was the "special and exclusive soil from which luxuriantly grow up these parasites of the human mind and intellect."[26]

His friendship with Felton, Longfellow, and Lowell remained unbelievably steadfast. Their frequent correspondence is a record of mutual fellowship and common interests. Library chatter was their usual theme, and when Gurowski or one of the Cambridge group wrote a book, mutually congratulatory letters inevitably followed. On one occasion, the Count requested that Lowell send a volume from the Harvard College Library. An intimate personal element was another aspect of the relationship. Gurowski never failed to send his sentiments in letters to the families and to express appreciation for many generous favors of the past. "Adieu from my heart, my dear poet, for all the friendly things in your last letter. My warm and sincere respects to Mrs. Longfellow and I embrace the children." In true Old World spirit he wrote Felton: "I kiss Mrs. Felton's hand."[27]

Solicitous replies came to the Count inquiring of his activities and his somewhat precarious health. "But," Longfellow wrote inquiringly, "have you all you need? Let me know if I can contribute in any way to your comfort or your cure."[28] Moments were not infrequent in the future when the exile longed to return to Cambridge and its friendly firesides, but time did not bring so much as a single visit. The sting of Gurowski's criticism over the years often hurt other friends and acquaintances, but for Felton, Longfellow, and Lowell he had only praise and understanding.

5

In late November, 1851, Gurowski retreated to New York City, where he soon found employment on the editorial staff of Horace Gree-

---

[26] Longfellow to Gurowski, November 30, 1852, in author's possession; Gurowski to Longfellow, February 27, 1853, in Longfellow Papers; *Diary*, III, 233 (May 19, 1864).

[27] Gurowski to Lowell, May 19, 1857, in Lowell Papers; Gurowski to Longfellow, [1858], in Longfellow Papers; Gurowski to Felton, December 16, 1859, in Felton Papers.

[28] Longfellow to Gurowski, November 30, 1852, in author's possession.

ley's *Tribune*. He wrote primarily on foreign politics and frequently on his favorite theme, the advocacy of Russia's Slavic leadership. Charles T. Congdon, Greeley's assistant, translated many of the illegible articles the Count wrote in French and corrected those in English, as did James S. Pike, the *Tribune's* associate editor and Washington correspondent.[29] The European was in his element among the able and considerate staff of this important daily, and for nearly a decade he spent many a pleasant hour in the company of Pike, Charles A. Dana, managing editor, George Ripley, literary critic, and William H. Fry, music editor. The Count's relations were never intimate with Greeley himself, whose personality he did not understand or trust. Also Gurowski borrowed from the editor three hundred dollars, which was probably never repaid, a situation that did not make for the best of relations. Moreover, Greeley sometimes changed the meanings of Gurowski's articles, with the Count's ensuing rage inevitably punctuated by a "Damn him!"[30]

The *Tribune* staff, with Fry leading the sport, liked nothing quite so much as occasionally to get Gurowski into a frenzy. A disrespectful or contradictory remark concerning his Panslavic ideas would be made and cause him to explode in a salvo of broken English, while he walked, stamped with his great boots, and waved his arms. Fry's knowing smile seemed not to appease him and evidently passed unnoticed. When he calmed somewhat, thinking the argument won, Fry or another tormentor would disagree once more with but several words, and the harangue would commence again. Eventually the staff would drift away, and Gurowski would conclude he had convinced his listeners.[31]

While Gurowski worked for the *Tribune,* it approached its peak of national influence, which far surpassed that of any rival at the eve of

---

[29] Congdon, *Reminiscences of a Journalist*, 237; Gurowski to Pike, June 14, 1854, in Pike, *First Blows of the Civil War,* 254. The Count's rhetorical difficulties in writing are further explained in Gurowski to W. T. Robinson, Tuesday, no date, in bequest of E. J. Wendell, Houghton Library, Harvard University, and in "Nebulae," *Galaxy*, Vol I, 269.

[30] Gurowski to Horace Greeley, October 1, 1861, in Horace Greeley Papers, New York Public Library, New York City; Gurowski to Greeley, no date, in *ibid.;* William Harlan Hale, *Horace Greeley: Voice of the People* (New York, 1950), 187, 269–70; Waters, *Career and Conversation of John Swinton,* 15.

[31] Congdon, *Reminiscences of a Journalist,* 238.

the Civil War. Although its total circulation numbered but slightly over 287,000, it was in many parts of the North a political bible. By 1854 its staff consisted of eighteen foreign correspondents, twenty American correspondents, fourteen local reporters, and a financial unit in addition to its administrative officers.

During the summer of 1854, Greeley sent Gurowski as part of a contingent of the *Tribune* staff to the Middle West to sound out and shape public opinion against Stephen A. Douglas' Kansas-Nebraska act. He traveled with Dana and other colleagues as far west as Rock Island, Illinois, where he enjoyed a view of the Mississippi, but because of his health, the crowded steamers, and "some other reasons peculiar to an old and spoiled European," he left the party and returned to New York by way of Niagara Falls and Montreal. At Chicago he found himself in mud, cold, and rain, as he talked squatter sovereignty with the "thick-soled, ragwearing part of the population, mostly strong Democrats." Gurowski fathomed a strong pro-Douglas sentiment, based on the idea that the act recognized the authority of the people. He recommended that the *Tribune* "destroy this fallacy" by several impressive editorials, and thereby cause the country papers to fall in line with Greeley's mouthpiece, before Douglas' squatter sovereignty program became more deeply implanted in the conviction of the voters.

On the same theme the Count conversed for several hours in a Chicago hotel lobby with William Alexander Richardson, the Democratic successor to Douglas' seat in the House of Representatives. Gurowski attempted to argue him away from squatter sovereignty and Douglas. At a heated point in the discussion, Richardson declared that if the final issue should be between the slave South and the free North, he would join the South. Gurowski noticed that during the twenty-four-hour period he observed and talked with Richardson, very few people spoke to the congressman except to assail his support of the Kansas-Nebraska act.[32]

Another *Tribune* excursion took Gurowski up the Hudson River to the United States Military Academy at West Point. He spent some

---

[32] Gurowski to Pike, June 8, 1854, in Pike, *First Blows of the Civil War,* 253–54.

time there in the company of Robert E. Lee, superintendent, and William Henry Talbot Walker and William Joseph Hardee, both instructors. These future military leaders of the Confederacy confided to him their opinion that Winfield Scott, general in chief of the army, was without exceptional talents and that there were many men of equal ability in every Continental army.[33]

6

But Russia and other foreign issues were of much greater interest to Gurowski while he worked with the *Tribune*. His many articles, unsigned and usually so revised as to be almost unidentifiable, began to establish his reputation among his journalistic colleagues. He came to be respected even more by his associates because of his book and two pamphlets published during the fifties, dealing with Russia and the Crimean War. By the middle of that decade the *Tribune's* management considered him its leading authority on Russian and Slavic affairs. When Greeley's paper was accused of being pro-Russian, Dana, the managing editor, without betraying Gurowski, replied emphatically that no Russian had ever written a line for the paper or had ever been on the staff. Yet by 1855 it had generally become known in New York literary circles that the Count responsible for shaping and promoting the *Tribune's* sympathetic point of view toward the czar's empire.[34]

Gurowski retorted with an emphatic *no* when the Paris correspondent of the *Tribune* reported in 1854 that Russia would soon cede Alaska to the United States. The Count, then at a resort in Newport, regretted that he was away from his office and unable to squelch this periodic rumor. He was sorry the *Tribune* had made this blunder and felt certain that the managing editor, whom he had warned against this error, would react in the same way. He explained to a colleague that the Russian legation considered the whole affair a hoax. In Newport he became increasingly impatient over people's innumerable questions concerning the alleged cession, and to stave off further questions, he prepared a brief

[33] *Diary*, I, 80 (August, 1861); Gurowski to Miss Lynch, October 8, 1854, Unclassified Manuscripts, Lincoln National Life Foundation, Fort Wayne, Indiana.

[34] New York *Tribune*, April 23, 1854; N. Rjasanoff (ed.), *Gesammelte Schriften von Karl Marx und Friedrich Engels 1852 bis 1862* (2 vols., Stuttgart, 1920), I, p. XLII.

article for the local newspaper, positively denying the story. "Everybody will find out," the Count added with no little egotism, "that I gave the information, as otherwise an insignificant village paper would not have dared to contradict several of the biggest guns of the American press."[35] Said the Newport *News:*

> We have the most authoritative reasons in the world to deny absolutely the wide spread rumor about a proposition said to have been made to our administration in Washington, concerning the cession of Russian territories extending along the north western coast of the Pacific, of which the establishment at Sitka forms the knot.—Such a proposition was neither made nor thought of by the Russian legation in this country; and well-informed persons consider it as a hoax invented in England and readily swallowed by the press in America. We doubt that this matter was for a moment seriously considered in St. Petersburg, as it is wholly contrary to the character of the Russian Government and of the Czar. Such a cessation of territories made by him would be an avowal of a despairing condition of affairs on his side, a condition to which until yet he is not driven, as show the last accounts from Europe. Once more, whatever may be said to the contrary, the whole affair is a pure invention, and soon the public will find it so likewise.[36]

Gurowski's prominence as a Russian authority had approached its peak several months earlier with the publication of *Russia As It Is,* which appeared when the Crimean War assumed threatening proportions. In this conflict, Turkey, France, Great Britain, and Sardinia had allied against Russia to prevent her from assuming leadership in southeastern Europe and especially from conquering Turkey. The book sold well, because Russia was in the news, and because it dared predict the Crimean War's outcome. At one dollar a copy, the 312-page publication went through three American editions in the first year, and was reprinted in Great Britain under the title *Russia and Its People.* The volume was one of many books and pamphlets appearing at the time on Russia and Turkey. A reviewer declared it the most able and original of the lot, abounding "in rare and valuable information, in comprehensive gen-

[35] Gurowski to Pike, July 30, 1854, in Pike, *First Blows of the Civil War,* 256.

[36] Newport *News,* July 31, 1854. In 1867, the year following Gurowski's death, the United States purchased Alaska from Russia.

eral statements, and in copious statistical accounts of the resources of Russia." The style he considered clear and vigorous, and its author "a thinker of great depth and penetration, profoundly versed in the civil and military affairs of Europe." Czar Nicholas also liked the book, and he requested one of his staff to thank the Count for his favorable account of Russia.[37]

Gurowski's study resulted from years of scholarly research, observation, and reflection, and was not a hastily written potboiler. The ideas and themes of the Count's volume had long been his topic of conversation in the drawing room of the New York home of George Templeton Strong, who became thoroughly bored by Russian Panslavism and Turkey.[38] Gurowski drew heavily on his earlier studies published in Europe in preparing the book.

It treated Russian institutions from the standpoint of economics, government, history, sociology, and culture in a critical attempt to evaluate and point out national features and characteristics. The Count contended that Russia's people were judged externally, whereas its citizenry and not its government were the real measure of its worth. The czaristic system arose from unavoidable necessity and, although obsolete, at times had benefited Russia. Beyond the autocracy of czardom, there existed in Russia a people with a destiny reaching beyond the curtain that shrouded it. Not the existing government, not the aristocracy, but the uncultured and uneducated lower classes, contained the promise of the future. The people would eventually change Russia's autocracy for democracy and ultimately prevail throughout Asia.

Predicting Russia's future in detail, Gurowski maintained that her destinies, as well as those of all Slavs, pointed towards Asia. Force would be necessary to achieve the goal, but with Europe there would be no hostility, since her aspirations were not in that direction. Although the des-

---

[37] *Harper's New Monthly Magazine,* Vol. IX (June, 1854), 137; Count [?] to Gurowski, November 14/26, 1854, in Gurowski Papers. The volume was published by the prominent New York firm of D. Appleton and Company. Gurowski's relationship with this concern cannot be traced because of two serious fires, which destroyed most of its records. The book's favorable reception is noted in Gouverneur, *As I Remember,* 248.

[38] Nevins and Thomas (eds.), *The Diary of George Templeton Strong: The Turbulent Fifties, 1850–1859,* 169 (April 17, 1854).

potism of czarism momentarily thwarted expansion into Asia, the impulse of the people toward that continent would be vigorous because of population growth. Only Russia and the Slavs could fulfill the mission of stirring the solitudes of Asia to civilization. "To electrify these regions," said the Count, "an uninterrupted contact and friction, exchange and excitation are absolutely necessary. . . . Those instructed . . . with this mission ought to be conterminous . . . with the East. This is the case with the Slavi, and principally the Russians. . . . An active mass is to press against an inert one. Such a labor can in nowise be accomplished by scattered commercial factories, not even by religious or political missionaries: but only by the concentrated activity of a mighty people."

Focusing his attention on Turkey, Gurowski prognosticated that the Crescent was rapidly approaching its end. In time the Russian flag would wave in Constantinople. For more than a hundred years, Russia had penetrated closer and closer. Turkey could not avert her doom, since she did not embody the fundamental principles of modern civilization "which cannot justly be named otherwise than Christian."

But Russia, the Count continued, would face complications when she acquired Constantinople and its Turkish dependencies. Turkey would not be governed as an independent state of Russia but as an integral part of one empire. The Russian court, the cold and misty capital of St. Petersburg itself, would be attracted by the unrivaled beauty of the Bosphorus and transplanted to Constantinople. If this were done, the heart of Russia would slip from the grasp of the czars, and the institution itself would collapse. The people of Russia, however, would find in Constantinople a mighty opening valve, for through this channel the nation would be connected with Europe and the world, for the first time, both commercially and culturally. Western ideas would stimulate the empire, and the masses would no longer be isolated and suspicious of everything foreign. Through the gateway of Constantinople, Russia would receive the cultural, educational, and economic nourishment and momentum to lead them to their destiny in Asia.[39]

The very month Gurowski completed his *Russia As It Is,* England and France threw in their lot with Turkey. This was the impulse the

[39] Gurowski, *Russia As It Is,* 268–71, 274–77, 279–87.

Count needed, combined with his rabid Anglophobia, to take up vigorously the cause of Russia in a pamphlet of forty-three pages titled *The Turkish Question.* Echoing the theme of his book, he charged England and France, but especially England, with supporting a reckless minority in oppressing the majority. He believed it consistent with England's national character, which he considered treacherous and hypocritical, that she should become knight-errant of the Turks.

The Count predicted that, doomed by her history and Darwinism, the Crescent would be shattered: "Whatever in the realm of nature shrinks and can exist no longer by its own essence . . . dies out, dissolves to make room for or nourish new creations. The process of history is similar . . . . As long as the Ottomans breathed even a ferocious but strong spirit, history was on their side. In the present issue . . . —admitting that both parties are barbarians—the one is increasing, growing, expanding and tending onward; the other diminishing, withering, and sinking down both morally and physically."[40]

Gurowski observed strong pro-Turkish sentiment among congressional leaders. Believing that his pamphlet would help them to see the other side of the problem, he sent copies to his friend, Charles Sumner, to William H. Seward, and others. The Count commanded Sumner not to go "sympathetically crazy" over the Turks.[41]

Early in 1855 the resolute Pole published a second pamphlet on the Crimean conflict, *A Year of the War,* selling at thirty-eight cents. In its 116 pages he gloated over the accuracy of the predictions in his earlier pamphlet and credited his prognosis to correct interpretation of historical facts. He prophesied again that Russia would win, because history supported her and the future of the Slavs depended on her. Jumping to Russia's defense, he wrote that Russia had been forced into war, else she would not have been so unprepared to meet the challenge. England and France, on the other hand, had allied against Russia for purposes of power. Without Russia acting as a buffer and guardian of the weaker states of Europe, they would fall prey to the "arrogant, over-

[40] Gurowski, *The Turkish Question,* 18, 25, 42–43.
[41] Gurowski to Sumner, April 27, 1854, in Sumner Papers.

whelming behavior" of England. Moreover, Russia never encroached on Europe and, consequently, never disturbed its balance of power system. Thus possession of Constantinople would not necessarily be dangerous to the rest of Europe.[42]

Despite Gurowski's cheering for Russian success, the conflict drifted into a stalemate, and Russian defenses at Sebastopol finally collapsed after a siege of eleven months. Russia was worsted in the treaty that closed the war and compromised its issues. The powers of Europe admitted Turkey to their great-nation club and promised to respect her independence and boundaries. The Count's Darwinian idea that a weak power must fall before a stronger remained unchanged, however, as evidenced by his opinions on the Polish Insurrection of 1863 and the American Civil War.

His efforts in Russia's behalf in *Tribune* columns and in his three publications were significant in shaping public opinion in America and maintaining the friendship of the United States and Russia, which had originated in mutual hatred of England. The exile's pro-Russian writings, especially his *Tribune* articles, were regularly translated and reprinted in journals of St. Petersburg and Moscow during the Crimean War.[43]

7

At this period, one of Greeley's corps of foreign correspondents was Prussian socialist Karl Marx, living in a hovel in London's Soho district. The Count watched the weekly letters of the author of the *Communist Manifesto* with special interest as they arrived at the *Tribune* office, since they were often concerned with Russia and the Slavs. He at first read and criticized with meticulous care the Marx essays, often prepared with the assistance of Friedrich Engels. Then he ventured even further in his treatment of Marx during the absence of Greeley in Europe, in the West, and in Washington in 1855–56. Dana, nominally the *Tribune*

---

[42] Gurowski, *A Year of the War,* 10, 20–21, 25, 26, 31, 58, 109.

[43] Bing, "Life of Gurowski," Pt. 2, p. 180, in Gurowski Papers; Frank A. Golder, "Russian-American Relations During the Crimean War," *American Historical Review,* Vol. XXXI (April, 1926), 462–76.

managing editor, took over Greeley's work during this period and con-trolled the newspaper's opinions and points of view.[44]

The influence Gurowski exercised over Dana came into action when Marx and Engels submitted the first two of a series of nine articles on Panslavism. *Tribune* contributions of Marx and Engels were sometimes submitted to Continental journals for simultaneous publication, and these appeared also in *Neue Oder-Zeitung*.[45] Exclusively the work of Engels, they painted Russian Panslavism as a menace to Europe, dedi-cated to war against Germanic peoples who controlled Turkey, Hungary, and a large part of Germany. Thus Europe could either submit to the Slavic impact or destroy Russia. Cited as proof was Czar Alexander II's statement that, if Austria allied herself with the West or committed an overt act of hostility against Russia during the Crimean conflict, he would place himself at the head of the Panslavic movement. With a show of intense German nationalism, Engels argued that Austria had discovered Panslavism, for the Russians were too barbaric to originate the concept.

Gurowski rewrote the two Engels articles, including additions, omissions, and some reinterpretation before they appeared in the *Trib-une*.[46] Czar Alexander's announcement concerning Austria was calmly accepted as a new turn in Panslavism, and the threatened subjugation of Europe by Russian-led Slavs regarded as a matter of course. Gurowski boldly inserted his own philosophy of Panslavism and complimented himself and the Czar in a paragraph of Engel's second article:

> Panslavism as a political theory has had its most lucid and philosophic expression in the writings of Count Gurowski. But that learned and distinguished publicist, while regarding Russia as the natural pivot around which the destinies of the numerous and vigorous branch of the human family can alone find a large historical development, did not

[44] Hale, *Horace Greeley: Voice of the People*, 154–55; Rjasanoff (ed.), *Gesammelte Schriften von Karl Marx and Friedrich Engels 1852 bis 1862*, I, p. XLVII; James Harrison Wilson, *The Life of Charles A. Dana* (New York, 1907), 141–48.

[45] *Neue Oder-Zeitung*, April 21 and 24, 1855. These articles are translated in full in Paul W. Blackstock and Bert F. Hoselitz (eds.), *The Russian Menace to Europe: A Collection of Articles, Speeches, Letters and News Dispatches by Karl Marx and Friedrich Engels* (Glencoe, Illinois, 1952), 84–90.

[46] New York *Tribune*, May 5, 1855, "The European Struggle," and May 7, 1855, "Austria's Weakness."

conceive of Panslavism as a league against Europe and European civilization. In his view the legitimate outlet for the expansive force of Slavonic energies was Asia. As compared with the stagnant desolation of that old continent, Russia is a civilizing power, and her contact could not be other than beneficial. This manly and imposing generalization has, however, not been accepted by all the inferior minds which have adopted its fundamental idea. Panslavism has assumed a variety of aspects; and now, at last, we find it employed in a new form, and with great apparent effect, as a warlike threat. As such, its use certainly does credit to the boldness and decision of the new Czar.

Gurowski's effort to reorient the ideas of Marx and Engels on Panslavism were far-reaching in their effect. The two revised *Tribune* articles were in later years reprinted separately or together in at least three languages and were presented as the authentic Panslavic thinking of the two socialist collaborators.[47] The seven additional articles on Panslavism sent to the *Tribune* went unpublished, because the Count suppressed them. For reasons unknown, Marx and Engels did not submit these to European newspapers, and after Dana ultimately returned them to Marx, they disappeared. Thus the picture of their thinking on Panslavism for the period of the Crimean War is incomplete.[48]

Gurowski studied Marx and Engels' seven rejected articles and commented in the margins. He also went over others of their articles and withheld publication because he disagreed with their basic attitudes toward Russia. During the winter of 1855–56 the *Tribune* printed none of the weekly Marx and Engels contributions. The rejected articles, a sizable accumulation, were not returned for months, however, for Dana was so busy performing Greeley's duties that he did not even write Marx a letter of explanation until June, 1856. Dana then pointed out that since the end of the Crimean War, domestic events had been of greater interest, and Panslavian articles could not be used "because the

[47] Eleanor Marx Aveling and Edward Aveling (eds.), *The Eastern Question: A Reprint of Letters* [by Karl Marx] *Written 1853–1856 Dealing with the Events of the Crimean War* (London, 1897), 542–50; Luigi Mongini (ed.), *La Questione Orientale: Lettere di Carlo Marx (1853–56)* (Roma, 1903), 378–84; Karl Marx, "Oesterreichs Schwäche," *Die Zeit,* Vol. XIII (October 2, 1897), 1–2.

[48] Rjasanoff (ed.), *Geseammelte Schriften von Karl Marx und Friedrich Engels 1852 bis 1862,* I, p. XLVII; Blackstock and Hoselitz (eds.), *The Russian Menace to Europe,* 250–51.

theme was not interesting enough for our public to justify our putting back other matters and making room for you." Two months later Dana finally got around to returning the unwanted articles.[49]

Then Marx discovered what he believed to be the correct explanation why his articles were rejected. He concluded, after studying Gurowski's marginal notations, that their spirit was Russian, that the poor French and English in which they were written could not have come from a Frenchman or a Yankee. He also believed that Dana's original plan had been to print all the articles before Gurowski sabotaged them. Marx knew of Gurowski's pro-Russian stand and his work on the *Tribune* through Frederick Law Olmsted, an agent of *Putnam's Monthly Magazine,* who visited him while traveling in Europe. Olmsted, a resident of New York, told Marx that Gurowski had great influence over Dana and that the Count received cash contributions from the Russian embassy in Washington. Marx confided to Engels that Gurowski had been the real source of their difficulty with the *Tribune,* for he "represents Panslavism against us . . . . We thus have also the honor that our articles are, or rather were, directly watched over and censored by the Russian embassy."[50]

Marx reasoned accurately when he concluded that his articles had been carefully gone over by Gurowski. He was likewise sound in assuming that the Count had been instrumental in withholding them from publication. He erred, however, in believing Olmsted's report that Gurowski was in the pay of Russia. Available evidence does not point to this, although Marx believed Olmsted because of the Count's widely known Russian sympathies and his own knowledge that the Russian government had agents abroad.[51]

8

Gurowski's second full-length book during his years with the *Tribune* was *America and Europe,* which appeared in New York in 1857

[49] Rjasanoff (ed.), *Gesammelte Schriften von Karl Marx und Friedrich Engels 1852 bis 1862,* I, p. XLVII–XLVIII.

[50] Marx to Engels, October 30, 1856, and February 7, 1857, in Karl Marx and Friedrich Engels, *Briefwechsel* (4 vols., Berlin, 1949–50), II, 193–94, 211–212.

[51] Rjasanoff (ed.), *Gesammelte Schriften von Karl Marx und Friedrich Engels 1852 bis 1862,* I, p. XLIX.

from the press of D. Appleton and Company. This comparative account, based on study and observation, was welcomed by a leading journal as "the profoundest and most comprehensive survey of America since de Tocqueville's work. It is, in truth, a more perceptive and philosophical treatise than de Tocqueville's; for . . . Gurowski pierces and exposes the very genius of our character and civilization. We commend the work to the thoughtful study of every one of our readers who loves his country . . . and who believe in its good destiny." Moreover, the Count "says sharp things of us sharply; but he, also, says sweet and true things well." This reviewer appreciated particularly the scholarship of the book, "of a scope beyond our usual standard."[52] Another reviewer also ranked the book with de Tocqueville's study, but concluded that its cardinal sin was failure to appreciate and understand Anglo-Saxonism.[53]

On the pages of *America and Europe,* Gurowski emphasized and explained the dissimilarities of the United States and the Old World. Man's individuality, he declared, appeared to be normally fixed and established, and his rights realized for the first time in free America. Qualities of social independence and domestic liberty produced in the people of the United States an element making it impossible for them to become servants of kings or victims of social caste. "To an Americanized, and therefore a reinvigorated European," said Gurowski, "a return to the past worn-out conditions of existence would prove unbearable."[54]

He saw in the nation's progress the solution to the age-old question of authority versus liberty. America was the incarnation of liberty, Europe the embodiment of authority. America proved that liberty, in superseding authority, did not result in disorganization. Authority continued to be the backbone of dominant ideas and actions in Europe, even for her reforming, revolutionary elements, but in the United States authority seemed to be wholly subordinate to liberty: "Here liberty alone cements the social structure, it is a central hearth, towards which gravi-

---

[52] *Putnam's Monthly Magazine of American Literature, Science, and Art,* Vol. IX (June, 1857), 659. "The short notice," said Gurowski, "written either by Park Goodwin or [George William] Curtis—both so independent, makes me proud." Gurowski to Sumner, May 27, 1857, in Sumner Papers.

[53] "Nebulae," *Galaxy,* Vol. I, 270.

[54] Gurowski, *America and Europe,* vi, 62.

tate elements, passions, interests, activities . . . . Until the apparition of the American social state, the like elements have been considered as chaotic, dissolving, disorganizing, fit only to be compressed, to be held sternly, and directed by authority. Liberty, not authority, gathers, classifies, combines, adjusts, imparts to them healthy vitality, regulates their orderly association . . . . Guided and inspired by liberty, America moves with stately impetuosity, and shall so move undisturbed in her luminous onward course."

The American mind, Gurowski observed, tended toward the objective. Receptive and daring, it was less disciplined and routine than the English mind. Although the American intellect grappled willingly with problems, it sometimes would not be patient or persistent enough to solve them, particularly when the answer lay in abstract thinking. The American mind, because of its early struggles with the forces of nature in the New World, had been trained to make on-the-spot decisions, to act at once, and not to contemplate.

In literature, the Count contended, the United States had not been original to the degree of the life of its citizens and its political institutions. In this sense, the nation remained an English colony, since there did not exist an original American literature, but only an imitation or continuation of England's literature. There had been, he said, a few exceptions, such as Longfellow's "Evangeline," but over all, American literature continued to be a grafted product and not an outgrowth of the nation's vitality.[55]

9

Concurrent with his work on the *Tribune,* the Count early in 1857 accepted employment on the editorial staff of *The New American Cyclopaedia,* an extensive undertaking sponsored by D. Appleton and Company and designed to supplant the then obsolete *Encyclopaedia Americana.* The project was a *Tribune* by-product, since Dana and Ripley were engaged as editors, and used *Tribune* employees for editorial work. Gurowski's articles appeared in the first four volumes and were, among

[55] *Ibid.,* 333–34, 340–41, 410–11.

others, on Alexander the Great, Attila, the Borgias, the Alexanders of Russia, Robert Bunsen, and aristocracy.[56]

After a second brief excursion to the Middle West, the Count spent the summer of 1857 working on biographical sketches for the *Cyclopaedia,* a task he characterized as "sending to immortality various dead and living individuals." At times he viewed the entire project with disgust. The first two volumes he believed poorly edited and far from scientific. "The people," he declared on the appearance of Volume Three, "ought to be warned and preserved from such a heap of stupendous ignorance. ... In many articles the Cyclopedia is a lie, and as such could be published in Rome by the Jesuits."[57] The break came in 1858 when he refused to make additional contributions, unless the project's standards were set higher. "It is not a question," he said, "of giving something good but to catch the pennies of a confiding people." The old grumbler even prepared an article attacking the low scholarly standards of the *Cyclopaedia.*[58] Although most reviewers agreed with him in his estimate of the undertaking, the sixteen volumes of the set were printed by 1863 and enjoyed a substantial sale.[59]

Dana was so angered that he called Gurowski "a G. d old brute and disagreeable in the bargain," and wished never again to see him. The two men were reconciled some months later when the Count promised to stop denouncing the *Cyclopaedia,* but with Ripley, who had consistently befriended him, a reunion never came.[60]

10

Gurowski's resignation from the editorial staff of the *Cyclopaedia* caused a serious financial situation to become unbearable. In the pre-

[56] Carter, "Gurowski," *Atlantic Monthly,* Vol. XVIII, 632.

[57] Gurowski to Pike, July 16, 1857, in Pike, *First Blows of the Civil War,* 375; Gurowski to Pike, August 19, 1858, in Pike Papers.

[58] Gurowski to Longfellow, [1858], in Longfellow Papers; Gurowski to Pike, [April, 1859], in Pike Papers.

[59] *Living Age,* Vol. LVII (May 15, 1858), 551–54; Octavius Brooks Frothingham, *George Ripley* (Boston, 1882), 218–23; Wilson, *The Life of Charles A. Dana,* 158–59.

[60] Charles A. Dana to Pike, November 15, 1858, in Pike Papers; Dana to Pike, June 23, 1859, and September 1, 1859, in Pike, *First Blows of the Civil War,* 441, 444.

vious year, when the Panic of 1857 had struck, the *Tribune* could no longer afford to continue the Count on its payroll, and income from the *Cyclopaedia* alone did not provide adequate support. Writing his faithful friend, James Russell Lowell, Gurowski pleaded for work of any nature in Boston or Cambridge, if only at forty or fifty dollars a month. He excused his request on grounds of health and complained that the New York air was unbearable, as he did not wish to admit financial embarrassment. In addition to his desire to live in Harvard's atmosphere, he probably sought a position on the staff of the *Atlantic Monthly,* recently organized under the editorship of Lowell. But to Joseph Green Cogswell, superintendent of the John Jacob Astor Library in New York City, he confided his actual condition: "I am thrown upon the streets and workless." He suggested that in the Astor Library, which he had used frequently in his studies, work of any type would be satisfactory, since the important thing was to find employment: "All what I request is work in any way, as not to starve and not to freeze."[61]

His meager needs were soon met with the annual allotment from his confiscated estate and a small income from articles he contributed to the *Messenger of Industry* periodical in Moscow. At the same time, he planned a book in French to be published in Paris concerning the Polish policy of Czar Nicholas I. Since the Count thought himself to be largely responsible for this policy, he considered the study a kind of autobiography or memoir. Although he collected the materials, he never composed the manuscript.[62]

Gurowski also busied himself at this time with a book-length study of the history of Roman law, an outgrowth of his Cambridge lectures. For the next two years he sought the aid of friends to locate a publisher. Refused on every hand, he finally attempted subscription selling, which also came to nothing. Because this was the only study of its kind in English, he had hoped for many subscribers in the Boston area, where he enlisted the assistance of friends. Simultaneously he had worked on an

[61] Gurowski to Lowell, October 5, 1857, in Lowell Papers; Gurowski to Joseph Green Cogswell, October 15, 1857, in Mellen Chamberlain Collection, Boston Public Library, Boston.

[62] Gurowski to Pike, August 19, 1858, in Pike Papers; Rjasanoff (ed.), *Gesammelte Schriften von Karl Marx und Friedrich Engels 1852 bis 1862,* I, p. XLIX.

antislavery book published in 1860 under the title *Slavery in History*.[63]

During his New York years Gurowski spent most afternoons in the Astor Library in study and research. His demands on the library staff were not excessive. His presence did not attract special attention during winter months, but on the hot days of summer he frequently spread himself across two chairs in one of the alcoves. As the heat mounted while he intently read, he inevitably removed his coat, unbuttoned his vest, threw open his shirt collar, and eventually took off his necktie.[64]

Despite paucity of income the Count managed to spend the summer months of the 1850's at resorts. For some seasons he went to fashionable seaside establishments at Newport, Rhode Island, but later forsook them for the healing waters of Saratoga Springs, New York. Efforts to restore his always fragile health, even after painful but successful hernia surgery in the summer of 1854, also took him to "water cure" businesses in the resort town of Brattleboro, Vermont. Longfellow warned him against using the water treatments as a remedy and recommended them solely for pleasure.[65]

Newport impressed the Count as "full of beauty, fashion, . . . snobism, absurdity, sham, affectation, would-be something, poor attempts at distinction principally by the means of liveries, carriages, horses, crests, apish overdressing, exclusiveness of fashion." On the crowded and sprawling porch of a Newport hotel, a Rhode Island United States senator and state militia general, Albert C. Greene, worsted the vacationing European. A mutual friend introduced the two men. Gurowski

[63] Gurowski to Henry C. Carey, March 6, 1858, in Edward Carey Gardiner Collection, Historical Society of Pennsylvania, Philadelphia; Gurowski to [?], February 12, 1859, in author's possession; Gurowski to Felton, December 16, 1859, in Felton Papers. The complete Roman law manuscript is in the Gurowski Papers. *Slavery in History* is treated in Chapter XI.

[64] Frank H. Norton, "Ten Years in a Public Library," *Galaxy*, Vol. VIII (October, 1869), 531.

[65] Gurowski to Pike, July 30, 1854, July 16, 1857, and August 19, 1858, in Pike, *First Blows of the Civil War*, 255–57, 375–76, 423–24; Dana to Pike, July 17, 1854, June 24, [1856], and July 22, [no year], in Pike Papers; Gurowski to Sumner, October 3, 1854, May 17, 1855, and May 19, 1856, in Sumner Papers; Nevins and Thomas (eds.), *The Diary of George Templeton Strong: The Turbulent Fifties, 1850–1859*, 289 (Brattleboro, August 13, 1856); Longfellow to Gurowski, September 23, 1858, in Henry Wadsworth Longfellow Papers, Boston Public Library, Boston.

made no courteous acknowledgment, but glanced over his blue glasses and quietly remarked, "I believe you have a great many generals in this country." "Yes," answered Greene, bowing, "almost as many as counts in Europe."[66]

In New York City, Gurowski often relaxed and dined in Pfaff's restaurant on Broadway, a favorite hangout of journalists, artists, stage people, and comedians. There in the middle-late fifties, he congregated with Walt Whitman, journalist, poet, and author of the scandalous *Leaves of Grass;* Albert Brisbane, American advocate of Fourierism and author of books on the subject; brothers John and William Swinton, antislavery-minded journalists on the staff of the New York *Times;* and Fitz-James O'Brien, the complete Bohemian, contributor to the New York *Times* and mainstay writer for *Harper's Magazine.* Of this group, John Swinton came to the Count's rescue by editing the jargon in the manuscripts of his books and pamphlets published during the 1850's.[67]

Gurowski also found amusement and companionship at the Athenaeum Club, a men's boarding group frequented by New York literary and business men. He was one of the first to join the club and regularly spent his meal hours and evenings in its quarters. Here on the night of February 27, 1860, he met Abraham Lincoln, the group's honored guest, in town for an address at Cooper Institute.[68] Two weeks later the Athenaeum rooms were in an uproar when the Count entered a quiet conversation between James H. Van Alen, a wealthy New York City merchant, and Charles F. Briggs, an editor of the New York *Times.* Gurowski vehemently disagreed with Van Alen on a point concerning the Constitution and called his opponent an ass. Van Alen angrily stamped from the room. Next evening in the Athenaeum the Count and Van Alen met face to face. Van Alen lashed at Gurowski with a

[66] Gurowski to Pike, July 30 and August 12, 1854, in Pike, *First Blows of the Civil War,* 255, 257; "Nebulae," *Galaxy,* Vol. VIII (July, 1869), 146.

[67] Waters, *Career and Conversation of John Swinton,* 14–15.

[68] Bing, "Life of Gurowski," 199–202, 205; *Constitution and By-Laws of the Athenaeum, with a List of the Members* (New York, 1859), 16; *Charter and Constitution of the Athenaeum Association, with a List of the Members* (New York, 1863), 16. For the Cooper Institute address, see Roy P. Basler (ed.), *The Collected Works of Abraham Lincoln* (9 vols., New Brunswick, New Jersey, 1953–55), III, 522–50.

strip of cowhide, and the Pole grabbed a nearby carving knife. Neither hit, since friends restrained and cooled the infuriated pair.[69] But neither Gurowski nor the Constitution were put to rest. On each the fates were soon to release unrelenting fury.

[69] Dana to Pike, March 15, 1860, and Thursday night, no date, in Pike Papers.

CHAPTER IV

WASHINGTON JACOBIN

I

THE COUNT CAME TO THE FEDERAL DISTRICT soon after South Carolina seceded from the Union, and while Mississippi, Florida, Alabama, Georgia, Louisiana, and Texas were passing secession ordinances. Hailed by a correspondent as a "wet nurse of revolutions," he was attracted by the activities of a wartime capital and the national issues at stake.[1] He hoped also to find employment growing out of his loyalty to Republican Party principles, contribute wisdom from his years of education and experience in Europe, and associate with political leaders as he had in Poland, France, and Russia.

Imminent war was only the immediate cause of Gurowski's move to Washington. The capital had pleased him since he first reached the United States. When he visited the city in 1852, he came ostensibly to escape New York's severe climate, but he brought letters of introduction to Secretary of State Daniel Webster and President Millard Fillmore. A year later he went again to Washington because of its mild climate and the fascinations of the capital's political figures and social life. He believed the city reflected American democracy at its best. People were accepted or rejected, he imagined, on the basis of their intrinsic values and not on their money. Individuals of artistic and intellectual accomplishments found the city a haven, he said, and those interested in politics, heaven.[2]

---

[1] Unidentified newspaper clipping, February 8, 1861, in Gurowski Papers; Gurowski to Pike, August 30, 1861, in Pike Papers.

[2] Edward Everett to Daniel Webster, January 30, 1852, in Everett Papers; Everett to Millard Fillmore, January 30, 1852, in *ibid.;* Gurowski to Sumner, February 23, 1853, in Sumner Papers; Gurowski to Longfellow, February 27, 1853, in Longfellow Papers; Gurowski, *America and Europe,* 406.

On his Washington visits the Count had found congenial fellowship in the Charles Eames home. Located on the northwest corner of Fourteenth and H streets, this unpretentious house was a gathering place of the city's political, intellectual, and social personages. No other private dwelling in Washington attracted so many people of distinction.[3]

When Gurowski returned to Washington to live, he became at once a frequent visitor at the Eames residence. He spent hours talking politics with Senator Charles Sumner, Congressman Henry Winter Davis of Maryland, Senator Preston King of New York, General Nathaniel Prentice Banks, and Attorney General Edward Bates. Others with whom he also visited in the Eames home were Senator Zachariah Chandler of Michigan, Secretary of the Treasury Salmon P. Chase, Congressman George W. Julian of Indiana, Lincoln's private secretary John Hay, and such out-of-town visitors as Julia Ward Howe, currently in the spotlight because of her "Battle Hymn of the Republic," and John A. Andrew, governor of Massachusetts.

Eames himself, Harvard educated, was winning prominence as a counsel of the Navy and Treasury departments. He was widely recognized also because of his knowledge of international law and his brilliant conversation. No less capable than her husband, Mrs. Eames had a sixth sense for understanding Washington society and for making their drawing room the city's most inviting, if not the most elaborate.[4]

No one experienced their hospitality and understanding more than Gurowski. Almost a daily caller, he visited and dined there often. The Eames fireside became a refuge of understanding and consideration, as he tormented and provoked many a friend and enemy. On one of his evening calls he was suddenly taken ill with cholera morbus—acute gastroenteritis characterized by vomiting, diarrhea, intestinal pain, and cramps—was put to bed by the master of the house, and nursed to recovery by Mrs. Eames. Some months later, when his fragile health

[3] Gurowski to Sumner, February 23, 1853, in Sumner Papers; Howe, *Reminiscences, 1819–1899*, 224; Gouverneur, *As I Remember*, 178.

[4] *Ibid.*, 178–79; Herbert Francis Wright, "Charles Eames," *Dictionary of American Biography*, V, 592–93; Howard K. Beale (ed.), *Diary of Gideon Welles, Secretary of the Navy Under Lincoln and Johnson* (3 vols., New York, 1960), III, 67–68 (March 16, 1867).

seemed even more delicate, Eames invited him to live with the family, and at once he moved in. He gladly deserted his rooming-house life with its lack of regular meals.[5] Mrs. Eames warned her friends that the Count must be treated with respect in her home, and in general acted as placater in the inevitable quarrels. He returned the warm friendship by usually making himself agreeable, and particularly by entertaining and often caring for their small daughter Frances.[6]

In the Eames home and elsewhere in Washington, Gurowski's activities centered in the Radicals, the extremist, abolitionist-minded wing of the Republican Party. Lincoln and his administration were the moderates—the Conservatives—whose purpose was to make the restoration of the Union the one war objective, to be accomplished at any cost and, if possible, without abolishing slavery. Beginning with secession, the party had gradually divided over the conduct and purposes of the conflict. Although practical considerations often caused the wings to compromise and co-operate, their over-all points of view clarified during the war and came to sharp focus in the mind of Gurowski. No man saw the lines of demarcation more distinctly than he. No man labored more tirelessly to strengthen the Radicals, dubbed by Hay "Jacobins," after a leftist faction of the French Revolution.[7]

[5] *Diary, II,* 261 (July 8, 1863); Gurowski to Longfellow, July 23, 1863, in Longfellow Papers; Gurowski to Andrew, November 13, 1863, in Andrew Papers.

[6] Gouverneur, *As I Remember,* 249; Howe, *Reminiscences, 1819–1899,* 224; statement by Laurence G. Hoes, December 26, 1950, in author's possession; unidentified newspaper clipping, in author's possession; Gurowski to Lee and Shepard, February 20, 1864, in Lee and Shepard Papers, American Antiquarian Society, Worcester, Massachusetts.

[7] For a thorough account of Radical and Conservative objectives, see T. Harry Williams, *Lincoln and the Radicals* (Madison, 1941), especially Chapter I. The impact of the Radical program on Lincoln's policies is evaluated in James G. Randall, *Lincoln the Liberal Statesman* (New York, 1947). The conflict between Lincoln and the Radical governors is the keynote in William B. Hesseltine, *Lincoln and the War Governors* (New York, 1948). While these authors generally picture Lincoln as opposed to the Radicals, David Donald maintains in his *Lincoln Reconsidered: Essays on the Civil War Era* (New York, 1956), Chapter VI, that the President tried to win their political support. Donald does not picture the Radicals as an organized anti-Lincoln clique, as do the above scholars, nor as a group that held common ideas beyond simple antislavery zeal. Eric L. McKitrick's *Andrew Johnson and Reconstruction* (Chicago, 1960) agrees with the Donald point of view.

2

The attitudes and approaches of the Radicals in preventing compromise while secession snowballed are well illustrated by Gurowski's relations with the Peace Convention, which assembled at Willard's Hotel on February 4, 1861. Meeting at the call of the Virginia legislature, all states were represented except Arkansas, Michigan, Wisconsin, Minnesota, California, Oregon, and the seven of the lower South. Although the convention assembled too late to be a controlling factor, its activities proved all the more futile, because Radicals insisted that its Republican members maintain an uncompromising stand. The convention's seven proposed amendments to the Constitution, presented to Congress on February 27, evoked negligible support. Both Radical Republicans and secessionist hotspurs rejoiced at this failure.[8]

Gurowski was quick to acquaint himself with the Northern delegates, and within a week of the opening of the convention he was conversing freely with a large number. He did not have access to the convention itself, which met behind closed doors, but he managed with uncanny accuracy to discover what was occurring. Realizing that negotiations were taking an unsatisfactory course, he unassumingly appeared before an informal group of Northern members one evening at Willard's, suggested a course of action, and related plots to seize the Union.[9]

He told them they would "make a mess of it," and impetuously questioned: "Are you lambs to be eaten up unresistingly by the wolves

[8] Robert Gray Gunderson, *Old Gentlemen's Convention: The Washington Peace Conference of 1861* (Madison, 1961); Jesse L. Keene, *The Peace Convention of 1861* (Tuscaloosa, 1961). Special aspects of the convention are in Lucius E. Chittenden, *Recollections of President Lincoln and His Administration* (New York, 1891), Chapter IV, and the same author's *A Report of the Debates and Proceedings . . . of the Conference Convention . . . held at Washington, D.C., in February, A.D. 1861* (New York, 1864).

[9] Chittenden, *Recollections of President Lincoln and His Administration*, 27–30. Gurowski's purported words before the Northern delegates as recorded by Chittenden are probably not accurate in every detail, but the remarks are substantially correct. It is likely that Chittenden recorded contemporaneously Gurowski's comments as he did the proceedings of the Peace Convention, although he was a delegate and not an official recording secretary.

of secession? Or are you fishes with blood so cold that it cannot be stirred to action?" Then he unfolded the plots. After Lincoln's election, pro-Southern governmental leaders had conspired to keep the electoral vote from reaching a count. Lewis Cass, secretary of state, would be jockeyed from the cabinet, while President James Buchanan, it was thought, would be controlled by the remainder of the cabinet. Federal property would be transferred as rapidly as possible to the South. South Carolina would secede immediately and be followed by other states in rapid order. Armed Southerners would pack Washington when the electoral votes were counted in the House of Representatives on February 13. They would start a riot, then seize the executive departments and the capitol and establish a confederacy with Jefferson Davis as president.

But the plot, Gurowski explained, had already failed. Disloyal activities of John B. Floyd of Virginia, secretary of war, and Howell Cobb of Georgia, secretary of the treasury, had been discovered; they were dismissed and replaced by John A. Dix and Edwin M. Stanton, two staunch Unionists. Cass, according to plan, was dismissed (actually he resigned) from the cabinet, but Buchanan stiffened and replaced him with Jeremiah S. Black, who favored coercion and holding Fort Sumter. Rheumatic old General in Chief Winfield Scott, contrary to expectations, collected a small number of army regulars in Washington and gave notice that he would shoot without trial, delay, or mercy those who used force against the government.

Then Gurowski revealed a second plot. This time Jefferson Davis was its head and general manager, with full authority to assign special duties, and he alone determined the extent to which others should be admitted to the conspiracy. In a meeting at Davis' home in Washington on the night of January 5, 1861, the Count maintained, Senators Stephen R. Mallory, Judah P. Benjamin, John Slidell, and James M. Mason, agreed to the broad outline of the plot. The electoral vote would be counted and results announced without interference. Senators and representatives would remain in Congress, drawing their pay, until their states passed secession ordinances. The states of the lower South would be urged to secede without delay. In the meantime Slidell and Mallory would work out a plan for a confederacy and call a seceded states convention for its adoption at Montgomery, Alabama, not later than the middle of February. The border states could not possibly be brought to secession by the date set to seize the government—March 4, Lincoln's inaugural day—but they would provide the necessary men to effect the *coup d'état*.

Now, said Gurowski, appeared the most treacherous scheme of the entire plot. Mason had been charged with the duty of enticing the North into peace negotiations. He had influenced the legislature of his state, Virginia, to invite the states, North and South, to meet in Washington to agree on terms of compromise and peace. The North was expected to respond favorably, and the South, pretending co-operation, planned the conference to occupy the attention of the government and its loyal citizenry until March 4. So while the South mobilized its strength for armed conflict, the North would sleep on, to be awakened only by the roar of insurrectional cannon on inauguration day.

"Here," said Gurowski, "you are permitting yourselves to be used as the instruments of a treasonable conspiracy, when you ought to be at home, organizing and drilling your regiments, preparing to defend the only government worth living under left upon the face of the earth." With this advice, he departed. James S. Wadsworth of the New York delegation, who heard the Count, commented that he wished there were not so high a degree of method and intelligence in his talk. "If he is half right," said Wadsworth, "our position here deserves the contempt of the world . . . . I begin to think it is time we held a caucus, and found how many members we have upon whom we could absolutely rely." Wadsworth's suggestion was agreed to and a caucus arranged the following evening. But several Southern delegates dropped in and the conversations abruptly halted.[10]

Radical propaganda spread by Gurowski and supported by Wadsworth and other Republicans, together with the opposition of secession leaders, was instrumental in the breakdown of the Peace Convention. When Northern delegates heard of the Count's alarms, they doubted their efforts. Fears increased, and the spirit of compromise sank deeper and deeper as hate flared in the convention's debates.

[10] *Ibid.*, 30–31.

3

Another example of Gurowski's Radical agitation, followed this time by Conservative reaction, occurred in the period after Lincoln's inauguration and before the attack on Fort Sumter. During these weeks of uncertainty by the Lincoln administration, the idea developed that if the government could not prevent military men and supplies from going South, it could not maintain itself. Out of this came a tendency for individual force to assert itself.

Late one evening Colonel Charles P. Stone, inspector general of the District of Columbia armed forces, received a message directing him to go immediately to General Scott's headquarters, where some hours earlier he had made his usual evening duty call. When Stone entered Scott's room, he found Secretary of State William H. Seward in conversation with the aged veteran. Scott asked Stone if he knew Gurowski, and when Stone replied that he did not, Seward remarked, "Why Colonel Stone, to say that you do not know the Count is to argue yourself unknown." Seward then described Gurowski's appearance and told Stone he could be found at Mrs. Ulrich's boarding house. Scott informed Stone that the Count was "playing the demagogue" by inciting individuals to make depredations on the property of such wealthy people as William W. Corcoran, well known for his Southern sympathies, and George W. Riggs.[11]

Scott gave Stone orders to go to Gurowski and to inform him that law would be preserved in the District, that attempts at violations would be suppressed by military force, and that men of his type known to have "advised or insinuated" violence would not be tolerated. Stone was, moreover, to tell Gurowski that his "movements and words had been well noted, and that a repetition of some of his incendiary propositions, made in supposed privacy, would place him where such conduct should place

[11] Gurowski also lived and boarded at Mrs. Ulrich's house, corner of Fifteenth and G streets, northwest, with prominent political figures such as Sumner, when he visited Washington during the fifties. Gurowski to Sumner, April 27, 1854, in Sumner Papers. That Gurowski lived and boarded there at this time is substantiated in his letter to Lincoln, March 12, 1861, in Lincoln Papers. Gurowski described Corcoran as "a rich partisan of secession." *Diary,* I, 22 (April, 1861).

him." After a "curious interview" with Gurowski, Stone reported to Scott and Seward that he had completed his assignment.[12]

Seward initiated this warning to Gurowski. Stone received no order from Scott to visit the Count, as he made his routine nightly report, and when Stone was called later in the evening, Seward was present and discussed the European.[13] Moreover, from the time of Lincoln's inauguration the Radicals severely attacked Seward for his conciliatory measures. The sting of these assaults was never felt more keenly by the Secretary than when they came from Gurowski.

At the approximate time of his reprimand, the Count learned from those who were in a position to know that Seward offered Southern leaders in the Senate concession and compromise to assure his confirmation to the State Department. The Radicals, said Gurowski, were "terribly scared" of Seward's policy toward the South and were accusing him of subserviency to the seceded states.[14] Seward's complaint concerning the Count was in a sense aimed at the entire Jacobin movement.

4

When the electrifying news of the fall of Fort Sumter awakened Washington, wild rumors circulated that the Confederates would seize the city and make short work of the North. To protect the capital, two volunteer groups were organized. One was led by Cassius M. Clay, a picturesque and swashbuckling Kentucky abolitionist, recently appointed minister to Russia by Lincoln. Without official sanction he recruited approximately three hundred men, a variegated group of office-seekers, composed mainly of ex-congressmen, professors, and governors, most of whom chanced to be at Willard's Hotel or elsewhere in the city.[15]

[12] Charles P. Stone, "Washington in March and April, 1861," *Magazine of American History*, Vol. XIV (July, 1885), 4–6. Stone, a West Point man, became the Jacobin victim of the federal defeat at Ball's Bluff, October 21, 1861, in investigations of the Joint Congressional Committee on the Conduct of the War. He was imprisoned and later released and assigned insignificant military duties. In 1864 he resigned his commission in disgust. Thomas M. Spaulding, "Charles Pomeroy Stone," *Dictionary of American Biography*, XVIII, 72; Williams, *Lincoln and the Radicals*, 46–47, 94–104.

[13] "It is said that Seward rules both Lincoln and Scott." *Diary*, I, 34 (April, 1861).

[14] *Diary*, I, 14–15, 20 (March, 1861).

[15] Stone, "Washington in March and April, 1861,"*Magazine of American History*,

The Count was among these patriots, found encamped one evening by Colonel Stone in the East Room of the White House. Stone noticed the youthful delight of the guards, as they examined their government-issued muskets. These warriors, high in spirit, allegedly were there to protect Lincoln, although regular guards were in and around the White House. Gurowski experienced several days of patrolling and drilling with the Clay guards and spent the nights sleeping on a hard floor. The organization reminded him of the humorous regiment of ragged ne'er-do-wells organized by Sir John Falstaff, but he believed that they would have made a splendid showing in battle. "I do not mind a brush," said the Count, "or even a little lead in my old carcass if it must come to that. But bitter were the feeling to fall and pay for the imbecility of a Lincoln, a Seward and Company."[16]

Panic in Washington passed with the arrival of troops, and the Clay volunteers were honorably discharged. Each member received a handsome testimonial certificate, but Gurowski arrogantly refused to accept his, since the organization had not fought. With little more than a week of military service, he gladly laid down his musket, "good for others to play at Soldiers under cover—not for an old stagge as me."[17]

A fortnight later Gurowski sensed inactivity and uncertainty in the capital, and his passions soared. "I wish ardently that the traitors," he bellowed, "may decide to attack Washington. I am in a rage and want to kill at least one rebel. This my craving can only be satisfied in a quiet manner, in a defense of a spot, as my damned 56 years, still more damned belly and weakened supporters of the body prevent long marchings; but they will prevent me likewise from running should it come to a brush."[18]

Vol. XIV, 8; Cassius Marcellus Clay, *The Life of Cassius Marcellus Clay: Memoirs, Writings, and Speeches* (Cincinnati, 1886), 259. Title page indicates 2 vols., but only one appeared.

[16] Stone, "Washington in March and April, 1861," *Magazine of American History,* Vol. XIV, 8; *Diary,* I, 24 (April, 1861); Gurowski to Sumner, April 23, 1861, in Sumner Papers.

[17] *Diary,* I, 24 (April, 1861); Gurowski to Sumner, April 23, 1861, in Sumner Papers.

[18] Gurowski to Sumner, May 10, 1861, in *ibid.*

5

Although Gurowski enjoyed his brief military service, a major purpose in coming to Washington had been to obtain government employment as a civilian. Since severing relations with the *Tribune* in 1857, he had not had regular work, and his income from contributions to a Russian periodical for the three following years ceased when the journal failed. His financial plight became even more critical because the annual sum of four hundred dollars from his confiscated estate failed to reach him in 1860 and 1861, and for the reason that the publisher of his *Slavery in History* unscrupulously held back royalty payments.[19]

Gurowski hoped to win an advisory position in the State Department, where he intended to serve as an interpreter of reports sent in by United States ministers in Europe. Mrs. Eames implored Senator Sumner to arrange the position with Secretary Seward, and the Count wrote President Lincoln and his old friend, Pike, soon to be named minister resident to The Hague, concerning the appointment. At the time that Sumner first approached Seward concerning Gurowski, the Secretary broke out, "G—— d—— you, don't you know he is always abusing me."[20]

When it appeared the Count had little hope of employment in the State Department office, Mrs. Eames asked Sumner to have him made minister resident to Venezuela, a post Eames himself had held from 1854 to 1857. "I should write all about him to my friends there," Mrs. Eames promised, *"translate* him and make him intelligible to the Spanish American mind. This would be of some value, for between their timidity and the Count's peculiarities, it would be a mere toss up if they did not consider him as equivalent to an earthquake."[21]

Gurowski did not want a South American mission. Sumner again approached Seward and after several visits slowly wore down his resistance. Weeks passed, but in the end Seward appointed the Pole to a

[19] Gurowski to Pike, [Spring, 1861], in Pike Papers; Gurowski to Greeley, October 1, 1861, in Greeley Papers.

[20] Mrs. Fanny Eames to Sumner, [March, 1861], in Sumner Papers; Gurowski to Pike, [March, 1861], in Pike Papers; Gurowski to Lincoln, March 12, 1861, in Lincoln Papers; Diary of Everett, December 6, 1862, in Everett Papers.

[21] Mrs. Eames to Sumner, April 5, [1861], in Sumner Papers.

temporary clerkship. Mrs. Eames immediately advised that he be affable and peaceable. "If it should so happen that some fine morning," she confided to Sumner, "or rather if it should *not* happen that in the course of a month, the Count should . . . tell Mr. Seward in his own manner 'My dear Mr. Seward you are an ass' then I shall believe the millenium is at hand."[22]

The irascible Radical went to work on June 4, 1861, on a job described by the New York *Tribune* as a "confidential position near the Secretary of State." With a salary of four dollars a day, and his own hours, he liked the job. He was not overworked, and accountable only to Seward, who treated him politely but without confidence.[23] His duty was to read foreign newspapers for items of interest to the State Department, and furnish Seward with translations or memoranda. An additional task, when necessary, was to provide opinions on international law and diplomatic questions. In Gurowski's judgment, his job seemed quite different. He believed his work was "to read the German newspapers and keep Seward from making a fool of himself." The first part of his job he thought simple, but the second part, difficult. Meanwhile, to Seward himself he pledged complete loyalty: "You considered me your political opponent, and such I was. But you treated me kindly . . . and now believe me henceforth as gratefull to you as . . . any of your friends of long standing. Savage animals, and I am one by nature—when tamed by kindness, become the most devoted."[24]

While employed in the State Department, Gurowski's opposition to his chief was open, caustic, and comprehensive, ranging from chuckles to sneers. The Secretary probably considered him a harmless growler who offered only quantities of unwanted advice. To friends, however, the Count openly bragged that his purpose was to spy on Seward. He

[22] Mrs. Eames to Sumner, June 4, [1861], in *ibid*.

[23] New York *Tribune*, July 5, 1861; *Diary*, III, 121 (March 2, 1864); Gurowski to Pike, August 30, 1861, in Pike Papers; "Nebulae," *Galaxy*, Vol. I, 270.

[24] Diary of Everett, December 6, 1862, in Everett Papers; Bing, "Life of Gurowski," 225–26; Carter, "Gurowski," *Atlantic Monthly*, Vol. XVIII, 632; Gurowski to William H. Seward, June 7, [1861], in William H. Seward Papers, University of Rochester Library, Rochester, New York.

carried confidential information from the Secretary's office to Radical cronies in Washington, recorded it in his diary which he regularly wrote at his departmental desk, and told it in long letters to Governor Andrew.[25]

In substance, Gurowski was a Radical agent in Conservative administrative quarters, where he guarded Jacobin interests and attempted to sabotage Seward's policies. Navy Secretary Gideon Welles could not understand why his colleague had given him employment, for the European's intimates were the Secretary's political enemies, and he himself always an "open, persistent, undisguised opponent of Seward and his course." The New York *World* commented that "of all the Tartars that ever were caught the most uncomfortable is unquestionably . . . Gurowski, captured . . . by Mr. Seward and by him let loose to ramble at his own will through . . . the offices of state at Washington."[26]

Before he began working in the State Department, Gurowski had commenced a diary, in which he mordantly attacked Seward and other Conservatives in the Lincoln government. He was careless of the manuscript and sent loose pages to be bound into a volume by the State Department bookbinder, Henry Chase. But Chase noticed the many derogatory remarks concerning Seward, and carried the manuscript to Seward's son Frederick, assistant secretary of state, who laid it before his father. Soon the diary was returned to Gurowski and his salary paid to date. On September 18, 1862, a terse letter signed by the Assistant Secretary was sent to the Count and the press: "I am directed to inform you that your services in this Department will not be required after this day."[27]

[25] Dana to Pike, May 28, 1862, in Pike Papers; Beale (ed.), *Diary of Gideon Welles,* I, 326 (June 8, 1863); *Diary,* I, and Gurowski's letters to John A. Andrew, in Andrew Papers.

[26] Beale (ed.), *Diary of Gideon Welles,* I, 188 (December 4, 1862); New York (weekly) *World,* December 13, 1862, editorial.

[27] *Ibid.;* Gouverneur, *As I Remember,* 247; press copy of a letter, Frederick W. Seward to Gurowski, September 18, 1862, in Records of the Department of States, National Archives; New York *Tribune,* September 19, 1862. Gurowski was paid a total of $680.00 in salary while in the employment of the State Department. Department of State account book entitled "Newspapers and Extra Clerks, 1857–1867," in Records of the Department of State.

Dismissal came as no surprise. Almost a year earlier he had told his friend Felton, president of Harvard, that his employment was unstable because of personal and political reasons.[28]

Following his State Department job, Gurowski did not again hold a salaried position. He lived off royalty monies from his *Diary* volumes, small annual remittances of income from his confiscated Polish estates, and the charity of Mr. and Mrs. Eames. Governor Andrew's efforts to convince Secretary of War Stanton to employ him as a literary man came to nothing.[29]

6

The Count's relations with Sumner illustrate in many respects his personal wartime contacts with Radicals in Washington. Each day or evening Gurowski would spend several hours conversing on politics in Sumner's apartment. His intimacy with the Massachusetts senator was a carry-over of an association dating back to the early fifties. Throughout that decade he had served as a kind of political barometer for Sumner by sounding out opinion. "You will become," he predicted, ". . . not a politician but a real loftier Statesman." The Senator's famous anti-slavery speech, "The Crime Against Kansas," elicited enthusiastic congratulations from the Count. After the attack by Representative Preston S. Brooks of South Carolina on Sumner in the Senate chamber, Gurowski wrote vehemently: "For four days my blood overboils, and more than ever I curse poverty who prevented me to go to Washington. Not to avenge you, as this will be done by a higher tribunal . . . than I. The crime against you belongs to history and will be avenged by her. But beasts of prey, . . . hyenas ought to be dealt with accordingly. They ought to be destroyed . . . . My gray hairs would not prevent me from it. Why must I write words instead of showing actions!"[30] His hearty support of Sumner continued, and as their interests became increasingly

[28] Gurowski to Felton, October 30, [1861], in Felton Papers.

[29] Andrew to Edwin M. Stanton, November 12, 1863, in Andrew Papers.

[30] Gurowski to Sumner, February 23, 1853, and May 25, 1856, in Sumner Papers; Gurowski to Sumner, no date, in Charles Sumner, *The Works of Charles Sumner* (15 vols., Boston, 1870–83), IV, 132.

similar, their friendship grew warmer and ripened into close association after Gurowski moved to the capital.

While Congress was adjourned during the spring and early summer of 1861, the Count wrote the Senator semiweekly, informing him of Washington developments, for the purpose of molding him into the master spirit of the hour. His faith in Sumner, however, gradually began to fade and approached the point of disgust, a condition which undoubtedly led to friction in their relations. "I think that he loves to *growl* over *you*," said Charles Eames to the Senator, hoping to bridge the widening gulf, "more than to talk even in . . . *praise* of *any body else*."[31] Politically the Count was becoming ultra-Radical, whereas Sumner's mind was turning to a middle-of-the-road, though still Radical, course. Sumner, Gurowski complained, lacked the "terrible decision" necessary for Radical accomplishment. The Senator, despite an admirable devotion to ideas, seemed to evaluate men and events or to appreciate the hour, and weakened the influence that he ought to wield, because he looked more to the outside effect of his actions than to their intrinsic values.[32]

A difference in views was only one cause of the break between Sumner and Gurowski. The Count's eccentric personality and customs were probably of greater importance. He came to Sumner's apartment at all hours of the day or evening, without consideration of time or circumstance. "When I left my sleeping-chamber in the morning," said Sumner, "I often found him in my study, seated at my table, perusing my morning paper and probably any other matter which might excite his curiosity." If the Count happened to drop in when a foreign minister or others of importance were visiting Sumner, he would stay during the entire conversation, as he did when the young and as yet undistinguished Henry Adams called. Annoyance was rapidly becoming unbearable. One evening Gurowski stayed for a long visit, leaving at a late hour. Presently he returned, refreshed and ready for another extended conversation.

[31] Gurowski to Pike, August 30, 1861, in Pike Papers; Gurowski to Felton, October 30, [1861], in Felton Papers; Eames to Sumner, marked "Private," September 5, 1861, in Sumner Papers.

[32] Gurowski to Andrew, August 10 and 28, 1862, in Andrew Papers; Gurowski to Pike, August 30, 1861, in Pike Papers; *Diary*, I, 154 (February, 1862), 222 (June, 1862).

Sumner ordered him to get out and stay out. When the astonished Count asked for an explanation, Sumner made none. With this incident in October, 1862, their associations permanently ended, and they were not even on speaking terms.[33]

Gurowski's opinions of Sumner for the remainder of the war were mainly unfavorable, though, like other Radicals, he could not ignore the senator's antislavery zeal. Sumner's re-election in February, 1863, the Count viewed as vindication of sound principle, since his opponents were all Copperheads and slavery supporters. The Pole noted with disgust, however, an affinity of Sumner for Seward, first indicated by news reports that numerous copies of Sumner's Cooper Institute oration were being distributed in Europe and throughout the world. In this address, said Gurowski, Sumner, as chairman of the Senate committee on foreign relations, suppressed facts so as not to hurt Seward. "Now," he predicted, "Sumner will find Seward an admirable statesman." Later, Sumner's efforts to give Henry Shelton Sanford, much disliked by the Count, full ministerial rank in Belgium, caused him to conclude that the Senator was definitely a tool of Seward: "Sumner caves in before Seward, and carries out Seward's bidding."[34]

Gurowski seemed annoyed even with the Massachusetts Senator's displays of erudition. Radical Senate colleagues, professing the same party principles as Sumner, he noticed, reacted in the same way and were often forced to put him in his place. Sumner himself thought envy the reason for his anomalous relations with fellow Radicals: "He cannot understand that it is his scholarly pretensions which render him unpalatable to his colleagues. His cold rhetoric falls powerless at their feet, and no Senator envies him his fertility of random quotations." But as Sumner labored for the abolition of slavery through the Thirteenth Amendment, Gurowski, like other Jacobins, rallied to his support:

---

[33] Howe, *Reminiscences, 1819–1899*, 223; Henry Adams to Charles Francis Adams, Jr., February 5, 1861, in Worthington Chauncey Ford (ed.), *Letters of Henry Adams (1858–1891)* (Boston, 1930), 85; Benjamin Perley Poore, *Perley's Reminiscences of Sixty Years in the National Metropolis* (2 vols., Philadelphia, 1886), II, 141; Gurowski to Andrew, October 19, 1862, in Andrew Papers.

[34] *Diary*, II, 126 (February 4, 1863), 334 (September 29, 1863), III, 174 (April 13, 1864); Gurowski to Andrew, March 27, 1864, in Andrew Papers.

"Never has Sumner been so really dignified, and one can only deeply regret he has not always been so."[35]

7

In the meantime, the Count transferred his hope for Radical leadership to Governor Andrew of Massachusetts. His admiration of the Governor began when he first heard of his unyielding antislavery attitudes during the fifties and increased with his decisive state militia activity early in the war. "Andrew," he declared when the conflict opened, "is the incarnation of the Massachusetts, nay, of the genuine American people." Meeting the Governor for the first time some weeks later at the Eames home, he found him as pleasing personally as in his Radical thinking. A man of forty-three, the youthful Governor was a brilliant conversationalist, strong and sturdy in appearance, unusually energetic and capable of uncommon endurance, truly, he thought, the man Sumner had not turned out to be. Andrew was at once sympathetic and understanding, with the result that he adopted the Governor as a special recipient of his Radical proposals. In scores of letters to Andrew, the Count hoped to bring action designed to force the Radical program on the Lincoln government: "I continue my work to warn you, as in my small position it is the only way to serve this brave, this noble and devoted, but by tricksters and imbeciles, so shamelessly betrayed people."[36]

To guide Andrew, Gurowski frequently favored him with inside knowledge of government politics: "Blair hates Stanton, so does Seward; that may serve to guide you; and Seward, Blair have a considerable influence over 'Abe' and both dabble in war and back MacClellan." All such information he communicated in confidence. What he wrote he wanted made public but "in such a smart way *that it never may be found out where it came from.*" Since newspapers were a ready means of dissemination, he recommended publication in Boston journals.[37]

At another time the Count advised Andrew to approach a problem

[35] *Diary,* III, 219–20, 234 (May 7 and 20, 1864), 137 (note, October 2, 1865).

[36] *Diary,* I, 42 (May, 1861), II, 321 (September 15, 1863); Gurowski to Andrew, August 10, 1862, in Andrew Papers.

[37] Gurowski to Andrew, May 12 and 30, July 7, and August 10, 1862, in *ibid.*

through Lincoln himself and to admonish the President "to have sense and not bring the people wantonly to the slaughter-block." He thought much could be accomplished by Andrew's presence in Washington, and to that end encouraged him to come down frequently, doubtless thinking that much additional information could be confided orally. At a period when Jacobin pressure on the Lincoln government was especially intense, he visited Willard's three or four times a day, hoping to find Andrew's name on the register.[38]

Frequent themes of Gurowski's letters to Andrew were depression over government policies and his faith in the Massachusetts governor. "At times such a dark spirit s[e]izes upon me," he wrote, "that I crave, even pray the devils from the South may storm Washington and I disappear in the midst of the bloody and fi[e]ry storm." All around he observed "the same double dealing, helplessness; the same men, the same doings, the same results as of old." Some days later the situation seemed even worse: "Here . . . the same small, mean intrigues as of old, and the more I see of it the less I make of exceptions. Littleness prevails in the thus called higher councils of the nation."[39]

And when abuse rained on Andrew for his unbending antiadministration stand, Gurowski came to his support: "Let the cowards, traitors, and weak minded howl; so do . . . all the beasts when the Lion roars." Andrew, he believed, had emphasized in a speech the inadequacies of the Lincoln government, "the terrible, reckless destruction of the most intelligent and the noblest population in the world." He contended that the Governor had become the leading civilian produced by the war. "In a certain sense," he told Andrew, "you are the civil Grant or Sheridan, and you make up for the general poverty and nothingness of civil productions . . . . You alone have grown in, amidst and with the events. Nobody else."[40]

His letters to Andrew brought replies equally intimate and outspoken. When the second year of the war was well along, the Governor

---

[38] Gurowski to Andrew, July 4 and August 10, 1862, and December 29, 1863, in *ibid.*

[39] Gurowski to Andrew, March 22 and April 10, 1863, in *ibid.*

[40] Gurowski to Andrew, May 7, 1862, February 1, 1864, and September 22, 1865, in *ibid.; Diary,* II, 111–12 (January 27, 1863), III, 90 (note, September 20, 1865).

wrote that in addition to performing the duties of his office, he was attempting to organize a movement to save Lincoln from ruining the country. Again Andrew pointed out that he was not at all certain that Lincoln even knew we were in a war. Gurowski received numerous other frank and confidential letters from Andrew during the war years. In fact, the Governor went to such extremes that he was hesitant about giving his consent to a postwar effort to publish the letters. "I may have, in my haste," he wrote, "said what might not stand the test of my own cooler judgment."[41]

8

The Count's views of the broad patterns of the Radical movement were unusually clear, not at all dimmed by daily concern over the intricacies of the intraparty conflict that surged about him in the capitol. He continued convinced, like his Jacobin friends, that the Lincoln government did not represent the will of the people. Because of this, an antiadministration Radical faction within the Republican Party had developed, its leaders "the true exponents of the character of the clear insight, of the soundness of the people." This group alone, he maintained, could avert national collapse and should prevail in the government without delay. As weeks turned to months and years with little obvious headway by the Radicals in taking over the Lincoln government or of imposing their principles upon it, he kept hoping and working for the hour of Jacobin authority.[42]

Meantime Gurowski saw that the Radicals could not do what they believed to be imperative, because "traitors as Seward, imbeciles as Lincoln who ought to be shortened by the head, they carry the day." He

[41] Andrew to Gurowski, September 6, 1862, in Henry Greenleaf Pearson, *The Life of John A. Andrew: Governor of Massachusetts, 1861–1865* (2 vols., Boston, 1904), II, 3, 48; Andrew to Julius Bing, November 2, 1866, in Andrew Papers. Andrew's letters to the Count, which should be in the Gurowski Papers, are not known to be extant. Copies of some of the originals, however, are in the Andrew letter books in the Massachusetts Historical Society, Boston. These are few in number and have been of little value in this study. The co-operative and conservative aspects of Andrew's relations with the Lincoln administration are emphasized in McKitrick, *Andrew Johnson and Reconstruction*, 215–23.

[42] *Diary*, I, 106 (October, 1861), 313 (November 9, 1862), II, 335 (September 30, 1863).

hoped that the Jacobins, "an honest and a patriotic opposition," would prune, dust, and shake the administration. "If it was possible," he conjectured, "to have an opposition strong enough to control the misdeeds of the Administration, . . . it would have forced the Administration to act vigorously and decidedly, it could have preserved the Administration from repeated violations of the rules of common sense, and in certain Administrative brains the opposition could have kindled sagacity and farsightedness:—such counterpoise would have spared thousands and thousands of lives, and thousands of millions of money." Before long he agreed with other Radicals that the war would be won by the North despite the administration, but he never receded from the conviction that countless lives and needless money had been "squandered by imbecility, by bad faith, and by incapacity."[43]

Republican Conservatives as well as Democrats, Gurowski contended, had been the principal cause of the war. When they offered the South understanding and compromise, an arrogant and overbearing attitude developed, contempt for the North grew, the idea of Northern cowardice arose, and these combined to bring about secession. The Conservatives at the helm of the government were, in effect, representatives of the slaveholders of the South, at times even emulating them with arrogant and domineering manners. More dangerous than the Copperheads, the Conservatives were perhaps a greater hazard to the Union than all other foes combined, particularly because they surrounded themselves with a halo of respectability and honesty in their support of the slow and the double-dealing.[44]

The Conservatives, said the Count, caused Republican defeats and the Democratic upsurge in the congressional elections of 1862. The problem had been Conservative leadership, the "Lincoln-Seward disorganizing . . . undecided, both-ways policy." Even worse, the Conservatives had put the Republican Party on the wane, perhaps beyond redemption, as Radical leaders had warned nearly a year earlier. "Lin-

43 Gurowski to Andrew, October 25, 1862, in Andrew Papers; *Diary,* II, 338 (October 4, 1863), III, 50 (December 20, 1863).

44 *Diary,* II, 130–31 (February 6, 1863), III, 126–27 (March 5, 1864), 261 (June 17, 1864).

coln-Seward politically slaughtered the republican party," the anguished Count wailed, "and with it the country's honor. The future looks dark and terrible. I shudder." On the other hand, the Democrats, flushed with victory and Republican confusion, were everywhere displaying revitalized energy to preserve slavery and the Confederacy, while pressuring Conservative Republicans for compromise with the South.[45]

Gurowski, nevertheless, was not completely pleased with Radical actions and attitudes. He complained that they usually did little more than protest verbally over slowness and indecision in the Lincoln government, which sometimes used appointive office to break Radical will. He did not agree with those Jacobins who showed patience with administration Conservatives, when they explained that the nation was great enough to withstand their blunderings. While Radicals sometimes argued that events should be relied upon to illumine and awaken the people, he retorted that this did not remove the need for vigorous and aggressive leadership, since events followed actions of men. For this reason, Radicals ought to point out and warn the people of the shortcomings of Conservative leadership.[46]

Whatever disappointment the Count experienced because of Jacobin attitudes was more than offset by his satisfaction with the Radicals in Congress. He envisioned them in an ever increasing majority in the national legislature throughout the war. Although this antiadministration group was hampered by Constitutional formulas in directing the war effort, he thought it palsied even more by the inefficiency and vacillation of the administration.[47] The position of the congressional Jacobins was difficult and at times disgraceful, because they frequently found it necessary to defend the Lincoln administration against attacks of ultra-Conservatives, Constitutionalists, Copperheads, and Democrats. They were also in the inconsistent situation of defending an administration which sometimes opposed measures they demanded and in the 1862 con-

[45] *Diary,* I, 300 (October 18, 1862), 312 (November 5, 1862), II, 23–24 (December 7, 1862).

[46] *Diary,* II, 187, 199–200 (April 4 and 17, 1863), III, 39 (December 6, 1863), 155 (April 2, 1864).

[47] *Diary,* I, 139 (January, 1862), 169 (March, 1862), 229–30 (June, 1862), 242 (July, 1862).

gressional elections disgraced or betrayed the principles of the party. "And thus the patriots have the dead weight to support," the Count complained, "and are wholly unsupported."[48]

But the Jacobins of Congress never faltered at any time during the war, he believed, despite administration opposition. He looked to the statutory record in judging accomplishments. There he found the "true" principles of the Republican Party, the "true" will of the people finally prevailing. A steady program of Radical legislation unfolded before the Count, a record pleasant to behold. Ahead he saw a glorious destiny for Radical legislation because of the overwhelming majority of "patriots" in the first reconstruction Congress, a body he viewed as destined to harvest and carry to fruition the Jacobin efforts of its predecessors and also "to sternly control and direct the Executive."[49] His one complaint of Congress was that it had yielded too much authority to the President on the ground of wartime necessity, thus establishing dangerous precedents that might ultimately lead to encroachment on civil liberties.[50]

Like other careful observers of his day, Gurowski saw certain common denominators and characteristics in individual Radical Republicans. The search for precedents, which generally plagued the American mind, he said, was not a concern of Jacobins, whom he considered resourceful enough to act in emergencies without example. Another trait, not evident in Conservatives, was a sense of righteous indignation combined with intense wrath and joy. Simple and quiet Spartan-like living was another quality, as was ability to resist temptation. Their patriotism, insight, devotion, and sacrifice were unprecedented in the history of the United States. Essentially abolitionists in the broad sense, they gave birth to and supported progress by clearing away prejudices and abolishing whatever inhibited the free and healthy impulses and activities of their minds and hearts.[51]

[48] *Diary*, II, 38–39 (December 22, 1862); see also 108–109 (January 25, 1863), and 159 (March 1, 1863).

[49] *Diary*, III, 393–94 (November 9, 1864); see also II, 278 (July 20, 1863), and III, 111–12 (February 16, 1864).

[50] *Diary*, III, 380–81 (October 24, 1864).

[51] *Diary*, I, 260 (Sepetmber, 1862, before the first daily entry of the month, September 3), 276 (September 20, 1862), II, 31 (December 31, 1862), III, 119 (February 29, 1864), 155–57, 185–86 (April 2 and 18, 1864), 377 (October 17, 1864).

Sidney R. Strober Collection
Photo by the Mathew B. Brady Gallery

ADAM GUROWSKI, who was described by Walt Whitman as an "almost phenomenal" man of "great keenness" and "splendid intellect." President Lincoln said of him, "So far as my personal safety is concerned, Gurowski is the only man who has given me a serious thought of a personal nature."

Mathew B. Brady Collection, Library of Congress

EDWARD EVERETT, statesman, diplomat, and president of Harvard, who befriended the immigrant Gurowski and invited him to lecture to Harvard law students in his home. It was Everett, not President Lincoln, who delivered the principal address at the dedication of Gettysburg National Military Cemetery.

Mathew B. Brady Collection, Library of Congress

HENRY WADSWORTH LONGFELLOW, Gurowski's staunch friend from the Harvard years, who said of him, "We all feel as if a huge garden-roller had gone over us." But in Gurowski's mind, Longfellow was always the "poet with generous heart."

Mathew B. Brady Collection, National Archives

THE CAPITOL as Gurowski saw it when he went to Washington in 1861. President Lincoln insisted that construction continue on the Capitol dome, which he considered symbolic of the preservation of the Union.

Courtesy of Laurence G. Hoes

MR. AND MRS. CHARLES EAMES and their son-in-law and daughter, Mr. and Mrs. Alastair Penrose Gordon-Cumming. Gurowski lived in the Eames home, where Washington's elite political, intellectual, and social personages gathered. Mrs. Eames acted as placator in the Count's inevitable quarrels.

L. C. Handy-Mathew B. Brady Collection, Library of Congress

JOHN A. ANDREW, the youthful governor of Massachusetts (1861–66) and Gurowski's confidant during the Civil War. Of the Count, Andrew said, "He *drew me* like a *magnet.*"

Mathew B. Brady Collection, Library of Congress

WARD HILL LAMON, Lincoln's bodyguard and former law associate, who quieted the President's assassination fear of Gurowski by strengthening security precautions. Lamon described the Count as "a revolutionist by nature, restless, revengeful, and of a fiery and ungovernable temper."

L. C. Handy Studios, Washington, D.C.
From the Handy-Brady Collection

WILLARD'S HOTEL, Pennsylvania Avenue and Fourteenth Street, Northwest, where Gurowski and other hotspurs helped to scuttle the Washington Peace Convention of February, 1861. The present Willard Hotel was constructed on this site during President Theodore Roosevelt's administration.

"A man inspired by conviction and glowing with fervent faith," the Count said of his Radical prototype, "thoroughly knows what he is about. Strong in his faith, and by his faith, he clearly sees his way, and steadily walks in it, while others grope hither and thither amidst shadows and darkness and bewildering doubts! Such a man boldly takes the initiative . . . for the signs of the times. The mere trimming and selfish politician is ever ready to swim with the stream which he had neither strength nor skill to breast."[52]

To Gurowski, Jacobins were also men of principle, impelled by pure, sacred, and patriotic motives. Christianity, he reasoned, had been established by men who were "absolute radicals," men who refused to compromise with heathenism and Judaism. In Jacobinism he found a sacred calling, in their kind a Christlike pattern. "Radicals—true ones—," he declared, "look to the great aim, forget their persons, and are not moved by mean interests and vanities."[53]

Gurowski should have known that most of the common denominators and characteristics assigned by him to the Radicals of the Civil War era would not stand the test of time. Many apply equally to the Conservatives of the period.

9

The Count was one of the most picturesque and one of the most exasperating characters in Lincoln's Washington. People could not fail to notice him because of his giant paunch, European-tailored clothing, blue goggles with side blinders, and semimilitary stride. He loved to talk with friends or strangers, and sometimes managed a little humor. Two army officers, new in the city, asked him where to find a theater. "In the White House," he replied, "where Lincoln is always performing." On another occasion, outside a government office building, he argued so forcefully with a friend that a policeman came up and asked if a fight was going on. When both said no, Gurowski asked the officer to loan him his club to better impress his companion.[54]

[52] *Diary*, II, 62–63 (January 2, 1863).
[53] *Diary*, II, 160 (March 2, 1863).
[54] Gouverneur, *As I Remember*, 246; Chittenden, *Personal Reminiscences*, 320; Mrs.

95

Quick to criticize, slow to give credit, the Count was unpopular for this alone. His habit of pushing around in Washington political, diplomatic, and social circles often caused him to seem wholly obnoxious. Politically, he usually confined his relations to Radicals, since Conservatives disgusted him. He did, however, attend most White House receptions for military officers and never missed Lincoln's annual New Year's levee. He also enjoyed the social functions of cabinet members and foreign ministers. In time, the political overtones of his *Diary* and conversations isolated him socially from the Conservatives, who refused to invite him. More and more he found himself acceptable to Radicals alone, and his visits increased with Secretary Stanton and other like-minded friends in the War Department and Congress.[55]

Remembering his European years, Gurowski felt that the revolutionary movements of 1831 and 1848 had failed precisely because the virtuous were not swift and drastic enough, while the wicked were fast and ruthless. He believed it high time for the righteous to function with a will. Although he had moved to Washington in hope of a civilian job, his basic and steadfast purpose was to work energetically for what he saw as "the victory of right and truth" in government and society. In Warsaw, Paris, and St. Petersburg he had labored for these ends through written and spoken political intrigue, maneuver, and propaganda, and his intention once again was to be heard effectively: "I wish I could speak from towers and roofs and awake the people." He considered his personal welfare unimportant, except as a means to mold and win national goals in which he believed. When these were endangered, he lost sight of "all earthly ties and relations." He had "no aim, no object in life, only the general success of our cause," which he interpreted as the prompt overthrow of the Confederacy and slavery. The North would also "vindicate self-government," he predicted, and would demonstrate "to the world that the apparently loose governmental ribbons are the strongest when everybody carries them in him, and holds them." For-

---

Eames to Sumner, September 1, 1861, in Sumner Papers; statement by Laurence G. Hoes, December 26, 1950, in author's possession.

[55] Beale (ed.), *Diary of Gideon Welles,* II, 101 (August 9, 1864); Dana to Pike, December 12, 1864, in Pike Papers.

tunately, thought he, a large and growing block of Radical Republicans viewed the problems much as he saw them. But the stumbling block to their solution was "Lincoln and Company."[56]

[56] Gurowski to Sumner, April 23, 1861, in Sumner Papers; Gurowski to Pike, August 30, 1861, in Pike Papers; Gurowski to Felton, October 30, [1861], in Felton Papers; Gurowski to Andrew, August 2 and 28 and November 9, 1862, and January 10, 1863, in Andrew Papers; Diary, I, 30 (April, 1861).

CHAPTER V

LINCOLN THE INCOMPETENT

I

Of criticism that plagued Lincoln, none was more caustic and bitter than that of Gurowski. The contemplative mind and relaxed attitudes of the President continually annoyed the combative European, who contended that the nation's head should be quick and grim, should hack and smash at the Confederacy.[1]

During the first year of the war, Gurowski remained hopeful that Lincoln would develop "energetic qualities" through the "shock of events," despite his "rather slow intellect" and "slow power of perception." Perhaps Lincoln would then wish for more than a war with blank cartridges, he said, and would no longer detest bloodshed. As weeks turned to months, he found a similarity between Lincoln's inaction and good will and the conciliatory political leadership of Pope Pius IX in the period preceding the outbreak of the Revolution of 1848. Lincoln, he said, also bore a "slender historical resemblance to Louis XVI.—similar goodness, honesty, good intentions; but the size of events seems to be too much for him." When Gurowski talked with Hay, he complained that the President showed no action or aggressiveness. Hay's reply that Lincoln was actually a man of unusual judgment and energy caused the Count to recommend to the Secretary that Lincoln should be more himself. "Neither pighead Lincoln nor the whole Cabinet," he snorted, "have been elected with the view of crushing a civil war."[2]

[1] Much of the material in this chapter was previously published under the title "Lincoln's Gadfly—Adam Gurowski," *Mississippi Valley Historical Review,* Vol. XXXVI (December, 1949), 415-34.

[2] Gurowski to Sumner, April 23, 1861, in Sumner Papers; *Diary,* I, 46 (May, 1861), 54 (June, 1861), 61 (July, 1861), 89 (August, 1861); Gurowski to Pike, August 30, 1861, in Pike Papers.

War events and pressures seemed not to spur the President to activity. Instead, he was pulled in all directions, thought Gurowski, and the Jacksonian qualities of energy, will, foresight, and prompt decision necessary in a war leader were not forthcoming. Moreover, Lincoln appeared to have had no experience in dealing with men and events, and no knowledge of the past. But the Count still hoped that he would become strong-willed and aggressive. "I wait and wait," he said, "for the eagle which may break out from the White House. Even the burning fire of the national disaster at Bull Run left the egg unhatched . . . . It looks as if the slowest brains were to deal with the greatest events of our epoch. Mr. Lincoln is a pure-souled, well-intentioned patriot, and this nobody doubts or contests. But is that all which is needed in these terrible emergencies?" "I still hope perhaps against hope," he commented doubtingly a month later, "that if Lincoln is what the masses believe him to be, a strong mind, than all may come out well. Strong minds . . . become inspired, and inspiration compensates the deficiency or want of information acquired by studies. Weak minds . . . become confused and dizzy. Which of the two will be Mr. Lincoln's fate?"[3]

Lincoln appeared more hesitant and bungling as the Radicals gathered strength during the second year of war. With their increase in power and influence came renewed cries for crushing the South. "And so Davis is making history," Gurowski roared, "and Lincoln is telling stories." Whatever Lincoln did he carried out under pressure of events and public opinion. These slowly moved the President in spite of his "reluctant heaviness" and opposition. Without doubt, Lincoln day after day "shows his want of knowledge of men and of things; the total absence of *intuition* to spell, to see through, and to disentangle events." The President did not even realize his responsibility for assisting in reckless squandering of life and treasure. But eventually Congress and history, the Count predicted, would bring him to a "terrible" account.[4]

To offset such Radical howls, Conservatives explained that Lincoln was a man of unusual wisdom and virtue, who proceeded with caution,

---

[3] *Diary*, I, 85 (August, 1861), 98 (September, 1861).

[4] *Diary*, I, 144 (January, 1862), 157–58, 162, 164 (February, 1862), 205 (May, 1862), 252 (August, 1862).

not wanting to hurt anyone. Gurowski conceded the claims made by Lincoln's eulogists and friends, but complained that these qualities, commendable in private life, were "transformed from positive into negative, since Mr. Lincoln's contact with the pulsations and the hurricane of public life." He found a good illustration in Lincoln's failure to remove General George B. McClellan from command. Lincoln preferred to sacrifice the best blood of the nation rather than offend McClellan and his friends by removing him. "I do not deny to Abe," he said, "all kind of good qualities, but they are *all negative,* and therefore unproductive and worthless." Honesty of purpose when not backed by "clear, strong brains" proved worthless in private life, but in the national leader became a "positive nuisance." The eventual success he predicted for Lincoln would come "not by his own merits but because a noble and devoted people carries him on its shoulders." He could not consider the President "a blessing to the people, to the cause of humanity and of freedom. At the utmost I fear him as I would an unavoidable evil, an original sin."[5]

Vainly, the Count said, he groped to find noble and energetic qualities in Lincoln. All that he found was "the stubborness of a mule." If Lincoln ever turned out to be a man and statesman, such an event would not occur until the country's political and material vitality had been exhausted. In harmony with other Jacobins, he grumbled after the Union disaster at Fredericksburg: "You can not change Lincoln's head, you can not fill his small but empty skull with brains; and when . . . brains are wanting, or soft or diseased the whole body suffers or is paralized, so with the nation." The truth was that Lincoln had come to represent no more than "the unavoidable constitutional formula." "For all other purposes," he said frankly, "as an acting, directing, inspiring, or combining power or agency, Mr. Lincoln becomes a myth. His reality is only manifested by preserving slavery, by sticking to McClellan, by disturbing offices, by receiving inspirations from Mr. Seward, and by digging the country's grave." He exclaimed in anguish that no gallows could be high enough for the President and predicted that history would erect them if the people did not.[6]

[5] *Diary,* I, 205, 207 (May, 1862); Gurowski to Andrew, May 7 and June 20, 1862, in Andrew Papers.

During the remaining years of the war Gurowski would assert that Lincoln could be spurred to action only by the people. "O, could I only win confidence in Mr. Lincoln," he lamented, "it would be one of the most cheerful days and events in my life. Perhaps, elephant-like, Mr. Lincoln slowly, cautiously but surely feels his way across a bridge leading over a precipice." Nothing that Lincoln ever did appeared to be accomplished in advance of public demands: "Lincoln acts when the popular wave is so high that he can stand it no more, or when the gases of public exasperation rise powerfully and strike his nose." Comparing Washington and Lincoln, he held that the first President vigorously had led the revolutionary forces when called on, but that the Civil War President "was, and is, always behind the onward march of the people, and is rather dragged by the people than beckoning it to follow him." The Count firmly believed that Lincoln was at best but a second-rate executor of what he considered the people's determined hope and will.[7]

Radicals agreed that the infirmity of the administration originated in its leader. Lincoln himself, Gurowski said, admitted that he never foresaw events and was always behind them and that when a government official acted ahead of events, he overruled him. He observed the same pattern in the President throughout the war and near the end of the conflict remarked: "Mr. Lincoln never yet boldly faced events and emergencies, never siezed the hour by the forelock or the bull by the horns. Mr. Lincoln was great in backing out to the last moment." On Lincoln's day of national prayer and humiliation in 1864 the Count felt that the people would probably propitiate Providence, but questioned whether atonement by the President and his Conservative associates would cause God to forgive them.[8]

[6] Gurowski to Andrew, September 2, October 19, and December 27, 1862, in *ibid.*; *Diary*, I, 262 (September 5, 1862), 303 (October 22, 1862).

[7] *Diary*, II, 153 (February 26, 1863), 328 (September 20, 1863), III, 40 (December 6, 1863), 100–101 (February 13, 1864), 389 (November 5, 1864).

[8] *Diary*, III, 182, 209 (April 16 and 29, 1864), 209 (August 4, 1864), 343 (September 13, 1864); Lincoln to Albert G. Hodges, April 4, 1864, in Basler (ed.), *The Collected Works of Abraham Lincoln*, VII, 281–82. Lincoln's proclamation of July 7, 1864, establishing August 4 as a day of prayer, is in *ibid.*, 431–32.

2

Seward, in Gurowski's estimation, was the most pernicious of the Conservatives influencing Lincoln. Even before the inauguration Seward had held Lincoln in the palm of his hand, proved by his bringing the President to the Senate and begging Southern Democrats to meet him, a sight "saddening, humiliating, and revolting" to Gurowski in the gallery. The extent of Seward's influence over Lincoln during the first year of the war seemed to be generally misunderstood: "More than ever Lincoln is under the t[h]umb of Seward; to a degree al[l] most ridiculous, Seward brings him out to take airing as were he Lincoln's nurse, who dares not a single mental or bodily move without his preceptor." When Lincoln attended a Seward reception, the Count observed that the President appeared much as a mannequin. The truth, as he saw it, was that Lincoln soon came to be completely overshadowed by Seward: "It is a positive fact that Seward exercises ⅘ of dictatorship. I say this not as an empty phrase, [but] as an unquestionable result of his allpowerful influence over Lincoln."[9]

The Secretary, according to Gurowski, nourished the Chief Executive's conceit as the easiest way to handle and dominate his "feeble mind." "If all the lies could only be ferreted out with which Seward bamboozles Lincoln, even the God of Lies himself would shudder." Worst of all, Lincoln did not realize the degree to which Seward wrongly influenced him, despite repeated warnings from those nearest him in heart and blood. After three years of this domination, Lincoln began to to assert himself, although he still at times caved in before Seward. The Count maintained that the more blunders the Secretary caused the President to make, the quicker the final emancipation would come. Yet Gurowski believed that the Radicals would dupe themselves by the hope that Lincoln, if re-elected in 1864, would sever his subservience to Seward. The Count sometimes thought that the Secretary then was stronger with the President than at any previous time.[10]

[9] Diary, I, 15 (March, 1861), 63, 66 (July, 1861), 89 (August, 1861); Gurowski to Sumner, May 1 and 14, 1861, in Sumner Papers; Gurowski to Greeley, October 1, 1861, in Greeley Papers.

[10] Diary, I, 205 (May, 1862), 244 (July, 1862), II, 89 (January 15, 1863), 242

3

To Gurowski and all other Radicals, control of Lincoln remained the major problem throughout the war, while Congress had been under their increasing influence since the beginning of the conflict. In an effort to guide and dominate the President, the Radicals directed at him a barrage of advice. Not only did Lincoln seem deaf, unmoved, and insensible to Radical direction, the Count maintained, but his response was peevish and irritable as well: "As the devil dreads holy water, so Mr. Lincoln dreads to be surrounded with stern, earnest, ardent, patriotic advisers." The only good that the President rendered the Jacobin cause, according to Gurowski, appeared to be his support of Secretary of War Stanton.[11]

As Lincoln continued to oppose the Jacobins and to baffle their plans, the Count looked to Congress for more stringent controls over the Executive. He heard from a group of congressional Radicals who visited Lincoln that he approved their views, promised to adopt them, and desired their counsel, but he doubted Lincoln's word. Instead of opposing Jacobin pressures covertly or openly, he reflected, the President ought to accept their guidance and be thankful for it. The Radicals of Congress initiated and pushed through all the legislation that had saved the country, dragged Lincoln into action, and then charitably drew a veil over his defects: "It is the work of the radicals that Mr. Lincoln stands today before the people and before the civilized world as the incarnation of the sacred Northern cause." He predicted in his *Diary* that the President would eventually collaborate with the Jacobins: "Well, well; the time will and must come, when either you will go overboard with all your varlets and advisers, or you will go on your knees to my friends the radicals, to be saved by them from Gehenna's fire. We will wait and see."[12]

(June 6, 1863), 267 (July 14, 1863), III, 149–50 (March 25, 1864); Gurowski to Andrew, March 27, 1864, in Andrew Papers.

[11] *Diary,* I, 267 (September 9, 1862), II, 85–86, 98–99 (January 10 and 20, 1863), 142 (February 14, 1863); Gurowski to Andrew, July 7, 1862, in Andrew Papers; Gurowski to Greeley, July 7, 1862, in Greeley Papers.

[12] *Diary,* III, 99, 113 (February 12 and 20, 1864), 136 (March 1, 1864), 171 (April 11, 1864).

Gurowski considered Lincoln's influence on military affairs objectionable. He complained again and again that the President kept generals in command simply because he did not wish to hurt their feelings or the feelings of their supporters. This was the case with McClellan, whom the Count believed Lincoln considered inadequate as commander of the Army of the Potomac. Gurowski observed that in any other country a military leader like McClellan would be dismissed, but here the nation's life blood was permitted to waste away. He reported that a few days after the Battle of Antietam, McClellan's father-in-law and chief of staff, Randolph B. Marcy, insinuated to Lincoln that the General wished to be relieved. Not even then did the President act. At last, on November 5, 1862, Lincoln removed him from command. Gurowski believed the President next wished to drop the General from the army, but lacked the courage.[13]

Lincoln, the Count said, also held stubbornly to General Joseph Hooker after he had led the Army of the Potomac to defeat at Chancellorsville. Similarly, the President stood by General Henry W. Halleck, the scholarly and pedantic general in chief, throughout his military blunderings, and defended the sinking star of General George G. Meade as he commanded the Army of the Potomac during its weeks and months of inactivity following the carnage at Gettysburg. When, in 1864, Lincoln reported that Halleck had been relieved at his own request, the Count retorted that the entire country knew the General in Chief had for all practical purposes been fired by Congress.[14]

Gurowski disliked what he considered to be Lincoln's undue interference in military affairs. "For several weeks," he wrote complainingly in the spring of 1862, "the President, God knows under what influences, *constantly* overrules Stanton, as to the conduct of the Virginia campaign." Considering Lincoln a man of small military ability, he accused him of directing tactics and battles from his office during McClellan's

[13] *Diary*, I, 161 (February, 1862), 250–51 (August, 1862), III, 171 (April 11, 1864); Gurowski to Andrew, July 4 and October 19, 1862, in Andrew Papers. McClellan resigned from the army on November 8, 1864.

[14] *Diary*, II, 234 (May 20, 1863), 240, 245 (June 3 and 14, 1863), III, 24 (November 1, 1863), 137–38 (March 17, 1864).

Peninsula campaign. Worst of all, there was no firmness in Lincoln's relations to military operations. Gurowski complained of the President's letter to McClellan in the autumn of 1862 concerning removal of troops from Harpers Ferry, although written "with ability and lucidity," and concluded: "This letter is in no sense an order."[15]

Lincoln's creation of generals also worried Gurowski. The President gave little consideration to the ability or intent of those he appointed, said the Count. Pushed into a corner by the demands of daring people, the Chief Executive created generals, and was in fact a "baker of generals." The Senate also became involved by its confirmation authority, with approval readily granted Lincoln's general-officer appointees, because various senators, Radicals excluded, had their own nominees. The Count sarcastically recommended that the many useless major generals nominated by Lincoln and later relieved of duty ought to be formed into a squadron with Halleck at the head and McClellan in the rear for the purpose of charging Lee's forces.[16]

Gurowski held the President responsible for battlefield disasters because he believed he failed during most of the war to provide the Army of the Potomac with adequate military leadership. When the North at last undertook extensive military operations, this time with success, and called for huge quotas of men to fill depleted ranks and build new armies, Gurowski sniped at Lincoln with this biting parody:

> A new call for 500,000 men. Lincoln ought to make his *whereas* as follows:
>
> *Whereas,* my makeshift and of all foresight bereaved policy—
> *Whereas,* the advice of a Seward, of a Blair, and of similar etc's—
> *Whereas,* my Generals, such as McClellan, Halleck, and many other pets appointed or held in command for political reasons, have occasioned a wanton slaughter of men; *therefore*
> I, Abraham Lincoln, the official Juggernaut, call for more victims

[15] Gurowski to Andrew, May 25 and 30 and June 11, 1862, in Andrew Papers; *Diary,* I, 299 (October 18, 1862); Gurowski to Andrew, October 19, 1862, in Andrew Papers; Lincoln to McClellan, October 13, 1862, in Basler (ed.), *The Collected Works of Abraham Lincoln,* V, 460–61.

[16] *Diary,* II, 267 (July 14, 1863), III, 34–35 (November 24, 1863), 55 (December 28, 1863), 67 (January 8, 1864).

to fill the gaps made by the mental deficiency of certain among my commanders as well as by rebel bullets.[17]

The Count rejoiced, however, when Lincoln was pressured by Stanton, the congressional Radicals, and public opinion to entrust Ulysses S. Grant with the command of all United States armies. Grant in turn, Gurowski pointed out, had brought in a brilliant group of new commanders, like William T. Sherman and Philip H. Sheridan, who were pleasing to the Radicals.[18]

4

The circumstances of Lincoln's re-election in 1864 posed a trying problem to Gurowski and most Radicals. A year and a half before the election the Count had reacted to the first ground swell in the President's behalf: "If Mr. Lincoln is re-elected, then . . . self-government is not yet founded on reason, intellect, and on sound judgment." Most distressing for Gurowski, however, was the gravitation of a few Jacobins to Lincoln before the close of 1863 and their belief that the President must be re-elected in order to save the country from the curse of McClellan and his Democratic supporters. When the Count saw and heard in Washington more than a year before the election that Lincoln was hard at work winning a second term, he hoped that the President would be as earnest in his efforts to destroy Lee's forces and to stamp out guerrilla activity.[19]

The degree of public sentiment favoring Lincoln's re-election in the early months of 1864 amazed Gurowski. He concluded that the people at large did not actually know the President, but judged him by his nickname, "Honest Abe," and by what politicians and newspapers said about him. The people erroneously credited to Lincoln, he said, the successes resulting from their own sacrifices and zeal. Those who truly knew the President because they worked with him—the senators and

[17] *Diary*, III, 168–69, 189 (April 11 and 19, 1864), 290 (July 18, 1864), Lincoln's proclamation calling for five hundred thousand army volunteers, July 18, 1864, is in Basler (ed.), *The Collected Works of Abraham Lincoln*, VII, 448–49.

[18] *Diary*, III, 365 (October 2, 1864).

[19] *Diary*, II, 237 (May 28, 1863), 298 (August 13, 1863), 320–21 (September 15, 1863), III, 43–44 (December 12, 1863).

representatives—realized his shortcomings, and a majority in both houses stood against his re-election. Unfortunately, he said regretfully, the people refused to listen to their representatives in Congress.[20]

As the movement to renominate Lincoln gained momentum, Gurowski observed that the President would be likely to reap the rewards of public sacrifice. The governors of the free states, pressed by the people, had showed more energy than the President and his entire administration and had breathed life into the ailing federal government. Thus the people and the loyal governors worked as early as the war's beginning to secure Lincoln's renomination and re-election in 1864.[21]

Vigorous Radical opposition should come immediately, Gurowski believed, if the tide for Lincoln was to be stemmed, because the people at large were heavily for him. Entreating Governor Andrew to come to Washington immediately, he wrote angrily: "Will you ever come to this sewer of meanness, subserviency, and . . . lack of manhood? Believe me, the Lincolnites make here progress and that *fallacy* the unanimity of the people in favor of Lincoln shuts up the lips of the true and honest men." "No body—no body," he wailed in his faulty English, "dares to speak out the truth and enlighten the public conscience concerning that sham Lincoln and as time runs quickly, the humbuged people may reelect him." A month later, well in advance of the Baltimore Convention, he conceded: "Lincoln's reelection is the triumph of meanness, of corruption, of the . . . *most* mediocre mediocrity, of lies, of bad faith triumphing over the noblest impulses of a generous people . . . . Oh! the people will curse for eternity all those who whip . . . and drag it into reelection."[22]

By late April other Radicals were submitting to the idea of Lincoln's renomination also, the Count said, but damning the expediency that drove them to it. His blood boiled, and he resolved to take the stump against the President, should he be renominated. The Radical delegates to the Baltimore Convention had their hands tied, Gurowski believed,

[20] *Diary*, III, 69–70 (January 12, 1864), 159 (April 4, 1864).

[21] *Diary*, III, 130–31 (March 6, 1864).

[22] *Diary*, III, 146–47 (March 22, 1864); Gurowski to Andrew, March 10, [1864], March 27 and April 27, 1864, in Andrew Papers.

since they had been pledged to Lincoln. All they could do, as they reluctantly supported the President, would be to carry the point in the convention that he be admonished to reform his ways and change his advisers.[23]

Even after Lincoln won renomination, the Radicals were anything but solidly behind the President. Gurowski observed that many were looking to the Democrats, that some would remain passive, and that others perhaps would call another Republican convention and insist on a Jacobin nominee. This condition appeared to be ominous for both Lincoln and the Republican Party, for it could mean defeat, resurgence of the Democrats, and the triumph of slavery. Although maintaining that the Radicals would not readily fall into the Lincoln re-election ranks, the Count contended that most would eventually yield because of the pressure of "unavoidable, imperious, life or death deciding necessity." Fellow Jacobins who reproved him just after the Baltimore Convention for not supporting Lincoln were answered that the time for that had not yet arrived. Three months later Gurowski revealed his change of heart: "In my small way I must support Mr. Lincoln . . . . I cannot politically separate myself from my best political friends, from men whom I truly respect, and between whom and me not a shadow of difference in principle exists."[24]

During high summer Lincoln's chances for re-election did not seem good, and the Count noted little popular enthusiasm for the President. He feared that the Democrats would nominate a candidate strong enough to win the election. With McClellan's nomination interest in Lincoln's re-election still lagged, but he hoped that public disgust over the Chicago platform would mushroom and buoy up the President's waning chances. On the other hand, thousands upon thousands could well vote for McClellan "only to overthrow Lincoln's hateful policy." How much more desirable a Radical candidate would have been, he mused, as he continued to hope Lincoln would be replaced at the

[23] *Diary*, III, 194, 200 (April 22 and 26, 1864), 246–47, 250 (June 5 and 7, 1864); Dennett (ed.), *Lincoln and the Civil War in the Diaries and Letters of John Hay*, 183 (diary, May 24, 1864).

[24] *Diary*, III, 251–53, 255 (June 9 and 11, 1864), 357 (September 21, 1864).

eleventh hour. Specifically, many a Jacobin senator, representative, or governor would be preferable to the President: "In one word, I could name hundreds more fit, more energetic, more clear sighted, and in every respect more proven and more eligible, and nevertheless the country, the people subside on a Lincoln!"[25]

Surprisingly, the Count sprang to the President's defense several times during the campaign. To those who criticized Lincoln for not being a classical scholar and therefore unfit for the Presidency, he replied that the American classical scholar was highly disgusting. He considered the President's mind luckily unbefogged by limited classical scholarship. He preferred "the railsplitter to any narrow, classical hairsplitter." Democratic criticism that Lincoln was a tyrant caused him to retort caustically that the President did not have nerve and mind enough to be a tyrant even in a righteous cause. For example, Lincoln did not hang Confederates nor imprison domestic traitors. Those who maintained that the President endangered freedom of the press were told by Gurowski that he wished Lincoln had courage enough to suppress newspapers such as the New York *World*, the Washington *National Intelligencer*, and the Boston *Courier*, because they "preach treason to right and to humanity, and poison the minds of the people."[26]

The Radicals who worked for Lincoln's re-election, thought the Count, labored for the principles of the Republican Party and not for its "accidental standard-bearer." By this reasoning the President's re-election was made palatable to them. A letter from Iowa Senator James W. Grimes provided in the Count's estimation the best qualification of Radical support. "Much as I disprove," wrote Grimes, "of Mr. Lincoln's irresolute indecisive policy and much as I despise many of the corrupt scoundrels by whom he is surrounded, yet I shall not hesitate to vote for him and against McClellan's Chicago platform. It is this Chicago platform that will elect Lincoln. Few now want to vote for him. He is very far from being a popular man today. He will only be accepted because the *public* are so genuinely loyal to the government, and they

[25] *Diary*, III, 304–305, 315, 322 (August 1, 11, and 24, 1864), 329, 335–36, 350 (September 1, 11, and 18, 1864).

[26] *Diary*, III, 348–50 (September 17, 1864), 382–83 (October 28, 1864).

are afraid to trust the men who concocted the Chicago platform and who they believe will surround McClellan should he be elected." Thus, maintained Gurowski, events and circumstances, rather than his own merits, caused the Radicals to accept and sustain Lincoln.[27]

As election day approached, the Count questioned whether the President would reform his ways. Had Lincoln learned from the past? Did he now know that it was useless to conciliate Copperheads, to spare Northern traitors, to pardon guerrillas, bushwhackers, and their cohorts? Had the President acquired some knowledge of men? Would he, re-elected, surround himself with Radicals? "I wish to believe it," Gurowski concluded hopelessly, "but my doubt is stronger than my faith. Lincoln is too old to bend, and may rather break under the weight of his old ways and mental habits."[28]

The Count viewed Republican victory at the polls as a triumph of justice, right, and humanity over the combined powers of hell. The victory of Lincoln was but incidental. The people voted, he believed, for the nation's honor and integrity. Their verdict called for an indivisible Union without slavery. Thus Lincoln had been reconsecrated to the task of crushing rebellion and destroying slavery, with the mandate that lost time be made up at once.[29]

5

The President undoubtedly thought Gurowski an eccentric person, whose letters to him were ample evidence for this opinion. These communications arrived frequently enough to be annoying, particularly at the beginning of the war. Foreign policy was a theme on which the European exile wrote in admonishing tones, for he felt himself unusually well qualified in this subject. The first letter reached the Executive Mansion after Lincoln's blockade proclamation of April 19, 1861. He explained that this "international demonstration" would evoke foreign recognition of the Confederacy as a belligerent. This in turn would lead

[27] *Diary,* III, 343, 358 (September 13 and 22, 1864), 375 (October 16, 1864), 388 (November 5, 1864); James W. Grimes to Gurowski, September 18, 1864, in Gurowski Papers.
[28] *Diary,* III, 390 (November 7, 1864); see also 386–88 (November 3–5, 1864).
[29] *Diary,* III, 392, 394–96 (November 9 and 10, 1864).

to recognition of Confederate privateers. To prevent such a development, he wanted Lincoln to enforce the blockade rigidly, thereby demonstrating to Europe that he intended to maintain "the fullest exercise of sovereignty." In a second letter he advised the President against subscribing to the Declaration of Paris of 1856. Hearing that Lincoln proposed using that instrument as a means of preventing Confederate ships from being recognized as legal privateers, the Count told him it would not serve.[30]

Next month Gurowski wrote a verbose letter on the recent recognition of the Confederacy as a belligerent by England and France. Of his guidance letters to the Chief Executive, this is the earliest now known in final draft.[31] He labeled this Roman numeral III, to set it apart as the third in his series of letters. This queer document is written in his best hand, as indeed are all his letters to Lincoln. Marked "strictly confidential," his advice is spread over seven large pages and is carefully itemized under sixteen major points with numerous subdivisions. The Count wrote of the growing unfriendly attitude of France and England and pointed out its causes. The blockade, tariff, threatened unemployment of cotton-mill workers in France and England, and schemes of Napoleon III of France he considered the factors involved. He also suggested that the government "be watchful of the barometer of Europe" because of the ominous condition of foreign relations and warned that the methods and attitudes of diplomats be carefully observed. But these problems, the Pole said in conclusion, would not have arisen if, instead of imposing the blockade, the government had merely suspended the Southern coastal cities as ports of entry and had used armed vessels to enforce its decision.[32]

Gurowski wrote other letters to Lincoln on the subject of foreign

[30] *Diary*, I, 27, 29 (April, 1861).

[31] The Lincoln Papers contain a final draft of an earlier Gurowski letter, March 12, 1861, in which he requested a job.

[32] Gurowski to Lincoln, May 22, 1861, in John G. Nicolay and John Hay Collection, Illinois State Historical Library, Springfield. For a brief mention of this letter, see *Diary*, I, 45 (May, 1861). This letter was apparently used by Nicolay and Hay in writing a chapter of their *Abraham Lincoln: A History* (10 vols., New York, 1890), entitled "European Neutrality" (IV, 266–80), for it is to be found among the Nicolay and Hay notes on that chapter.

relations. In one he warned of Seward's inability to understand Europe and European diplomacy: "Mr. Seward is held in utter contempt by European Cabinets, by European premiers and by European diplomacy. The reasons are obvious. European[s] . . . respect such men as show convictions and character but not such who shift with every wind, who instead of being statesmen are common intriguers. European premiers above all in England can not respect a Secretary of State who shows the draffts of his dispatches to a foreign itinerant newspaper repporter as did . . . Seward to Russel of the English Times."[33] Curiously, he also dispatched letters on the same subject to Mrs. Lincoln, hoping that she would sustain him.[34]

The Count also wrote Lincoln on military affairs. "Give my scribbling fife minutes of time, and patience . . . . I believe firmly that you will and can save the country notwithstanding the dead weights [the Conservatives] sodered to you." In this case, he urged the arming of Negroes and their use against Confederate guerrillas, who were harassing Union forces and loyal inhabitants in the border states. At another time he warned Lincoln against Seward's dabbling in military affairs and said that with "that half ass half traitor McClellan" the nation was being destroyed. These letters he held necessary because he understood that the Executive never read newspapers, or heard, except through Seward, what was going on outside the White House.[35]

Gurowski told Lincoln to get a staff of military experts when the Army of the Potomac under McClellan was accused of having developed the "slows" in the Peninsula campaign. To bring efficiency and action, he advised that the President make the influential German-American, Major General Franz Sigel, chief of staff. Simultaneously he urged that Lincoln himself take to the field and command his generals.[36]

[33] Rough draft of a letter, Gurowski to Lincoln, no date, in Gurowski Papers. With this and other unrevised rough-draft letters intended for Lincoln is an envelope endorsed "Letter to the President belonging to the *Diary.*" Gurowski evidently retained these first drafts in order to note each in his *Diary,* as he actually did, and as the endorsed envelope suggests. The "itinerant newspaper repporter" of whom Gurowski wrote was William Howard Russell, on assignment to cover the war for *The Times* of London.

[34] Gurowski to Andrew, April 10, 1863, in Andrew Papers.

[35] Rough draft of a letter in Gurowski's hand, intended for Lincoln, no date, in Gurowski Papers; Gurowski to Andrew, October 25, 1862, in Andrew Paper.

When on July 11, 1862, General Halleck became general in chief, Gurowski saw the nucleus of his recommended staff. He wrote Lincoln requesting an assignment to that body in whatever capacity the President should consider his services useful. Rank or kind of work mattered little, the Pole assured the President, for not even a colonelcy could raise his position in society! He suggested that his friend, General James S. Wadsworth, a leading Radical, also be attached to Halleck's staff. Calling himself an impartial observer of administrative management in Washington, he recommended Wadsworth, because much depended on the "intimate surroundings of men who are to act . . . upon the destinies of the country . . . . You are aware of it even better than I." Then he excused his letter: "I thirst for the success of my adopted country [and] . . . for that of the eminent general who is to be the head of our armies."[37]

The Count's thirst remained unslaked. Soon Halleck had demonstrated his incompetence by devoting himself to minutiae instead of strategy and had thoroughly irritated the Count, who could not tolerate an office general even at his best. By and by Gurowski's temper reached boiling point. As if to relieve the pressure, he treated Lincoln to a rash letter. He indicted the President for having appointed Halleck on the basis of a military treatise the General had written years before the war and denounced the book as superficial and of no value by European standards.[38]

In pointing out Halleck's lack of initiative, the Count emphasized that he himself was not an applicant for civil or military position, but "for God's and the country's sake read what follows. No personal interest dictates these here lines." Placing in Halleck's hands "a power

[36] *Diary*, I, 214 (May, 1862); see also Gurowski to Lincoln, May 26, 1863, in Lincoln Papers, for reference to this staff suggestion.

[37] Rough draft of a letter in Gurowski's hand, intended for Lincoln, no date, in Gurowski Papers.

[38] Halleck's book was *Elements of Military Arts and Science; or, Course of Instruction in Strategy, Fortification, Tactics of Battles, etc., Embracing the Duties of Staff, Infantry, Cavalry, Artillery, and Engineers; Adapted to the Use of Volunteers and Militia* (Third Edition, New York, 1862). The initial edition appeared at the outbreak of the Mexican War in 1846. Halleck, a member of Phi Beta Kappa and a graduate of the United States Military Academy, wrote books on mineral law and international law while in the military service.

which must ruin any country even if the man . . . were a genius, a genuine Napoleon," was extremely risky. But Halleck "literally never saw a fite . . . on a genuine field-of-battle; he possesses not . . . the first notion of what is a campaign . . . . His ignorance tells in the butcheries and defeats; Halleck wholly demoralizes the army."

Then the Count advised Lincoln that general-in-chief desk positions were taboo in Europe. Warming to his theme, he continued: "Gl Halleck is odious to the country, to all good and brave officers who are not spitlickers, he is envious to genuine military capacities and prevents such capacities to take in hand the salvation of the country." If Lincoln must have men such as McClellan or Halleck as commanding generals, he should return to McClellan, for he had been "the less destructive curse of the two." Halleck, he snarled, had not his heart in the cause, for his sentiments were "those of a hireling but not of a patriot."[39]

These anti-Halleck tirades calmed the Count's emotions, but did not kill his idea that Lincoln required a military staff. He reiterated this in a letter written when the war looked especially dark for the Union. Once more he urged the President to take the field command. The Count had recently visited an unnamed general of Radical sentiment, who had talked with Lincoln following the disasters of Fredericksburg and Chancellorsville. "The patriot observed," he noted, "that Mr. Lincoln wanted only encouragement to take himself the command of the Army of the Potomac." He suggested to the President that he fortify himself with a staff, for which he recommended General John Sedgwick as chief, to be aided by George G. Meade, Gouverneur K. Warren, Andrew A. Humphreys, John B. Turchin, John G. Barnard, and Colonel James B. Fry. As might be expected, Sedgwick was an enthusiastic Radical. Gurowski then explained that "the military disasters . . . can be traced to one cardinal reason, . . . the absolute ignorance and incapacity of their respective Staffs . . . . But this . . . condition of warlike success

[39] Gurowski to Lincoln, January 21, 1863, in Lincoln Papers; a rough draft of this letter, January 20, 1863, is in the Gurowski Papers. Gurowski records writing the letter in his *Diary*, II, 101 (January 20, 1863). A comparison of the rough draft and the final draft shows no verbal tempering.

is unknown to, and therefore despised by infatuated Westpointers."[40] His appeal went unheeded, and the staff of experts, modeled on the Prussian pattern, did not materialize.[41] Halleck, however, on March 12, 1864, was at last shelved, several days after Grant had been made lieutenant general in charge of the armies of the Union.

6

Did Lincoln read Gurowski's letters? It is probable that some came to his attention and that he glanced through their contents. Four are in the Lincoln Papers, and they may have been perused by the President. In one case a Gurowski envelope bears his endorsement. But John Hay, the Chief Executive's junior secretary, asserted that Lincoln read only one in fifty letters addressed to him; the senior secretary, John G. Nicolay, estimated the number at only one in a hundred. Another of Lincoln's helpers, William O. Stoddard, who screened much of the incoming White House mail, observed that the "larger number of the epistles belonged in one or another of . . . two tall waste baskets . . . , and their deposits were as rapid as my decisions could be made. It had to be swift work." This "river of documents" averaged approximately two hundred and fifty items daily, exclusive of newspapers, according to Stoddard.[42]

One can safely conclude that the letters held for Lincoln's attention by his secretaries must have been considered pertinent or of unusual interest. Consequently, it is probable that the clerical staff selected these four letters, which have been preserved, as of sufficient value to have

---

[40] *Diary*, II, 229 (May 17, 1863); Gurowski to Lincoln, May 26, 1863, in Lincoln Papers. The endorsement on the envelope in Lincoln's hand reads, "Gurowski, May 26, 1863." The Count records writing the letter in his *Diary*, II, 230–33 (May 17, 1863), and describes its background and content. The nine-day discrepancy in these dates cannot be satisfactorily explained; perhaps Gurowski took time to polish his original draft or to obtain staff suggestions from friends.

[41] In 1903, with defects of American military planning during the Spanish-American War fresh in mind, Congress belatedly passed a law authorizing a general staff. Until World War I the vicissitudes of this body were numerous and at times distressing. See Otto L. Nelson, Jr., *National Security and the General Staff* (Washington, 1946), 58ff.

[42] David C. Mearns, "The Lincoln Papers," *Abraham Lincoln Quarterly*, Vol. IV (December, 1947), 372; William O. Stoddard, "Face to Face With Lincoln" (ed. by William O. Stoddard, Jr.), *Atlantic Monthly*, Vol. CXXXV (March, 1925), 333.

their Chief read them. Gurowski was by no means alone in offering advice to Lincoln, for hundreds of letters of the same nature remain in the Lincoln Papers, most of them of doubtful value. Yet there is something of wisdom in the Count's opinions. Although sometimes amusing, they are sincere, earnest, and unsophisticated. No other unsolicited adviser wrote with a background like his.

During these years of letter-writing the Count frequently saw Lincoln, but his contacts seldom were personal. When the two met on the streets, as they often did, he observed that the President looked spiritless, exhausted, careworn, as if his nights were sleepless and his days without comfort. He happened to be in Lincoln's presence when a telegram arrived announcing a move of General John Pope's forces in Missouri. He remembered the occasion with disgust because of several "not very washed stories" which the President told after reading the dispatch. According to Gurowski, he thereby demonstrated lack of good taste.[43] Likewise, when at the beginning of the war the Count attended a reception at the White House for officers of the armed forces, he had been unimpressed by Mrs. Lincoln: "Nature refused to her ... flexibility, pliability of muscles, of nerfs, of mind, and of soul. Never I saw such hard woodden features. She lacks altogether, and most absolutely, the gracefulness of smile, this most beautiful and generous gift by whose spell even the most complete—nay often even repulsive—ugliness brightens into attraction. Her mouth is only an opening without any graceful, soft, light outlines. For the second time I watched her for more than an hour, and not one single time, not to any person, not an impression of any word spoken, her features even contracted into a smile."[44]

It is, unfortunately, not possible to determine Lincoln's complete opinion of Gurowski, for the Chief Executive never, so far as is known, mentioned him in writing. But there are two second-hand reactions. Hay reported the President much amused at a story which he told him about the Count airing his views on the 1864 Presidential contest in a

[43] *Diary*, I, 252 (August, 1862), II, 241–42 (June 5, 1863). On Gurowski's dislike of Lincoln's storytelling, see *Diary*, II, 29, 31 (December 14 and 17, 1862); Carter, "Gurowski," *Atlantic Monthly*, Vol. XVIII, 633; "Nebulae," *Galaxy*, Vol. I, 271.

[44] Gurowski to Sumner, May 10, 1861, in Sumner Papers.

barrage of faulty English, climaxed by calling Lincoln a coward and an ass for running a second time.[45] Lincoln's other known reaction to Gurowski was that he considered him to be his one potential assassin. The unpredictable European's background, nature, and behavior seemed to cast him perfectly in the murderer's role. Even his appearance suggested the part. Ward Hill Lamon, the President's marshal of the District of Columbia, said Lincoln frequently told him that Gurowski would perhaps try to take his life.[46]

Lamon is the only source for this opinion, but there is no reason full credence should not be given to it. Naturally, Lincoln would have confided such an opinion only to Lamon, for this burly man served as his unofficial bodyguard. He had accompanied Lincoln to Washington for the inauguration, and with doglike devotion guarded the President. When plots against Lincoln's life were especially numerous in 1864, he slept next to the Presidential bed chamber. Always heavily armed, Lamon's giant person was a threat to any assassin. He also supervised in great part the kind of precaution he thought Lincoln needed, but which he could not give in person. Lamon always regretted his absence from Washington (on an official errand to Richmond) on the night of the assassination. His personal efforts in Lincoln's behalf were more than exercise of a duty as marshal of the District of Columbia, for Lincoln had been a law associate, an intimate friend of long standing. Lamon did not indicate his own reaction to the President's fear of Gurowski. Although he personally disliked Gurowski on account of his Jacobin propensities, he probably did not consider him a potential assassin of the Chief Executive.

Lincoln had no real cause to worry, for while this expatriated Pole frequently thought and threatened rashly, he was only threat and fury. He would have disposed of Lincoln only by the Constitutional process of electoral defeat. He loved his adopted land too much to violate its legal procedures. "I do not preach or the like, the overthrow of the President," he confided to Governor Andrew, "but I shall never become

[45] Dennett (ed.), *Lincoln and the Civil War in the Diaries and Letters of John Hay*, 177 (diary, April 28, 1864).

[46] Lamon, *Recollections of Abraham Lincoln, 1847–1865*, 274.

friendly to a undeserved, unnecessary, and by circumstances unprovoked adulation."[47] Thus he described his role as a Lincoln critic.

Gurowski's harmless bark, threatening and trenchant, alarmed Lincoln and caused the Count to be misunderstood. Midstream in the war he wrote menacingly: "I, a thorough revolutionary man, I know more remedies, and if at times I wish I go to Europe, it is to escape horrible temptations. Lincoln and Company make me loose my mind." His later verbal threats were no less belligerent: "I shall fight to the last against Lincoln and all the shams, fight if even left alone."[48] The bite he did not possess the President feared because he was unfamiliar with this type of European theorist, but saw in him the embodiment of Radical purpose.[49]

[47] Gurowski to Andrew, June 20, 1862, in Andrew Papers.
[48] Gurowski to Andrew, August 2, 1862, and March 27, 1864, in *ibid.*
[49] Otto Eisenschiml, *In the Shadow of Lincoln's Death* (New York, 1940), 19.

CHAPTER VI

DISCOVERING A SECRETARY

1

Gurowski's search for Radical leadership extended beyond the White House. Various members of Lincoln's cabinet underwent observations by the Count, as did some prominent military men, but he did more than merely pass upon those in positions of leadership. Ever mindful of the impact of written and oral propaganda, he carefully proceeded either to build or to destroy the reputations of public men through his published *Diary* and by endless conversations in Washington's social and political circles. He meticulously defended from attack those on whom he placed the Radical crown, and with equal vigor and persistence denounced those he assigned to the Conservative limbo. He frequently sought to advise leaders, as he did Lincoln, by means of personal interviews, conversations, or letters. His purpose was to mold administrators into his Jacobin point of view.

The Count's quest was not without moments of frustration. As he viewed the situation, the Radicals were far outnumbered by Conservative civil and military administrators. "Vainly! vainly in all directions," he complained, "among the helmsmen, leaders and commanders I search for a man inspired, or, at least, an enthusiast wholly forgetting himself for the holiness of the aim." "In times as trying as ours are," he added, "men and not counterfeits are needed."[1]

2

Although Secretary of the Navy Gideon Welles openly detested the Radicals, Gurowski considered him far from hopeless. The strait-laced

[1] *Diary,* II, 206 (April 22, 1863), 235 (May 23, 1863); Gurowski to Andrew, August 5, 1862, in Andrew Papers.

Secretary seemed efficient and forthright to the Count in his administration of the navy, as demonstrated by Welles' orders in the opening
year of the war to provide naval protection for runaway slaves and to
allow their enlistment in the seafaring service. The depredations on the
Union navy by the Confederate ironclad *Virginia* Gurowski considered
to be the result of the delaying tactics of the army under McClellan, not
that of the alleged slowness of the navy. More praise for the Secretary
came from the Count, when Flag Officer David G. Farragut occupied
New Orleans in the spring of 1862. "The Navy fights without talk and
strategy," the Pole commented, "because it does not look to win the
track to the White House."[2]

In the hope that Welles might be converted, Gurowski sought him
out. He explained to the Secretary that his appointment to the cabinet
had been passively accepted by the Radicals, because they believed his
influence on Lincoln would be desirable and that he would counteract
the Conservative ideas and policies of Thurlow Weed and Secretary
Seward. When Seward realized that the Radicals were relying on Welles
to checkmate him, the Secretary of State set out to destroy the influence
of the navy head with Lincoln. So successful had Seward been in this
effort that the President went against Welles on significant measures
when the two were in actual agreement. By this means, Gurowski concluded, Seward firmly intrenched himself with Lincoln. This statement
convinced Welles that the Radicals intended that he offset the influence
of Seward and Weed. The rest of the Count's story Welles regarded as
a combination of truth and error.[3]

According to Gurowski, this scheme to play off Welles against Seward and Lincoln bore fruit. He observed that when Seward proposed
an extension of the Maritime League, Welles opposed it. In fact, he
believed that Welles was teaching Seward the principles of good behavior, common sense, and international law.[4]

Welles' administrative procedures withstood the test of the Count's
evaluation for a while: "Because Neptune has a white wig and beard,

[2] *Diary,* I, 168 (March, 1862), 198 (May, 1862).
[3] Beale (ed.), *Diary of Gideon Welles,* I, 325–26 (June 8, 1863).
[4] *Diary,* II, 263–64, 283 (July 8 and 26, 1863).

he is considered slow, when in reality he is active, unflinching, and progressive." But when repeated attempts of the navy to take Charleston, South Carolina, midway in the war ended in failure, Gurowski turned on Welles. Other ironclads in addition to the *Monitor* type were needed, he insisted, and also numbers of rams. The men who went to sea compensated for these inadequacies as best they could by their enthusiasm, energy, and enterprise. "It is not sufficient," he explained about Welles, "to be honest as a chief of Department; insight, promptness of decision, knowledge of the various subjects, and enthusiasm, are as imperatively necessary as is honesty." The people, Gurowski pointed out, were boiling over with new naval inventions and wondrous devices for the sea, but Welles resisted these because of his slow, undecided, backward attitudes and procedures. Not even well-intentioned contractors were able to cut through the red tape of the Navy Department: "I accuse not Neptune-Methuselah-Van Winkle of any ill-will; he has the most honest intentions, but a rather slow convolution of the *cerebellum*."[5]

Damage to Union shipping during the spring of 1864 by the Confederate ironclad ram *Albemarle* brought new Gurowski outcries. "During the time that Welles pondered," he growled, ". . . and while he pedantically cramped the SOAR of the people's inventive and constructive fertility and powers—the rebels built rams. For one ram that the rebels bring out we ought to have ten of various drafts and size; but we have Welles." When the *Albemarle* drove Union shipping from the Roanoke River, he suggested that the Secretary go down and butt the vessel with his wig. "He ought," the chiding continued, "to be daily stimulated with the whip of snakes in the hands of furies." The Count's dislike of Welles finally grew so intense that, when he approached the Secretary on a Washington street during the summer of 1864, he dropped his head, turned off, and went far around him.[6]

[5] *Diary*, II, 188 (April 4, 1863), 283 (July 26, 1863), III, 49 (December 14, 1863), 91–92, 102 (February 4 and 14, 1864), 183 (April 16, 1864), 264 (June 22, 1864).

[6] *Diary*, III, 207, 209 (April 27 and 29, 1864), 265 (June 23, 1864); Beale (ed.), *Diary of Gideon Welles*, II, 101 (August 9, 1864). The Radical attack on Welles by the Joint Congressional Committee on the Conduct of War in 1864–65 is treated in Williams, *Lincoln and the Radicals*, 359–60.

3

Secretary of the Treasury Salmon P. Chase, although a Radical, received little more applause. Gurowski's dissatisfaction arose not with the Secretary's financial measures, which he generally found acceptable and sometimes praiseworthy, but from what he considered a tendency to compromise with the Conservatives. His principal illustration was the role of Chase in the cabinet crisis of December, 1862. In this incident, he explained, the Secretary alone thwarted the Radical senators from expelling Seward from the cabinet: "And yet, from the first day of the official assemblage of this cabinet down to the day of the meeting of the present session of Congress, Chase was more vigorously vicious than any other living man in daily, hourly, *all the time,* denunciation of Seward,—of course, behind Seward's back!" His temper mounting, he continued: "Chase! Faugh! I hereby brand him, and leave him to the bitter judgment of all men who can conscientiously claim to be even *half honest."* He never completely forgave Chase for not abandoning Seward. Weeks after the cabinet incident, the Count and Chase attended the same evening party. The Secretary extended his hand, but Gurowski put his own behind his back and turned around.[7]

When a fellow Radical reported that the Treasury Secretary did not appreciate advice from the Jacobins, that element of the Republican Party which had mothered him, the Count predicted that Chase was on his way to ruin. He felt certain that the Secretary would do little or nothing to counteract a speech made in Maryland by Postmaster General Montgomery Blair attacking emancipation. Yet Chase, as a member of the cabinet, claimed "to represent there the aspirations, the tendencies, and the aims of the radicals and of the emancipationists."[8]

The efforts of Chase to win the 1864 Republican Presidential nomination disgusted Gurowski. He believed that the Secretary was carefully building up a reservoir of patronage second to none ever held by a President or even by a constitutional king. This was being done by depleting

[7] *Diary,* II, 44–45 (December 22, 1862); Dana to Pike, March 13, 1863, in Pike Papers; unidentified newspaper clipping [May, 1863] in volume titled "Scraps," in John Hay Papers, Library of Congress.

[8] *Diary,* II, 241 (June 5, 1863), 340 (October 6, 1863).

banks of their resources through government borrowing, by establishing the national banking system, by appointing vast numbers of new treasury officials, and by dealing in cotton. Thus people who benefitted could easily be turned into Chase political supporters.[9]

Actually, the Count observed, there appeared to be very little to recommend the Treasury Secretary for the Presidency. For example, he had desired the states of the South to secede and had made a loan of ten million for the United States government in April, 1861, instead of the fifty million offered by bankers, thinking the war would be brief. Even worse, he had been tricked and taken in by Seward. The Pole believed that, despite his personal honesty, Chase lacked knowledge of men and possessed a most disdainful pompousness. Yet he much preferred him to Lincoln or Seward for the Presidency. When late in the 1864 campaign, the Secretary threw his support to Lincoln, Gurowski lauded him for abandoning his personal interests and supporting the "people's cause."[10]

4

Of the oral and written attacks made by the Count against members of Lincoln's cabinet, the most vicious, venomous, and unrelenting were directed at Secretary of State Seward. The fact that Gurowski had been an employee of the State Department during most of the first two years of the war, and then was dismissed, undoubtedly heightened a dislike of the Secretary, which eventually grew into a raging hate. Nevertheless, weeks before the Count went to work in the State Department, he disliked Seward much more than any other member of the cabinet.

Gurowski despised Seward's conciliatory policy toward the South. Seward, he believed, betrayed the Radicals immediately after he became secretary of state, by offering concessions and compromise. Even after the war began, Seward still held to the idea that the conflict was a minor domestic disagreement which would last no longer than ninety days. To stiffen the Secretary's attitude, Gurowski warned him orally that the government was surrounded by "the finest, most complicated,

[9] *Diary*, II, 304, 305 (August 23 and 24, 1863), 329–30 (September 22, 1863).
[10] *Diary*, III, 26–27 (November 8, 1863), 376 (October 16, 1864).

intense and well-spread web of treason that ever was spun." Seward answered calmly that this would soon change, for when he had become governor of New York, a similar situation existed between two sections of the state, and that he had soon been able to adjust the difficulty. "What a Merlin! What a sorcerer!" exclaimed the Count. In the office of the State Department the garrulous revolutionist observed that Seward talked and acted as if he did not sense the seriousness of the war or the responsibilities of his job. "Often," said Gurowski, "I can scarcely resist answering him, Beware, Beware!"[11]

As the war dragged on, the unhappy Count pronounced Seward "beyond salvation" on the slavery question. Seward worked, he said, to preserve slavery on the plea that a Conservative Union party would re-establish the government as it had existed before the war. This Union party, which Seward purportedly worked to organize in both the North and the South during spring and summer of 1862, had, according to the Count, the additional purpose of combating the Radicals. Gurowski decried its program as offering liberal terms to the Confederates, including the protection of slavery, after the capture of New Orleans and Richmond. The Count said that Seward fully expected the Confederacy to be killed ultimately by the Southern wing of his Union party. Restoring the Union to its antebellum condition had for some time been a delusion of the Secretary's mind, since at the opening of the conflict he had advocated conciliation when it was imperative that quick, crushing blows be dealt rebellion to maintain the *status quo*. Hence Seward himself, the Count reasoned, helped to create a condition that made his Union party in the South impossible.[12]

Gurowski believed that Seward directed the whole Conservative movement, which the Count called Hunkerism, after the Conservatives of the New York Democracy of the forties. These Civil War Hunkers, he said, spoke of readmitting the South on the basis of the Constitution as adopted in 1789. He thought also that the Secretary directed an attack

[11] *Diary*, I, 14–15, 19–20 (March, 1861), 22 (April, 1861), 47–48 (May, 1861), 157 (February, 1862).

[12] *Diary*, I, 155 (February, 1862), 177–78 (March, 1862), 181, 184 (April, 1862), 222 (June, 1862), 240–41 (July, 1862); Gurowski to Andrew, June 6, 1862, in Andrew Papers.

by way of the New York *Herald* against an increasingly Radical Congress because of its anti-Southern legislation. Complaining that no New York paper would print the truth about Seward, he implored Governor Andrew to expose him in Massachusetts. Seward's policy, in the Count's eyes, appeared as nothing less than "rampant treason." Two years later Gurowski believed Seward continued to insult the Radical majority of Congress: "No English minister, not even the most powerful, would ever have dared in such a way to kick an English parliament. The fate of such a premier would have been sealed: impeachment, the tower, and the block." Outside of Congress, he said, Seward also worked hard attempting to crush the Radicals.[13]

The Radical opposition which Gurowski hoped would offset Seward seemed to be weak and unable to make effective attacks on the Secretary. He complained that this opposition was "not courageous, not open, not dignified," which revealed weakness and did not inspire respect. He challenged his Radical brethren to work against Seward effectively or not at all: "If he is bad and mischievous, then unite your forces and overthrow him; if he is not bad, or if you are not strong enough against him, do not cover yourself with ridicule, making a show of impotent malice." But Gurowski went further than to suggest Seward's overthrow. He would replace him by Senator William Pitt Fessenden of Maine or Representative George Sewall Boutwell of Massachusetts; thus the State Department would be carried for Radicalism.[14]

Viewing Seward apart from his political ideas and activities, the Count discovered in him several admirable personal qualities, but even these he qualified. The Secretary, he said, worked intently and produced in quantity. Seward's elastic mind was given to argument, but his ability to master information was questionable. He considered him true and devoted to those he liked, easy to associate with, and honest in money matters. Seward, he maintained, never spoke evil of others, unless to destroy; when it came to undermining a rival or crushing an enemy,

---

[13] Gurowski to Andrew, March 1 and July 20, 1862, in *ibid.; Diary*, II, 132–33 (February 8, 1863), III, 275 (July 6, 1864).

[14] *Diary*, I, 63 (July, 1861), II, 115 (January 30, 1863); Gurowski to Andrew, September 9, [1862], in Andrew Papers.

the Secretary used unlimited slander. In Washington a rumor had it that Seward was often drunk. This the Count contradicted. The reason for the hearsay, he explained, had been Seward's love of generalizations: "He goes off like a rocket. Most people hearing him become confused, understand nothing, are unable to follow him in his soarings, and believe him to be intoxicated. His devotees alone get in ecstacies when these rockets fly."[15]

Gurowski believed that Seward did untold damage to the national welfare. Not only had his control of Lincoln been well-nigh fatal, but he also influenced other departments, particularly during the first year of the war. He often saw Seward's hand cunningly at work in military matters. The Secretary's influence, the Count maintained, was greater than that of the President. Seward, he thought, considered himself the government early in the war and in its later phases believed he still had the authority of Lincoln. "Who ever knows a little of the things and affairs," Gurowski warned, "knows well,—or is an idiot—that every day that Mr. Seward remains in the cabinet, the country's ruin is accelerated with lightening like velocity." For an example, he pointed to the Secretary's declared intention to overcome the abolitionists as well as the secessionists.[16]

As weeks and months wore on, Gurowski became more firmly convinced that Seward had been the "great stumbling block" of the nation. "All the Copperheads fused together have done less mischief," he exclaimed, ". . . are responsible for less blood and lives, than is Mr. Seward . . . . Even McClellan and McClellanism recede before Seward and Sewardism, the latter having generated the former. In times of political convulsions, perverse minds and intellects at the helm more fatally influence the fate of the nation than do lost battles. Lost battles often harden the temper of a people; a perverse mind vitiates it."[17]

Then Gurowski threw down the gauntlet: "Let Mr. Seward show

[15] *Diary*, I, 62–63 (July, 1861), 96 (September, 1861), 214 (May, 1862), II, 45 (December 22, 1862), III, 82 (January 22, 1864).

[16] *Diary*, I, 43 (May, 1861), 63 (July, 1861), 96 (September, 1861), 147 (January, 1862), 156 (February, 1862), 226 (June, 1862), III, 334 (September 8, 1864); Gurowski to Andrew, August 2, October 25, and November 1, 1862, in Andrew Papers.

[17] *Diary*, II, 39 (December 22, 1862), 154–55 (February 27, 1863).

his patriotic record! To his ambition, selfishness, ignorance and innate insincerity he has sacrificed as much of the people's honor, of the people's interests, and the people's blood as was feasible." He concluded that the Secretary's damage to the country seemed to be almost as great as that of any prominent leader of the Confederacy.[18]

When the Count learned of Radical defeats in the congressional elections of 1862, which he believed had resulted from Seward's influence, he determined once again to expose the Secretary. Openly he stated that his purpose and "employment" would be to achieve this through the abuse of Seward. Some months later, as before, he wrote his confidant Andrew in hope that the Massachusetts Governor would find a means of getting his opinions of Seward published in newspapers: "only patriotism," he explained, "makes me hate that scoundrel, otherwise he is to low to deserve my hatred." However, he was never able to attack Seward through newspapers, for none could be found Radical enough to print his opinions. He remained confident, nevertheless, that Seward's end would come: "O, you will fall, and you will be covered with . . . . I shall not stain the paper." Eventually the raging Count implored Chase, by then Chief Justice, not to stand between Seward and the gallows if justice brought him to that end.[19]

5

Gurowski's opinions of Secretary of War Edwin M. Stanton ran to the opposite extreme. When Stanton became head of the War Department in January, 1862, the Count hailed him as "the awakening voice of the good genius of the people, almost as that which awoke Lazarus. This Stanton is the people; . . . perhaps he may turn out to be *my* statesman." "How he overtops in the Cabinet," he exclaimed, "those myrmidons with their many petty notions! One idea, but a great and noble one, makes the great men, or the men for great events. Would God that the people may understand Stanton, and that pettifoggers, im-

[18] *Diary*, II, 168 (March 8, 1863), III, 299–300 (July 28, 1864).

[19] *Diary*, I, 312–13 (November 5, 1862), II, 262 (July 8, 1863); Dana to Pike, March 13, 1863, in Pike Papers; Gurowski to Andrew, April 10, 1863, in Andrew Papers; Gurowski to Salmon P. Chase, December 7, 1864, in Salmon P. Chase Papers, Historical Society of Pennsylvania, Philadelphia.

beciles and traitors may not push themselves between the people and Stanton, and neutralize the only man who has *the one idea* to break, to crush the rebellion." If Lincoln, he reflected, had been in the hands of Stanton during the first year of war, nine-tenths of the opposition to the federal government in the South would have been overcome. After the Secretary had been in office a month, Gurowski declared: "He is the *statesman* so long searched for by me."[20]

Stanton's vigor, conviction, and antislavery beliefs impressed the cantankerous Pole from the outset. The fact that he had been a Democrat made his antislavery stand all the more amazing and commendable to the Count, who viewed his actions as a refreshing contrast to the compromising attitudes of Secretary Seward and Postmaster General Blair, both early Republicans. As Gurowski contemplated the administrators known to him, no one seemed to be as free of mean, personal, petty influences, or so fortunate in the selection of his departmental employees as Stanton. He selected men because of their proved abilities, such as Assistant Secretaries of War Peter H. Watson and Charles A. Dana. No selfish interest had prompted the Secretary to take his present position, for he had left a lucrative and eminent law practice to assume a burdensome office that was ruining his health and not increasing his fortune. Gurowski admired Stanton also because he refused to resign his post in the face of opposition and asked for no defense from critics. "But if he were to retire," the Count pointed out, "he could not . . . reveal to the people the cause of such a step, and by remaining at his post, Stanton prevents still greater disasters and disgraces." "In the higher councils," he extolled, "Stanton is the *only and the last true Roman*."[21]

Gurowski never wavered in his support and defense of Stanton. When the Secretary was new, the Count sensed that cabinet Conservatives were at work to undermine him. Stanton lobbied for the direct land approach to Richmond in launching 1862 military operations, but when this plan was changed to the strategy of the Virginia Peninsula,

[20] *Diary*, I, 145 (January, 1862), 162 (February, 1862), 179 (March, 1862).

[21] *Diary*, I, 179 (March, 1862), 238–39 (July, 1862), II, 243 (June 7, 1863), 300–301 (August 16, 1863), III, 114 (February 23, 1864), 326 (August 26, 1864), 377–78 (October 18, 1864); Gurowski to Andrew, August 2, 1862, and September 9, [1862], in Andrew Papers.

the Count wailed that the rats of the cabinet had overcome his hero. A month later he lamented that, if Stanton's decisions had not been tampered with and weakened, Richmond would already have been taken, along with Charleston and Savannah.[22]

The Pole defended the Secretary of War on the ground that his orders had been overruled by Lincoln, when censure for the failure of McClellan's Peninsula campaign was heaped on the war office head. He demanded the gallows for the editor of the Boston *Advertiser* because of his editorials making Stanton the scapegoat. "Where he within my reach," he said of the editor, "I should not hesitate a moment to shoot him as I would a mad dog. I speak earnestly." Moreover, he explained, a military order signed by Stanton did not necessarily mean that the content originated with him, for in most cases the ideas came from Lincoln, making confused and palsied the Secretary's clarity of view.[23]

As McClellan's army succumbed to McClellan, Gurowski noted the restlessness and the despair of Stanton and explained that his "healthful activity" and "broad and clear perception of almost all exigencies of the critical times" were constantly frustrated and neutralized by Conservative elements. To critics of the Secretary who complained that he did not send reinforcements to McClellan, the Count snorted that the General had "exhausted and devoured" all that once existed. Conservative pressure on Stanton over the Peninsula failure caused Gurowski to stress that "strong and infamous intrigueurs are at work to upset Stanton." Momentarily expecting the Secretary to be forced from the cabinet, he wrote with a ray of hope: "Stanton is still in, and God give that he may remain. He is the only one, whatever may be his few mistakes."[24]

Gurowski believed that events justified the Secretary's opposition to the strategy and execution of the Peninsula campaign. He fully acquitted Stanton and shifted the blame to the Conservatives:

> If Stanton could have had his free will, far different would be the condition of affairs. Stanton's first appearance put an end to the prevailing

[22] *Diary,* I, 164 (February, 1862), 169 (March, 1862), 184 (April, 1862).

[23] Gurowski to Andrew, May 29 and 30, 1862, in Andrew Papers.

[24] *Diary,* I, 227, 228–29 (June, 1862), 236 (July, 1862); Gurowski to Greeley, July 7, 1862, in Greeley Papers; Gurowski to Andrew, July 12, 1862, in Andrew Papers.

lethargy, and marked a new and glorious era. But, ah! how short! The rats and vermin were afraid of him, and took shelter behind the incarnated strategy. Stanton embraced and embraces the *ensemble* of the task and of the field before him . . . . If Stanton had been left undisturbed in the execution of his duties . . . , McClellan would have been obliged to march directly to Richmond, and the brainless strategy in the Peninsula would have been crushed in the bud. If Stanton had not been undermined, not only the people would have been saved from terrible disasters, but McClellan, Lincoln, Seward, and Blair would have been saved from reproaches and malediction.[25]

Gurowski realized that if Union arms continued unsuccessful, Stanton would be discredited. The Radical movement itself suffered from want of victory. As always, the Count urged as a remedy a competent general staff modeled after the Prussian pattern and headed by an able chief of staff. After the Battle of Antietam, he included in a lengthy letter to Stanton several pages translated from a recent German book on army staffs. He desired to give Stanton some idea of the qualities, knowledge, and duties of a chief of staff. "I explained," he pointed out, "that the staff and the chief of the staff of an army are to it what the brains and the nervous system are to the human body."[26]

The necessity of a staff again loomed up when General Joseph Hooker's Chancellorsville campaign ended in defeat. Gurowski wrote to Stanton, explaining that the failure had resulted from inadequate staff. He pointed out that Halleck attempted to engage an army of more than a hundred thousand men virtually without a staff, a feat even Napoleon would not have dared. He directed the Secretary's attention to illustrations from military history on the importance of staff planning in major battles.[27]

The Pole grew impatient as Hooker took no action on reworking his staff, and implored Stanton "to compel Hooker to reform his staff, and not to allow science to be any longer trodden under foot." He repeated once more that either the Secretary of War or the President

[25] *Diary,* I, 238 (July, 1862), 247–48 (August, 1862).

[26] *Diary,* II, 110 (January 26, 1863). Gurowski's translation was from Hubert Oscar Friedrich von Boehn, *Generalstabsgeschäfte. Ein Handbuch für Offiziere Aller Waffen . . . Mit Vielen Figuren in Hochzinkguss* (Berlin, 1862).

[27] *Diary,* II, 222 (May 10, 1863).

should select a chief of staff after the European pattern rather than permit the commander to appoint his own, the American procedure. He excused Stanton for not acting in this matter, for although the Secretary realized the need, he was thwarted by military regulations and "another will."[28]

Gurowski favored the Secretary of War with all varieties of advice, written and oral. He told Stanton on one occasion to organize "honest, ignorant, useless military big men" into "an honorary military counsel, to counsel nothing." This group should occasionally handle such unimportant tasks as directing recommendations and advising on military goods. To clinch his idea, he declared that a similar council existed in Russia. Another suggestion came jointly from him and Governor Andrew. This called for regiments of "flying infantry" and discussed their equipment. But Stanton was not interested in this bizarre idea, countered by Gurowski's explanation that "the gentlemen in power dislike when the initiative comes from the outside, from men of brains and not of routine." When one of General Ambrose E. Burnside's commanders, William B. Franklin, intrigued against his chief following the Fredericksburg disaster, the Count went to the Secretary and unfolded details of the affair.[29]

Similarly, Gurowski rushed to Stanton at the time of Lee's 1863 invasion to tell of a conversation with a passive Washington secessionist. According to the report, a Copperhead from the capital city had visited with President Davis to make the request that the Confederate commander be instructed to devastate. The Count also pointed out that the invasion had come at the urging of Copperheads. Even when Gurowski was at his favorite health resort, Long Branch, New Jersey, he kept the Secretary posted. "Of the many tales which you say you hear respecting myself," Stanton wrote in reply, "you need give credence only to such as you believe consistent with the character of a man who has no other object in view than to serve his country to the best of his ability, happen what may." Congratulatory letters came also from the European. "The

[28] *Diary,* II, 240 (June 3, 1863).
[29] *Diary,* II, 85 (January 10, 1863), 176 (March 23, 1863); Gurowski to Andrew, December 21 and 29, 1863, in Andrew Papers.

commendation of noble minded men," the Secretary responded gratefully, "is an ample recompense for the toil and vexation of public life."[30]

Gurowski at other times troubled Stanton with requests for the
appointment of friends to military service—or demanded the cashiering
of enemies. To a solicitation in behalf of a fellow Pole, the Secretary
replied: "I have the pleasure to enclose the appointment you requested
for Captain [Baron Władisław] Leski." Another of Gurowski's letters,
this time asking Stanton to revoke a military appointment, brought more
action: "I found that the appointment was one with which I had nothing
to do, and, upon investigation, the officer was consigned to Old Capitol
Prison, where he now awaits his trial." Other requests came also. One
recommended the colorful Prussian soldier of fortune, Prince Felix zu
Salm-Salm, as capable of carrying out a plan to levy troops in Europe.
Another was an appeal to place Baron Rudolf de Wardener, an Austrian army officer, in the Union Quartermaster Corps. Still another requested that Captain Alfred de Waterville, a Swiss on a scientific mission under the direction of the Smithsonian Institution, be permitted
to accompany a military expedition to Idaho.[31]

The Count's concern over Stanton's welfare continued throughout
the war. When rumors reached him that the Secretary was breaking
down mentally and physically, he denied it, but added that only an
iron constitution could survive the machinations of Conservative civil
and military administrators. In the wake of defeat at Fredericksburg,
he had word that the Secretary supported his vanquished commander.
This Gurowski refused to believe. If true, Stanton, ruined by bad company, ought to be removed.[32]

The unsuccessful effort of Radical senators to remove Seward from
the cabinet in December, 1862, caused more apprehensive moments. "I

[30] *Diary,* II, 253 (June 27, 1863); Stanton to Gurowski, September 9, 1863, in Gurowski Papers; Stanton to Gurowski, March 1, 1862, copy, Bing, "Life of Gurowski," 239.

[31] Stanton to Gurowski, May 1, 1862, and September 9, 1863, in *ibid.;* Gurowski to
Stanton, July 9, 1862, in Lincoln Papers; Gurowski to Stanton, July 24, 1863, and March
14, 1864, in Records of the War Department, Office of the Adjutant General, National
Archives.

[32] *Diary,* II, 21 (November 30, 1862), 35 (December 18, 1862).

wish, yet dread," said the Count, "to hear the exact particulars of Stanton's behavior during the crisis in the cabinet." A few hours later the news filtered through: "I am told that Stanton took sides with Seward. I deny it; Stanton remained rather passive. But were it true that Stanton, too, is *Sewardized*,—then, Oh Mud, how wonderful thou art!" "It is repulsive to me," intoned the discouraged Count, "to include Stanton with the others; but Stanton too begins to fail, he begins to show signs of exhaustion produced by his unceasing fight against imbecillity and intrigue; the unclean reptiles have eaten him up."[33]

The rumored Seward-Stanton alliance typified further Gurowski's concern over Stanton. When the Count first heard that this combination had been worked out by Senator Edwin D. Morgan of New York, Weed, and William Whiting, War Department solicitor, his uneasiness was over Stanton, for he firmly believed Seward would not compromise. "Is Stanton," he questioned, "dragged down by the infuriated fates?" His recommendation to Governor Andrew was that the rumor of the alliance be published, his hope being to produce confirmation or denial.[34]

Within three days, Gurowski had cleared the fog. In a personal interview with him, Stanton explained that his reported alliance with Seward was the invention of Postmaster General Blair, and arose because he united with Seward in advocating letters of marque against England, a step opposed by Blair and Sumner. "So at least says Stanton," Gurowski confided, "and I gladly believe him because it is a bitter horrible pang to lose faith in manhood."[35]

In the long run, the Count considered Stanton's record outstanding. His relations with General McClellan illustrated his qualities as an administrator. When Stanton became secretary of war, he had tried by friendship and devotion to cause McClellan to fight. Only when the Secretary realized that the General dodged combat "under false pre-

[33] *Diary*, II, 48, 51 (December 24, 1862); Gurowski to Andrew, January 10, 1863, in Andrew Papers.
[34] *Diary*, II, 175 (March 22, 1863); Gurowski to Andrew, March 22, 1863, in Andrew Papers.
[35] *Diary*, III, 176 (March 25, 1863); Gurowski to Andrew, March 25, [1863], in Andrew Papers.

tenses" did he become disappointed and force him to give battle: "Stanton was a friend of McClellan, but sacrificed friendship to the sacred duty of a patriot."[36]

Another service the Secretary performed, Gurowski pointed out, had been to prevent McClellan from being elected President in 1864. Only the "energy, the prompt and daring decision" of Stanton turned the tide. "If he is sincere," he predicted, "the future historian of that ominous epoc will establish the above assertion beyond doubt or cavil." Still another act of heroism had been the purification of the Army of the Potomac of the McClellan "plague," and the elevation of General Grant to the command of all Union armies. Without a doubt Napoleon's administrative task, Gurowski concluded, had not been as great as Stanton's, nor had he performed it as well. "Stanton," the Count acclaimed, "is equal to every emergency."[37]

[36] *Diary*, II, 204 (April 21, 1863); see also III, 315–16 (August 15, 1864).
[37] *Diary*, III, 292 (note, July, 1865), 398 (epilogue, April 15, 1865); Gurowski to Andrew, March 27, 1864, in Andrew Papers.

CHAPTER VII

UNCOVERING A GENERAL

I

GUROWSKI'S SEARCH FOR MILITARY LEADERSHIP centered in the Army of the Potomac, which he observed from Washington. This fighting force, strictly speaking, was based in the capital, and at no time were its battles with the Confederates at any great distance from the city. Moreover, the making and breaking of its commanders were in large part engineered by Radicals in the federal district, operations in which the Count himself usually participated by serving as a communication medium for their propaganda.

Gurowski's quest began during the discouraging days just after the Union rout at Bull Run in midsummer, 1861. The forces that had retreated to Washington were, to his thinking, in obvious need of vigorous leadership. The youthful General McClellan, fresh from minor victories in western Virginia, received the Count's welcome to the capital city as the man of the hour. The reorganized army under McClellan's leadership soon began to look truly military: "God grant that McClellan may preserve his western vigor and activity, and may not become softened and dissolved by these Washington evaporations." He "is organizing, working hard. It is a pleasure to see him, so devoted and so young. After all, youth is promise."[1]

To assure the General's success, the European immediately sent McClellan a reorganization plan. He outlined in detail what he thought would be required to produce an effective fighting force. His theme called for the dispersion of units of the regular army into the new military machine made up largely of volunteers. To have adequate numbers of good noncommissioned officers, he advised the promotion of

[1] *Diary,* I, 76 (July, 1861), 87 (August, 1861).

privates from the regular army to corporals and sergeants and their placement throughout the ranks. The need for additional commissioned officers should be met by granting commissions to noncommissioned regulars.[2]

Less than two months later Gurowski's faith in McClellan began to wane. The Count became increasingly annoyed as the General delayed operations. "The army is in sufficient rig and organization to take the field," he complained, "but nevertheless McClellan has not yet made a single movement imperatively prescribed by the simplest tactics, and by the simplest common sense, when the enemy is in front." "When will we deal blows?" he questioned impatiently, then answered with sarcasm: "Not under McClellan, I suspect." It was his contention that, if the commander knew military history, he would not keep the army in camp: "He would know that after recruits have been roughly instructed in the rudiments of a drill, the next best instructor is fighting." The Confederate P. G. T. Beauregard at nearby Manassas, Virginia, Gurowski explained, shared the campfires of his men, whom he knew individually. McClellan, by comparison, lived comfortably in Washington and appeared before his troops only "as the great Lama on special occasions."[3]

The Count's complaint that McClellan lingered in the capital was but one of his objections. He also thought, after viewing troop maneuverings, that the commander was wrong in not distributing artillery among infantry regiments: "When the rank and file see the guns on their side, the soldiers consider them as a part of themselves and of the regiment; they fight better in the company of guns, they stand by them and defend them as they defend their colors." He further complained that he did not know of a single serious reconnaissance made by McClellan to determine the enemy's strength at Manassas.[4]

The General's alleged preference for army regulars over volunteers caused the Count's blood to boil. Because McClellan specialized in engineering, he believed he turned automatically to the defensive and could not be the proper leader for offensive operations. The General soon

---

[2] *Diary,* I, 75–76 (July, 1861).

[3] *Diary,* I, 104, 114 (October, 1861), 142, 144 (January, 1862).

[4] *Diary,* I, 99–100 (September, 1861), 104–105 (October, 1861).

passed beyond redemption, the European said, for whatever humility he possessed that would lead him to listen to reason had been turned by the adulation of Washington officials and crowds. Late one afternoon, wearing his battered broad-brimmed hat, blue goggles, and long, gray overcoat, Gurowski followed a mass of people returning with McClellan to Washington after a review. In contrast to the cheers and happiness of applauding military officers, civil officials, and idlers, the Pole looked downcast and dispirited. Coming up beside his friend, General E. D. Keyes, he pointed to McClellan and remarked that the head of a popular favorite had never been turned so quickly as his.[5]

When Gurowski met McClellan, his initial hope faded completely. All McClellan said in a lengthy conversation, held at the commander's headquarters, was "altogether unmilitary and inexperienced." The consultation revealed, thought Gurowski, a lack of confidence in the troops, no knowledge of how battles are conducted, and no understanding of or confidence in the use of the bayonet. The Count pointedly told the General that he would take his worst infantry brigade and, after two weeks of drill, challenge and defeat any Confederate brigade. McClellan quickly turned the subject to Washington's defenses, and pointed with pride to one of the forts as having a longer profile than the celebrated Malakoff defense point at Sebastopol during the Crimean War. "What a confusion of notions," the Count moaned in his *Diary*, "what a misappreciation of relative conditions!"

Next Gurowski spoke of the necessity of dividing the army into corps. The General responded favorably and displayed the names of the generals to whom he intended to give these commands but said Scott prevented him from taking action. "I cannot express my sad, mournful feelings," Gurowski intoned, "during this conversation with McClellan. . . . It made me sick at heart to hear him, and to think that he is to decide over the destinies and the blood of the people." Even in the eyes and features of the General the Count discovered a "soft, insignificant inexpressiveness" foreshadowing no good. "My enthusiasm for

[5] *Diary*, I, 108–109 (October, 1861), 127–28 (November, 1861); E. D. Keyes, *Fifty Years' Observation of Men and Events: Civil and Military* (New York, 1884), 441; A. B. Johnson to Sumner, October 3, 1861, in Sumner Papers.

him, my faith," he exclaimed, "is wholly extinct." McClellan loomed now as a positive menace. To checkmate him on Scott's retirement, the Count talked with Secretary of War Simon Cameron and warned him against making McClellan general in chief.[6]

The youthful General, however, fell heir to Scott's post in early November. Gurowski believed the moment appropriate to hand him additional advice. The Army of the Potomac, the Count said in his best French—none too good—ought to be under McClellan's immediate command. Even after the division of the army into corps had materialized, commanders of these new units should be solely responsible to him. "Once again," he said in concluding, "I beg you, General, to pardon me for this audacious but very respectful step. Its motive is the most absolute devotion to my new country."[7]

McClellan's embarkation in March, 1862, for the Virginia Peninsula at last put the army in the field. But Gurowski denounced the strategy as unsound and ineffective, because he preferred the direct land route to the Confederate capital. "Common sense," he explained, "shows that the rebels ought to be cut off from their resources, that is, from railroads, and from communication with the revolted states of the interior, and to be precipitated into the ocean. To accomplish it our troops ought to have marched by land to Richmond, and pushed the enemy towards the ocean. Now McClellan pushes the rebels from the extremity towards the centre, towards the focus of their basis—exactly what they want." Even this could be corrected by decisive and adventurous campaigning, he thought, but predicted that McClellan would "stick in the marshes" before Richmond. Watching the army embarkation at Alexandria, he considered it poorly organized and slow.[8]

Disembarking at Fortress Monroe, McClellan encountered the Confederates at Yorktown and began an elaborate siege. "If McClellan could know anything," the Count said critically, "then he would know this—that nothing is so destructive to an army as sieges, as diggings,

[6] *Diary*, I, 106–108 (October 6, 1861), 117 (November, 1861).

[7] Gurowski to McClellan, November 3, 1861, in Archives and Museum, Polish Roman Catholic Union of America.

[8] *Diary*, I, 169–71 (March, 1862).

and camps, and nothing more disciplines and re-invigorates men, makes them true soldiers, than does marching and fighting." As the army bogged down before Yorktown, he asserted that but for McClellan's generalship Richmond could have been taken in three weeks. Around Washington, nevertheless, he found the "infamous, impure elements" giving unlimited support to the General. "Only a disaster," he lamented, "can cure the country from MacClellanomania." He then wrote Mrs. Seward concerning the uselessness and harmfulness of McClellan's strategy and sent along a book on military history with pages marked for her enlightenment, doubtless hoping she would influence her husband.[9]

After a month of siege, the Confederates abandoned Yorktown. "Traitors, intriguers, and imbeciles," Gurowski complained, "applaud, extol the results of the bloodless strategy. McClellan is used by the rebels only to be fooled by them." Union pursuit of the Confederates as they withdrew up the Peninsula toward Richmond was frustrated by a stubborn rear-guard action at Williamsburg. Although the Count believed that Radical Generals Samuel P. Heintzelman and Joseph Hooker emerged from the engagement heroic and impeccable, McClellan could not be excused, for he had ignored the battle and the circumstances surrounding it: "MacClellan is responsible for blood spilt so stupidly and infamously." The first main engagement of the campaign soon followed at Seven Pines (Fair Oaks), just outside Richmond. In this Union victory McClellan, the Pole contended, disgraced Radical General Silas Casey's division by reporting its action unfavorably. McClellan had turned out even worse than he expected. "Any one sustaining MacCln," he moaned in a fit of anger, "is a unmistakable ass ass 3, 4, 5, 6, etc etc and a traitor to boot."[10]

The renewed pleadings of McClellan for reinforcements during and following the indecisive Seven Days, Gurowski considered as additional excuses for the General's inadequacies. "After all," he reflected, "McClellan is not the greatest culprit. It is not his fault that he is without mili-

[9] *Diary,* I, 191 (April, 1862); Gurowski to Andrew, April 21, 1862, in Andrew Papers; Gurowski to Mrs. William H. Seward, April 6, 1862, in Seward Papers.

[10] *Diary,* I, 201, 202 (May, 1862), 219–20 (June, 1862); Gurowski to Andrew, Washington, May 7 and 12, 1862, in Andrew Papers.

tary brains and without military capacity. He tried to do the best, according to his poor intellect. The great, eternally-to-be-damned malefactors are those who kept him in command after having had repeated proofs of his incapacity; and still greater are those constitutional advisers who supported McClellan against the outcry of the best in the Cabinet and in the nation. A time may come when the children of those malefactors will be ashamed of their fathers' names, and—curse them."[11]

The long casualty lists and the many sick and wounded pouring into Washington drove the revolutionary to the depths of despair. His heart bled, he said, for these victims, all sacrificed to McClellan by Conservatives in the government. "The beautiful army now on the James," he advised, "ought to be brought back here; united with what Pope commands now, it will make an army which in the course of two months will not only take Richmond but reach the Gulf. But all for a fighting, enterprising commander." McClellan must be replaced immediately, he told Governor Andrew, calling on him for assistance: "For the peoples' and country's sake, stimulate: *down with the imbecile MacClellan,* and do not loose time." The Count rejoiced when the troops were ordered back to Washington in early August, 1862, but wailed as the General continued in command.[12]

2

McClellan's forces, however, were detached from him and assigned to General John Pope's new Army of Virginia. Gurowski, like other Radicals, welcomed Pope as a leader capable of winning battles. The test soon came. Advancing to meet invading Confederate forces under General Robert E. Lee, the new commander failed miserably at the Second Battle of Bull Run. The Count immediately accused McClellan of deliberately withholding troops from Pope, contrary to orders. As the defeated forces fell back on Washington, Gurowski's discouragement once more became despair, for Pope was relieved of command and his troops reassigned to the Army of the Potomac under McClellan: "The

[11] *Diary,* I, 237–38 (July, 1862).
[12] Gurowski to Andrew, July 12, 1862, in Andrew Papers; *Diary,* I, 249, 254 (August, 1862).

people's honor, the country's cause are nearly entombed. The diggers of the grave are the imbeciles, the intriguers and the traitors who have been grouped around and supported MacClellan. Rage and pain make me shead tears."[13]

With Lee crossing the Potomac into Maryland, little time could be lost in meeting the foe. Troops streaming west out of Washington cheered as they passed McClellan's residence, much to the dismay of Gurowski, who watched through his blue goggles. "Such shouts," he explained, "would cheer up the mind but for the fact that they were mostly raised for the victory over those who demanded an investigation of the causes of *slowness* and insubordination—those exclusive causes of the defeat of Pope's army. Those shouts were thrown out as defiance to justice, to truth, and to law. Those shouts marked the inauguration of the *pretorian regime*."[14]

According to Gurowski, the ensuing Maryland campaign under McClellan's leadership proved anew the commander's lack of generalship. As in the Peninsula, McClellan never caused the enemy to commit its total force or brought his combined units to bear on them. In fact, the Confederates would have retreated into Virginia without being attacked, and since McClellan did not destroy the invader at South Mountain or Antietam, he accomplished little or nothing. When Lee entered Maryland, "the *fighting* generals, as Heintzelman, advised to mass the troops between the rebels and the Potomac, cut them off from their bases and communications, push them towards the North without a possibility of escape, instead of throwing them back on the Potomac . . . . But this bold plan of a *fighting* general could not be comprehended by pets and pretorians. Since, daily and daily occasions occur to destroy the rebels; but that is not the game."[15]

McClellan, the Count believed, had been kept in command after

---

[13] *Diary,* I, 231 (June, 1862), 256 (August, 1862), 258 (September, 1862); Gurowski to Andrew, September 2, 1862, in Andrew Papers.

[14] *Diary,* I, 264 (September 7, 1862); David Donald (ed.), *Inside Lincoln's Cabinet: The Civil War Diaries of Salmon P. Chase* (New York, 1954), 123 (September 7, 1862); Gurowski to Andrew, September 9, [1862], in Andrew Papers; and Benjamin Perley Poore to Sumner, September 11, 1862, in Sumner Papers.

[15] *Diary,* I, 274, 275, 287 (September 19, 20, and 28, 1862), 309 (October 30, 1862).

Antietam by Conservative supporters to give him an opportunity to redeem himself at last by winning a great battle. This he would never do, but would instead call for more men, use up the people's vitality, and further show his incapability at handling troops strategically and in combat. When the General finally moved across the Potomac into Virginia weeks after Antietam, Gurowski continued to be dissatisfied: "The horizon brightens not. It is the sixs day of MacClellan's great movement and the enemy is still where he was and nobody hurt." As McClellan's army massed for attack, Lincoln relieved him of command. In the Count's first genuinely happy moment since McClellan came to defend Washington, he exclaimed: "Great and holy day! McClellan gone overboard! Better late than never."[16]

3

The joy of Gurowski and the Radicals turned out to be brief, for the command of the Army of the Potomac went to General Ambrose E. Burnside, a Democrat and admirer of McClellan. The Count considered Burnside well-meaning and goodhearted, but something beyond his capacities he thought necessary in an army commander. Gurowski called for daring and quick action in the march on Fredericksburg, and, as the advance moved slowly in the mud of fall rains, he complained that "bold conceptions, and energetic movements to match them, are just about as possible to . . . Burnside as railroad speed to the tedious tortoise." The General would not likely be successful at Fredericksburg, for nothing was being done to prevent the enemy from constructing well-nigh impregnable fortifications. The faultfinding Radical answered Burnside's complaint that the War Department was causing his delay by failure to supply pontoons for bridges to span the Rappahannock at Fredericksburg with the suggestion that a twelve-year-old schoolboy could have found in the ranks thousands of workmen capable of building on the spot the necessary pontoons and bridges.[17]

On the eve of Fredericksburg, Gurowski still had no confidence in

[16] *Diary*, I, 289 (October, 1862), 313 (November 9, 1862); Gurowski to Andrew, November 1, 1862, in Andrew Papers.

[17] *Diary*, II, 14, 17, 19 (November 19, 25, and 27, 1862), 23, 25 (December 6 and 7, 1862).

Burnside's military skill: "But I have *full* confidence in our soldiers, in many of the generals and the fullest in Hooker; so if the traitors fight they may be annihilated even under Burnside." Instead, the Army of the Potomac was severely defeated. The Conservatives, Gurowski agonized, when they had given Burnside the command, promised that he would take care of the Union army, but rather he had taken care of the Confederates. He placed the blame squarely upon Burnside and Halleck, the general in chief. "The curse of the people," he cried out, "ought to rest for centuries upon the very names of the authors of such frightful disasters. They are fiends, yea, worse, even than the very fiends themselves."[18]

Gurowski severely criticized Burnside's wish to lead in person a last hopeless charge of his old corps across the masses of dead and dying bodies: "If all this is true, then Burnside is weaker headed than I had judged him to be; but I will not do him the injustice to say that he really intended to play a mere farce. What, in the name of common sense, could he do with a single corps, when the whole army was repulsed?" Burnside's official report on the battle also angered the Count, who considered it unsoldierly, fussy, and inane, although he was impressed with the manly letter to Halleck, in which the defeated commander assumed entire responsibility for Fredericksburg. If Burnside had complied with the orders of the General in Chief, instead of being manly, the letter would be almost treasonable, reasoned the Count, for in not divulging Halleck's orders, he had given the General in Chief authority to repeat the slaughter and ensure the failure of the Union armies.[19] Radical pressures and growing discontent among Burnside's subordinate generals momentarily put an end to Gurowski's growling, for General Hooker became commander of the Army of the Potomac late in January, 1863.

4

The Count and his fellow Jacobins were delighted with Hooker, who seemed to them to possess all the requisites of a fighting and win-

[18] Gurowski to Andrew, December 12, 1862, in Andrew Papers; *Diary,* II, 30, 31, 32 (December 15 and 17, 1862).
[19] *Diary,* II, 41–43 (December 23, 1862).

ning general. Gurowski had found his record good enough to warrant giving him the Potomac command in place of McClellan following Antietam. At Williamsburg his bravery, determination, and energy had won from his troops the sobriquet "Fighting Joe," and he had never once been worsted in battle. When Burnside followed McClellan, the Count's choice still had been Hooker, who "alone has the sacred fire and the inspiration of the god of battles." But the Conservatives had embarrassed him by revealing questionable aspects of the new commander's California life. "What of it if true; Bluecher was trunkered and gambler," the Pole retorted, "but fought well and saved his country." "Hooker, because he alone is a *captain,*" he explained, "cannot be in command. Infamous intriguers, traitors, and imbeciles, prevent Hooker from being intrusted with the destinies of our army."[20]

While the news of Hooker's appointment caused Gurowski to exclaim, "patriotic hearts thrill with joy!" he believed there were still herculean problems at hand. Hooker's inheritance consisted of demoralization, winter and mud, loss of precious time, and vast casualties. Few commanders in all military history had ever taken charge of an army under such ominous circumstances: "If Hooker succeeds, then his genius will astonish even his warmest friends." The Count thought that the new head of the army had acted unwisely in selecting as chief of staff General Daniel Butterfield, whom he believed to be untrained for the job. "All this," he said, "is a very bad omen, very bad, very bad." Others, even Radicals, disagreed with his judgment of Butterfield. But he recalled hopefully the promise that Hooker had made him about organizing a flawless staff, when the new commander had lain wounded in a Washington military hospital following Antietam.[21]

When Hooker started to reorganize the army, Gurowski advised him concerning his staff and sent along a current book on military science, written by the Austrian, Emil Schalk.[22] "Well, Count," said Hook-

<hr />

20 *Diary,* I, 276 (September 20, 1862), 313 (November 8, 1862), II, 57–58 (December 28, 1862); Gurowski to Andrew, November 9, [1862], and December 12, 1862, in Andrew Papers.

21 *Diary,* II, 109–11 (January 26, 1863).

22 *Diary,* II, 173 (March 18, 1863). The book sent was Emil Schalk, *Summary of the Art of War: Written Expressly for and Dedicated to the U.S. Volunteer Army* (Philadelphia, 1862).

er, in thanking him for the volume, "I feel that I have fought my great battle, which was to acquire the confidence and the respect of the Army of the Potomac and to it the splendid confidence—the feeling of invincibility, which it carried with it, when we entered upon the Campaign of the Peninsula a year ago. I believe it to be now better than ever." Gurowski seemed to be encouraged also when he observed that the strongest McClellanites admired Hooker's activity and were astonished at his success in rebuilding the fighting machine. "To reorganize a demoralized army," he emphasized, "requires more nerve than to win a battle." But with the military force revitalized, the time had arrived to move from camp, give battle, and crush the enemy. To prod Hooker and to help keep a clean name, the Count recommended that an end be put to carousing in camp, by ordering away all women, "be they wives, sisters, sweethearts or the promiscuous rest of crinolines."[23]

Gurowski considered Hooker's army to be in a poor strategic position as it moved out to meet Lee's hosts, but when this was rectified by Hooker's success in throwing his forces across the Rappahannock in the face of the enemy, Gurowski was elated. "The patriots feverish. One might easily become delirious," he exclaimed, as unfavorable rumors of the ensuing battle at Chancellorsville filtered back to Washington. Then the truth reached the capital. Hooker, the darling of the Radicals, had been defeated. "Are the Gods against us?" questioned the anguished European: "Or has imbecility exasperated even the merciful but rational Christian God to that extent, that God turns his back on us?"[24]

To Gurowski's disgust, Hooker had committed the errors of his predecessors and proved a complete failure as army commander: "After all that he said, after all that we said and repeated in his favor, to turn out an awful mistake!" Hooker had hesitated, shown no vigor, had not maneuvered skillfully, and had lacked the support of a trained staff and chief of staff. Although the General's defenders called Chancellorsville inconclusive, Gurowski believed it to be not only a lost battle but "a

[23] Hooker to Gurowski, March 29, 1863, copy, Bing, "Life of Gurowski," 262, in Gurowski Papers; *Diary,* II, 180 (March 30, 1863), 199 (April 15, 1863).

[24] *Diary,* II, 200 (April 18, 1863), 216, 217, 218 (May 2, 3, and 6, 1863).

miscarried, if not altogether lost, campaign." "Poor Hooker. Undoubtedly he has a soldier's spark in him. But adulation, flunkeyism, conceit, covered the spark with dirt and mud. I pity him, but for all that, down with Hooker!"[25] This time, however, the Pole was out of tune with the Radicals, since few of them demanded the removal of the defeated commander.

If the Jacobins must retain Hooker, the Count determined at least to point out how he believed a successor ought to be selected. In a paper prepared for Benjamin F. Wade and Zachariah Chandler, the two leading Radicals of the Senate, he recommended that the President, the Secretary of War, and the senators go to the Army of the Potomac and call together all corps and divisional commanders. To this assembled group Lincoln would explain "the impossibility of making a new choice." The President would then request them on the spot to elect by secret ballot one of their number. Gurowski also told the two senators his opinions about Hooker's staff and gave other reasons for the Chancellorsville disaster. A few days later he propagandized Wade further by explaining in a letter the high degree to which he believed Hooker incapable of commanding a large army, asserting that the commander was ruining the morale of his men and suggested that he be removed and assigned to command a unit of not more than two army corps.[26]

On the heels of Chancellorsville, Lee again invaded the North and rolled unmolested into Pennsylvania. Hooker followed in a parallel direction, much to the dismay of the Count, who believed Hooker ought to cut Lee's line; here was more proof that "Fighting Joe" had lost his old dash and certainty. By a single hard blow, said Gurowski, Hooker could now retrieve his fortune, but this would be unlikely because he had refused to reform his staff.[27] At last other Radicals began to agree with the Count, and when Hooker was relieved on the eve of Gettysburg, most Jacobins reflected bitterly that he likewise had turned out to be a dud.

[25] *Diary,* II, 218–19, 220–21, 226 (May 7, 8, and 13, 1863); Gurowski to Horatio Woodman, May 9, [1862], Massachusetts Historical Society, *Proceedings,* Vol. LVI, 237.

[26] *Diary,* II, 226–27, 234–35 (May 14 and 22, 1863).

[27] *Diary,* II, 247–48, 252 (June 17 and 25, 1863).

5

Hooker's successor was the reticent and austere George Gordon Meade, known to the Radicals as friend of McClellan and member of the Democratic clique. Although their leaders were not pleased with his selection, some even labeling him a Copperhead, Gurowski defended him on the basis of his successful, skillful, and daring battlefield record. He pitied Meade for having to take over the army at so critical a moment and suggested that he should have been assigned to the post a month earlier.[28]

After Meade had held the reins but three days, he met Lee in the titanic struggle at Gettysburg. As news of the encounter reached Washington, Gurowski believed that the plan demonstrated boldness and that it was being carried out with bravery and rapidity. At last a general appeared to be in command! But the Count's delight turned to dismay when he learned that the Union forces were not on Lee's heels as he began a retreat. Surely, Meade would not permit him to recross the Potomac: "Oh for a general who understands how to maneuver against the enemy!!!" Then word came that Lee's forces successfully had recrossed the swollen Potomac River. "And our brave soldiers again baffled," the Count continued, "almost dishonored by domestic, know-nothing generalship. We have lost the occasion to crush three-fourths of the rebellion." Lincoln, he believed, ought to dismiss Meade for failure to pursue Lee vigorously.[29] The President, equally exasperated, agreed completely.

While Meade stayed a cautious distance behind the Confederate army, Gurowski thought perhaps the plan was to keep Lee at bay and not give battle. Meade, he complained, did "nothing beyond feeling his way." The Chickamauga struggle of late September, 1863, which took troops from Lee's command, brought again a superb opportunity, Gurowski believed, to strike the enemy, but it appeared that "a conception of a plan of campaign or of a military operation is altogether beyond the reach of Meade's *cerebellum*." Like McClellan, Meade had no sense of attack, but only delayed, hesitated, retreated, and remained inactive dur-

[28] *Diary*, II, 228 (May 15, 1863), 254 (June 28, 1863), 258 (July 1, 1863).
[29] *Diary*, II, 259, 266, 267–68, 273 (July 2, 13, 16, and 17, 1863).

ing good weather. When the army fell back to the vicinity of Washington, after its snail-like pursuit of Lee's forces, Gurowski recommended that the "President had better order Meade to bed, and put *a man* in his place." He concluded that the General must be in direct communication with McClellan, recognize him as his chief, report to him all campaign plans, and execute his orders rather than Lincoln's. The Count went to Stanton about "this treasonable intercourse."[30]

In early November, 1863, Meade crossed the Rappahannock and the Rapidan "to search," declared Gurowski, "what he does not wish to find." "Meade under Lincoln, is like a boy whipped by his father, and sent in search of stolen cattle." Concerning this campaign of Mine Run, without significant engagements or important results, the European wittily remarked that Meade "went to find out about Lee's health, found it good, and—returned, and dutifully reported to the headquarters, to the White House, and to McClellan." He scoffed at the report spread by Meade's supporters that the Mine Run affair had been a successful reconnaisance of the Virginia Wilderness. All that Meade had accomplished during the winter of 1863–64 had been to let Lee collect his scattered forces.[31]

Grant's appointment to the command of all Union armies in March, 1864, did not remove Meade from the head of the Army of the Potomac, much to Gurowski's dismay: "How can Grant abandon to Meade the execution of any military movement of the army?" Meade, he thought, ought to be most grateful to Grant, because he received credit for his superior's achievements and no blame for the difficulties or mishaps of the Wilderness campaign. "I expected that he would be a good Chief of the Staff under Grant," he complained of Meade, "and execute Grant's combinations well, but he is not even good for this." As Grant's campaign bogged down before Richmond in late summer, 1864, the Count agreed with fellow Radicals that Meade must be relieved if the Con-

[30] *Diary,* II, 284 (July 27, 1863), 303 (August 21, 1863), 328, 331 (September 20 and 24, 1863), 338–39, 340–41, 342 (October 6, 7, and 12, 1863), III, 20, 22 (October 21 and 27, 1863).

[31] *Diary,* III, 25, 27 (November 5, 9, and 11, 1863), 38, 52 (December 4 and 23, 1863), 94 (February 7, 1864).

federate capital was to be taken.[32] The commander, however, remained the titular head of the Army of the Potomac until Appomattox.

6

Meade and McClellan were to Gurowski the military curse of the North, but the squat, bearded, sloppily dressed Grant seemed to him the incarnation of Union success, the savior of the people's cause. He admired Grant from the time of his victory at Fort Donelson in February, 1862. The General's ability to strike blows and gain objectives appealed to him, and like his fellow Jacobins, he engaged during the spring of 1863 in an avalanche of praise, while Grant brilliantly executed the Vicksburg campaign. "Grant is an eminent man as to character and as to capacity," lauded the Pole during the build-up, and the news of the city's capitulation brought this grateful exclamation: "Vicksburg taken! No words to glorify Grant . . . *and the army of heroes on land and on the waters.*" "Grant has overpowered men, soil—and elements," the praise continued. "GRANT, PORTER, FARRAGUT, and their men overpowered land and waters. They overpowered *the Mississippi*."[33]

The formidable river bastion capitulated, rumor reached Gurowski that Grant had been offered command of the Army of the Potomac. "If Grant accepts," the Count reasoned, "he will be a ruined man. Grant ought to have Pope in memory. Grant soon will see stained his glorious and matchless military record. He will not withstand the cliques and the underground intrigues of craving, selfish and unsatisfied ambitions." When he heard authoritatively that Grant had declined the Potomac command, he commented apprehensively: "They cannot ruin Grant— they will neutralize him."[34]

In the wake of the Vicksburg triumph, Grant's army was scattered, as had been the fate of his forces the previous year. "It could be considered a crime against the people's cause," wailed the Count, "—but—

[32] *Diary*, III, 221 (May 7, 1864), 254 (June 11, 1864), 331 (September 3, 1864), 367 (October 5, 1864).

[33] *Diary*, I, 164 (February, 1862), II, 236 (May 25, 1863), 261, 267 (July 8 and 14, 1863).

[34] *Diary*, II, 297–98, 309 (August 11 and 31, 1863).

hurrah for Lincoln." He rejoiced that the Radicals had their way in October, 1863, when the West was concentrated under Grant's command, a development due to Stanton's insistence. He also reasoned that Grant had decided to become a Radical and followed their program even to the point of advocating the use of Negro soldiers. At the same time Jacobins saw in him a general of dazzling success, a leader they could use to control military patronage by smashing the influence of Meade and his coterie in the Army of the Potomac.[35]

Gurowski applauded when Grant took to the field in the campaign to relieve beleaguered Chattanooga: "Oh, why has not Grant the command of the noble and fated army of the Potomac!" The relief of Chattanooga and route of the besieging Confederate forces brought more praise: "Grant again victorious. No *ifs* with Grant, and Meade and his clique stick in the—to them congenial—mud." Gurowski and his Radical associates continued into 1864 their praise of Grant and their denunciation of Meade. "Whatever I hear from and about Grant and the generals in the western army," the Count exclaimed, "all of them behave differently from Meade, and are altogether the opposite of our Potomac McClellanised heroes. I mean Meade and his clique. It seems to be the curse of the Potomac army to be the prey of intriguers."[36]

The Radicals were now ready to bring Grant east to take command of all military operations. Claiming him as their property, the Jacobins pushed through Congress a bill making the hero of the West a lieutenant general, the highest military rank, and one held only by George Washington and Winfield Scott. Gurowski, however, had not justified Grant's blunders at Shiloh. When the Confederates published their report of the battle, he reasoned that, because Grant had resisted their superior numbers on the first day, he turned out to be the true hero of the engagement. While the Grant promotion bill was on the threshold of becoming law, the Count explained that the "question of making Grant a Lieutenant General—urged by the patriots in Congress, urged by the people, urged by Stanton—is hanging fire because Lincoln cannot get rid of his incubus Halleck, and wishes to save him. Grant will have a hard time with

[35] *Diary*, II, 328 (September 20, 1863), III, 20 (October 21, 1863).
[36] *Diary*, III, 21 (October 26, 1863), 35 (November 26, 1863), 68 (January 9, 1864).

Lincoln's pets." "Grant's elevation," he maintained, "was forced upon Lincoln . . . by Stanton, by public opinion, by the Congress. Lincoln, as always, was reluctant. Now if Grant is successful that Sham Lincoln will have all the credit of it."[37]

Gurowski and the other Radicals welcomed Grant to Washington with open arms, when he came to assume supreme command in March, 1864. Grant on arrival pleased the Count immensely by publishing an order of six lines and refusing three dinners: "If that is not significant of a man then nothing is." Little time slipped away in searching out the new commander. "Grant is the most shy, bashful, simple and natural man that ever I have met," he confided to his friend, Andrew, "and this may be as well as not a sign if not of a genius at least of an eminent capacity." Grant alone, of all generals in Washington, avoided the "various corrupting allurements," and only he retained freshness of mind and ingenuity. Here was a new breed of commander, a man who traveled with a small trunk, which he forgot in his room, and then to save time, went off without. With the spring campaign in the offing, the Pole said, Grant sent his wife to her father's home in Missouri: "If all this . . . is not Roman, Cincinnatus, . . . then I am at a loss for precedents and for historical illustrations." Every time he saw the General, he admired "his truly Republican simplicity. He must have the sacred fire in his heart and brain." There continued, nevertheless, apprehension for the commander: "Will Grant remain a diamond, resisting the dissolving Washington acids?"[38]

Gurowski hoped to purify Grant for the Radicals through several visits and innumerable letters. In one interview the conversation turned to Benjamin F. Butler, a political general loved by the Count and most other Jacobins because of his breezy, vigorous, and ingenious methods of dealing with Confederates. Grant told Gurowski that the flashy Butler pleased him more than any other new acquaintance. During other visits the Count warned Grant that Meade appeared to be under McClellan's

[37] *Diary*, III, 122, 133 (March 3 and 9, 1864); Gurowski to Andrew, March 27, 1864, in Andrew Papers.

[38] *Ibid.; Diary*, III, 138, 148 (March 18 and 24, 1864), 159–60, 164–65, 180, 181–82, 194 (April 5, 8, 15, and 22, 1864).

influence and in constant correspondence with him, and urged the removal of the Potomac commander. At another time the Pole suggested to Grant the idea of excluding newspaper correspondents from the army. Their dispatches confused public opinion and puffed up generals, who extended to these news writers' compliments and favors. Instead, all news should be edited and handled by Grant's military bureau, so as to give the Radicals opportunity to check Conservative sentiment.[39]

The Count looked on with misgivings while Grant prepared the spring campaign. The General had had no freedom of choice of commander for the Army of the Potomac, because Lincoln and Halleck insisted that he retain Meade. "It is a bad sign," Gurowski complained, "and a bad beginning." "God grant that the Lieutenant General may not bitterly regret having kept Meade in command of the army! Grant ought to have been more self-willed. Meade's hesitation, if not worse, will defeat the best plans, and may defeat the whole campaign." Nor was the army reorganized by Grant, as the Count had hoped. Nothing had been done to reform its spirit or to change much of its leadership.[40]

If Grant were unsuccessful, it would be because he had not "sufficiently purified" the army of Conservative leadership, which had been the chief purpose of Gurowski and other Jacobins in bringing Grant to supreme command. Rumors that he would not stand up to Lee were being spread by Meade and his Conservative supporters, thought the Count. Although he did not fear that Grant would be awestruck by Lee, "these malignant and cowardly insinuations demoralized the army, and that is the only aim of the clique." On the eve of the supreme commander's departure for the field, Gurowski chided: "Grant has the cursed inheritance of all the bloody, criminal faults and mistakes committed by his predecessors in command, and above all, the inheritance of the more than accursed McClellan and Meade's ungeneralship."[41]

When the Count probed for Grant's plan of campaign, he found it

[39] *Diary,* III, 160, 162 (April 5 and 6, 1864); George Gordon Meade to [?], April 8, 1864, in George Gordon Meade (ed.), *The Life and Letters of George Gordon Meade, Major-General United States Army* (2 vols., New York, 1913), II, 188.

[40] *Diary,* III, 151–52 (March 27, 1864), 155, 158–59, 160 (April 2, 4, and 5, 1864); Gurowski to Andrew, April 27, 1864, in Andrew Papers.

[41] *Diary,* III, 163–64, 200 (April 6 and 26, 1864), 211, 219 (May 1 and 6, 1864).

to be cloaked in complete secrecy. Slowly, nevertheless, he unraveled from talk about the capital what he concluded to be the pattern. "Grant does not go to Richmond," he wrote to Governor Andrew, "as did all the asses before him. Grant knows that Richmond and ¾ of secessia is in Lee's army; and Grant's [plan] seems to be not to force Lee back on Richmond, but either to cut him off and destroy him or precipitate Lee on the defenses of Washington and crush him there between the forts and our army. This last would be a master stroke, the boldest but the surest."[42] Gurowski did not accurately know the plan until early May, when Grant opened his co-ordinated campaign. Sherman in the West would push into the lower South and enter Georgia. The Army of the Potomac would lunge southward at Lee's host in front of Richmond. Grant would make his headquarters with Meade's army and give the orders.

In the dense, wooded region known as the Virginia Wilderness the Eastern armies clashed. Grant hurled his masses against inferior numbers, but again and again saw them fall back, bleeding and shattered. Anxiety grew worse in the North, with the Radicals providing the final touch, said the Count, by "agonizing for news" from the Wilderness. When information at last reached Washington, he concluded that Grant had "sustained his reputation for unrelenting stubbornness" and "forced Lee to retreat or to fall back on another impregnable position." He thought it a bloody and suicidally insane campaign, a slaughter that dwarfed Gettysburg, but for the first time during the war there seemed to be genuine achievement to show for the thousands of maimed and dead. "Step by step," he said while voicing the praise of all Jacobins, "Grant hammered and hammers Lee's army back." It appeared to Gurowski that the great dailies credited Meade with the Wilderness campaign achievements, but this did not detract from Grant's glory, for the public knew that Meade carried out the orders of his superior.[43]

If only Grant had been in the saddle in the spring of 1862, reflected the Count, his unrelenting and stubborn qualities would have undoubtedly ended the war long ago. "Grant the Hammerer," he said near the

[42] Gurowski to Andrew, April 27, 1864, in Andrew Papers.
[43] *Diary*, III, 220, 221, 226, 227 (May 7, 8, 13, and 14, 1864).

end of the first month of the campaign, "twenty-five miles from Richmond! And what a powerful hammer is the Potomac army!"[44] Yet after weeks of bloody battering, and despite the propaganda support of Gurowski and other Radicals, Grant had moved little farther than when he entered the Wilderness. He called off the attack on the night of June 12 and withdrew from Lee's front. Immediately he took his army over the James River and prepared to attack Lee and Richmond from the flank.

Grant's strategic withdrawal across the James was hailed by Gurowski as a brilliant military achievement because Lee had no opportunity to attack. McClellan's withdrawal to the James in 1862 had been unlike Grant's, the comparison continued, since in the earlier move the Army of the Potomac had been contested the entire distance and usually worsted. In fact, Grant had not committed a single error in the entire campaign down to the middle of June, 1864, except the monstrous sin of retaining Meade.[45]

A cloud of discouragement, however, settled on Gurowski by late June, when he concluded that the task of Grant and his forces was steadily growing heavier and more complex. "Will it be possible," he asked as the long siege of Petersburg commenced, "to Grant and to the army to correct now and make up for that criminal imbecility paramount in the conduct of the war which began with Scott, and culminated in McClellan and in Meade?" The investment of Petersburg appeared to the Count as a greater task than all recorded sieges from Troy to Sebastopol. The Battle of the Crater, following an effort by Grant to blast a gigantic hole in Confederate fortifications near Petersburg, ended as a dismal failure, he said, because Meade, the "true culprit" of the incident, was not on the spot as he should have been. But Grant would cope with the problem despite Meade, and he predicted that Lee would probably be unable to leave the trenches protecting Richmond. In autumn, with the siege still dragging on, he justified the delay by sarcastically complaining that Grant perhaps earlier could have strangled Lee were the enemy General not "so *ably* and so *efficiently* seconded by Meade."[46]

[44] *Diary,* III, 227, 236 (May 14 and 24, 1864).
[45] *Diary,* III, 260–61 (June 16, 1864).

Lee, contrary to Gurowski's prophecy, evacuated Petersburg on April 2, 1865, but time was running out for the beleaguered Confederates. Grant paralleled Lee's march and sent Philip H. Sheridan's cavalry ahead to intercept, and the end came a week later at Appomattox Court House. Meade, said Gurowski, had been altogether innocent of these brilliant and climactic actions. If Meade rather than Grant had directed these concluding movements, Lee would probably have escaped. Meade, the complaint continued, must be blamed for one third of Grant's killed, wounded, and disabled in the 1864–65 Richmond campaign. "Seldom, if ever," he said of Grant, "have such extensive military operations been conceived and centered in, or issued from, a single mortal brain."[47]

Grant's reports of the final campaigns impressed Gurowski favorably. These had few equals in military history in regard to modesty, simplicity, clarity, and breadth. The General, nevertheless, had judged inaccurately some subordinates in the report. The pompous darling of the Jacobins, General Butler, seemed to be handled "with unwanted and pointed severity." Meade, on the other hand, received Grant's "inexhaustible magnanimity." Sheridan, the Count agreed, truly deserved Grant's praise. But he held his ground on Meade even before the eye of Grant himself: *"forgive the accusation of to much magnanimity,"* he wrote the General, *"showed by you towards Meade*: who is—but never mind."[48]

When Gurowski reflected on Grant's four years of military leadership, he continued convinced that his quest for satisfactory military leadership had ended. He could find few parallels or precedents in history for such ability. He was delighted to have backed constantly the commander on the printed record from the day of his first significant successes in Tennessee early in the war. What satisfaction in choosing the winner! Grant ought to be informed of his constant and enthusiastic support, so unabashedly the Pole wrote: "Yours, my dear General: Not of to day, not since the capture of Lee, but since the first ray of glory at

---

[46] *Diary*, III, 265–66 (June 24, 1864), 294 (July 24, 1864), 312 (August 8, 1864), 390 (November 6, 1864), 401–402 (note, December 7, 1865).

[47] *Diary*, III, 348 (note, June, 1865), 400 (note, December 7, 1865).

[48] *Diary*, III, 400–402 (note, December 7, 1865); Gurowski to Ulysses S. Grant, March 23, 1866, in Brown University Library, Providence.

fort Donaldson." And Grant was not unappreciative of Gurowski's endorsement. At the close of the war the Count received a printed invitation to the Grant home in Washington for an evening of dancing.[49]

7

Although Grant turned out to be Gurowski's military beau ideal, the ostentatious and ingenious soldiering and political activities of General Butler won the Count's admiration and captured most other Jacobins. Gurowski and his companions early had adopted Butler as a favorite and thrilled to his antics throughout the war. The General's rash initiative first attracted Gurowski when he occupied Baltimore without orders a month after the fall of Fort Sumter: "General Butler . . . did what ought to have been done a long time ago." Butler next proposed to take Norfolk by a sea-land operation. The Count approved, of course, and verbally lunged at General Scott for squelching the idea.[50]

Butler's work as head of the occupation forces in New Orleans (May 1–December 16, 1862) pleased Gurowski, who saw much to compliment in his severe military rule of the city. The General's seizure of $800,000 in bullion left by the Confederates in the care of the French consul of New Orleans, however, he considered to be a mistake, for it taunted the French people and the consul himself, "who was not partial to Secesh." But with the over-all picture he continued pleased. When Butler was relieved of the command of the Department of the Gulf, he took farewell of his troops in a flamboyant proclamation relating his accomplishments in the Crescent City. The Pole described it as "the best and noblest document written since the war. It is good, because it records noble and patriotic deeds."[51]

Some days later Gurowski praised the General's parting words to the people of New Orleans, complimenting his own achievements and loaded with antislavery sentiments. In Butler's statement "rings the purest and most patriotic harmony. Compare Butler's with Lincoln's

[49] *Diary*, III, 403 (December 7, 1865); Gurowski to Grant, March 23, 1866, in Brown University Library; printed invitation from General and Mrs. Grant, in Gurowski Papers.

[50] *Diary*, I, 43, 45–46 (May, 1861).

[51] *Diary*, I, 255 (August, 1862), II, 58 (December 29, 1862). For Butler's proclamation, see *Official Records*, Ser. I, Vol. XV, p. 610.

writings. All the hearts in the country resounded with Butler." The effervescent Count could not contain his ecstasy, so he wrote the General: "I master not my feelings, my rapture, and bring to you my homage. You speak deeds not words; deeds of eternal honor of a noble and true patriot and citizen, a lofty minded and genuine statesman." Butler's removal from the New Orleans command, he said, resulted from a "serreptitious undermining" by Seward working through his agent, Reverdy Johnson. The former Maryland Senator had been sent by President Lincoln to New Oreanls to investigate complaints of foreign consuls that Butler had seized their property. Seward feared, the Count explained, that the "patriotic activity by which General Butler won, conquered and maintained the rebel city for the Union . . . as crushing out every spark of any latent Union feeling among the rebels."[52]

Gurowski's enthusiasm for Butler did not wane during the ten-month period when the General held no command. He would be ideal, he recommended, as general staff chief. Butler's speech at the Academy of Music in New York in early April, 1863, thrilled the man in the blue goggles. He described the General's abolitionist-scented remarks as "the paramount exposition of the whole rebellion in its social, governmental and military aspects. No President's messages, no letter, no one of the emanations of Seward's letter and dispatch-writing, corrosive disease, not an article in any press compares with Butler's speech for lucidity, logic, conciseness and strong reasoning. Butler laid down a law, a doctrine— and what he lays down as such, contains more cardinal truth and reason than all that was ever uttered by the administration." Butler was "the *only man,* emphatically the ONLY MAN who was always and everywhere equal to every emergency—who never was found amiss, and who never forgot that an abyss separates the condition of a rebel, be he armed or unarmed, (the second even more dangerous,) from a loyal citizen and from the loyal Government." He wrote unrestrainedly again to Butler: "I kiss your hands very fervently for your great speech. Patriotism, manhood,

---

[52] *Diary,* II, 65, 79–81 (January 3 and 9, 1863); Gurowski to Butler, January 3, 1863, in Jessie Ames Marshall (ed.), *Private and Official Correspondence of Gen. Ben-jamin F. Butler During the Period of the Civil War* (5 vols., Norwood, Massachusetts, 1917), II, 566. For Butler's address to the citizens of New Orleans, see *ibid.,* II, 554–57.

broad statesmanship, fearlessness, and the noblest civism pour from every word." Months passed before Butler received a command. Gurowski believed the General wholly fitted to deal with the bloody draft riots that racked New York in mid-July, 1863.[53] But the administration thought otherwise, glad to have "Bold Ben" neutralized.

Finally, in early November, 1863, the administration sent Butler to Fortress Monroe as commander of the Department of Virginia and North Carolina. "Good news," said the Count jubilantly, when adding a word of explanation: "The White House shakes before public opinion and before the coming Congress, and so appeals to *men* and *patriots* for support." He unfolded in his *Diary* his hopes for the General: "Ben Butler would make an excellent President. He has all the capacities of a statesman. Butler can destroy and build up, organize and administer. He is bold, with keen insight, and with prompt unerring decision. Could only Butler make some *coup d'éclat* before Richmond."[54] Two days later he wrote the General a confidential letter and unfolded a scheme, reminiscent of the days of his conspiracies for Polish independence, designed to make him President. He reminded Butler that "in the last hour the people will go for the ablest man, provided that man accomplishes some brilliant action, and accomplishes it in the *nick of time.*" Then he detailed the plan:

> The army of the Potomac is to begin operations early in the spring. It is to be supposed that Lee will draw to him all the available forces. Then a lightning-like blow dealt from Fortress Monroe on Richmond, putting you in possession of the nest of the rebellion, transforms you into an irresistible favorite, and a candidate for the Presidency.
>
> Of course Lincoln and his advisors will never put you in possession of sufficient means for such a *coup,* and still less would they assent that you should deal it.
>
> Therefore—if possible—and possible it ought to be for such fertile

[53] *Diary,* II, 174 (March 18, 1863), 187–88 (April 4, 1863), 268 (July 15, 1863); Gurowski to Butler, April 6, 1863, in Marshall (ed.), *Private and Official Correspondence of Gen. Benjamin F. Butler,* III, 53.

[54] *Diary,* III, 24 (November 2, 1863), 86 (January 28, 1864).

[55] Gurowski to Butler, marked "confidential of course," January 30, 1864, in Marshall (ed.), *Private and Official Correspondence of Gen. Benjamin F. Butler,* III, 348–49; see also *Diary,* III, 87 (January 31, 1864).

brains as are yours—you ought continually, slowly, but uninterruptedly increase your forces and resources; do it daily and hourly, and justify it by reasons plausible and palatable to our rulers.

When the hour comes, strike the blow without letting out your secret. ... the people will carry you into the White House. This people and this continent must be rescued from the curse to have Mr. Lincoln re-elected.[55]

Butler arrived at the same conclusion and collected troops for a raid on the Confederate capital. Meantime, the veil of secrecy lifted in federal command circles, and Butler openly requested assistance. He made the move toward Richmond with but six thousand men and simultaneously carried out a diversionary demonstration with a small unit of the Army of the Potomac. The effort turned out to be a complete fiasco, because the Confederates had wind of the plan.

But the General's political prospects and military reputation emerged unblighted, and his boom for the Republican Presidential nomination actually developed during April and May, 1864. Lincoln's fear of the Radicals progressed to the point during Butler's political rise that he offered the General the Vice-Presidency, which was declined. Butler wanted the Presidential nomination or nothing. Gurowski and other Butler supporters contended that, if the General were nominated and elected, the Confederates would give up immediately. By All Fools' Day the Count thought that the Radicals had let too much time slip away and that it would be well-nigh impossible to nominate Butler.[56]

In the 1864 offensive on Richmond, Grant planned for Butler to advance up the James, threaten the Confederate capital, break communications, and keep reinforcements from Lee. Perhaps in this Butler had another opportunity to win the Presidency, thought the Count: "Butler's activity creates great uneasiness in the White House and among the most ardent Lincolnites. Butler's genuine availability for the Presidency is recognized by all, and any, even the smallest *coup d'eclat* before Richmond, would carry him into the White House. *Of course,* the Lincoln crew in power will take care that Butler has no success."[57]

[56] William Frank Zornow, *Lincoln and the Party Divided* (Norman, Oklahoma, 1954), 64, 66–67; *Diary,* III, 154 (April 1, 1864).
[57] *Diary,* III, 199 (April 25, 1864).

But the coup never came to pass. Butler's failure before Richmond resulted from his military incompetence, and not from interference by the administration, and in the end made necessary the long siege of Petersburg. Blunder militarily as he would, Butler still held the Count's admiration, confidence, and hope for the Republican Presidential nomination. "I am wholly upset," Gurowski wrote to the General as the Presidential election approached. "I consider that the nomination of McClellan can easily be beaten to pieces, and that our party ought to nominate a man for the emergency. Your leaders ought to do it. I die from impatience . . . for a man of my choice as you. And if A. Lincoln is elected, what security have the true patriots that you will have a preponderating influence in his councils, and that you will have a broad and grand space for action? I am perplexed almost to despair."[58]

Butler's future career as a soldier must have perplexed Gurowski even more. The blustery General botched the attempt to capture Fort Fisher, guarding the mouth of Wilmington harbor in North Carolina, in December, 1864. Butler called off the attack by needless and hasty withdrawal of his troops. Soon afterwards Grant retired him from command. Although most Jacobins ranted and bellowed at this action, the Count said nothing. Even he no longer found in Butler the political Messiah for whom he had hoped so long and fervently.

---

[58] Gurowski to Butler, September 7, 1864, in Marshall (ed.), *Private and Official Correspondence of Gen. Benjamin F. Butler,* V, 126.

CHAPTER VIII

LIBELOUS BOOK

I

"I AM WRITING day after day the events and their philosophy," Gurowski told James S. Pike, Lincoln's minister to The Hague, during the first summer of the war. "It will be published here or in England, and pitiless I am for all the absurdities, stupidity and meanness that I witness now."[1] In a kind of preview, he quoted critical passages from his diary to Governor Andrew on the Battle of Seven Pines.[2] Commenced about the time of Lincoln's inauguration, the manuscript had grown steadily because of periodic, often daily, entries and during summer, 1862, reached the proportions of a medium-sized book.

Now was the time to search out a publisher, reasoned the Count, reflecting on the dreary and disheartening military situation and the administration's sagging political prospects. His diary would undoubtedly cost him his job in the State Department and make even more perilous his quest for food and shelter, but at all costs to himself he must be heard. Therefore in August, 1862, he visited the shop of William H. Moore, a Washington printer, and asked that the absent proprietor call on him at the State Department. At Gurowski's desk some hours later Moore agreed to print the diary and carted off its loose, disreputable, almost illegible pages. The printing establishment did not get to the typesetting immediately, so the irritated Count dropped by to hurry up the work. His plan, a customary procedure of that day, was merely to employ Moore to print a copy or two of the manuscript on wide-

[1] Gurowski to Pike, August 30, 1861, in Pike Papers; see also "Nebulae," *Galaxy,* Vol. I, 270.

[2] Gurowski to Andrew, marked "confidential," June 6, 1862, in Andrew Papers.

margin letter paper, for corrections and rewriting. The type, he said, would need complete resetting before book publication.[3]

Several weeks later Gurowski took his proof-sheet diary to Henry Chase, State Department bookbinder, for arranging and binding the loose pages. Chase glanced at the contents and noticed many derogatory remarks concerning his chief, Seward. He took the diary to a State Department official, who showed it to Seward himself, with the result that Gurowski was relieved of his duties as temporary clerk. Meantime, he had sent the concluding pages of his manuscript, not yet set in type, to Governor Andrew, with the request that it be "put in order and sew[n] together; if you like read it; if possible give it then for a few days to Edward Everett and tell him that I wish to have his opinion, provided he can go through this rough and unwashed language." When the proof sheets were returned by State Department officials, he dispatched them also to the busy Andrew, of whom he inquired a month later: "What about my book?"[4]

The problem of locating a publisher seemed acute by early November. "I am sure not to find a publisher bold enough for my *Diary,*" the Count feared, and explained that it was "not at all an affair of any literary ambition or personal vanity. I am not in need of it." The public criticism which publishers foresaw, as they read his censorious proof sheets, he would willingly take on himself. "Could I pawn—as it was done in former times—my soul and body to the devil," he wrote Governor Andrew, "I should do it cheerfully if by it I could procure means to print myself the book. I know that you have not much more than I. But could you not find some one in that wealthy community who would make me a loan of 700 to 800 dollars, for this business. One thing is certain: the book will sell and the coasts will be soon recovered."[5]

Andrew obliged. Within a fortnight he not only lined up a financial

[3] "Nebulae," *Galaxy,* Vol. 1, 270; Washington *National Intelligencer,* October 12, 1863; Washington *National Republican,* October 10, 1863; Washington *Star,* October 15, 1863.

[4] Washington *National Intelligencer,* October 12, 1863; Washington *National Republican,* October 10, 1863; Washington *Star,* October 9 and 10, 1863; Washington *Chronicle,* October 10, 1863; Gurowski to Andrew, September 16, [1862], and October 19, 1862, in Andrew Papers.

[5] Gurowski to Andrew, November 1, 1862, in *ibid.*

sponsor, but opened the way for a publisher as well. George Luther Stearns, a wealthy Bostonian engaged in abolitionism and manufacture of lead pipe, agreed to provide the money. Stearns had been one of John Brown's primary financial backers in both the Kansas bloodletting and the Harpers Ferry raid. When Andrew approached Stearns concerning the Gurowski diary, the Boston manufacturer was in the midst of a new publishing venture, the *Commonwealth,* a newspaper launched in September, 1862. On its pages Stearns boldly advocated removal of General McClellan, immediate emancipation of all slaves as a war measure, and re-election of Sumner to the Senate and Andrew as governor.[6]

Stearns went immediately to the office of the prominent Boston publishing firm of Lee and Shepard and made arrangements for bringing out the diary. Although the firm had not been established under its name until early in 1862, one of the partners, William Lee, had earlier been a junior associate in the old Boston publishing house of Phillips, Sampson and Company, which distinguished itself by bringing out Emerson's *Essays* and rejecting *Uncle Tom's Cabin.* Stearns' dollars and insistence on immediate publication caused Lee and Shepard to set type without delay. The Count reveled in the mass of proof that poured upon him and returned the sheets promptly. Work on the volume progressed with such dispatch, that late in November he told his publisher of his delight over the prospect of early publication. He requested copies to send abroad to personal friends, "but not to literary notabilities." As to review and publicity copies, he said he never sent his books to critics and public men, but suggested to Lee and Shepard the desirability of sending the new publication to the London newspapers.[7]

2

Before the middle of December, Gurowski's *Diary,* covering March 4, 1861, to November 12, 1862, was available in book shops in the East.

[6] Gurowski to Horatio Woodman, April 25, 1863, in Massachusetts Historical Society, *Proceedings,* Vol. LVI, 236; Gurowski to Andrew, April 10, 1863, in Andrew Papers; Frank Preston Stearns, *The Life and Public Services of George Luther Stearns* (Philadelphia, 1907), 268.

[7] Hellmut Lehmann-Haupt and others, *The Book in America: A History of the Making and Selling of Books in the United States* (Second Edition, New York, 1951),

At least four Washington booksellers promoted the volume, selling at $1.25, in a series of advertisements in the local newspapers. The big blurb, however, appeared in the sometimes Radical New York *Tribune,* where the *Diary* was advertised as the inside story of the Lincoln government. In a series of questions designed to indicate content as well as stir interest, Greeley's paper sought to popularize the book:

> Who Predicted that this Rebellion would be crushed in 60 days? Who parleyed with the Rebel Commissioners? Who incorporated and perpetrates the Fabian policy? Who has caused this nation to float upon an uncertain, tempest-tossed sea during 20 months? Who planned and Executed the Peninsular Campaign? What Great Military Chieftain kept 200,000 men watching a cordon of Quaker Guns during the entire Winter of '61 and '62? Who constantly and perseveringly disobeyed the orders of his superiors, and by doing so lost victories? Who displeased his great Generalship by ingloriously resting upon his oars and allowing the enemy to escape after the battle of Antietam? Gurowski Will Tell You That It Was Not Joe Hooker!

Readers were told that the Count divulged "The Whole Story" and advised to purchase the *Diary* and judge for themselves. Cincinnati, the book entrepôt of the Middle West, advertised the volume as "the Secret History of Lincoln's Administration."[8]

Two hundred and fifteen pages of truth, rumor, scandal, complaint, and approbation greeted Gurowski's readers. Handsomely bound in dark red ornamented cloth, the *Diary* was dedicated "to the widowed wives, the bereaved mothers, sisters, sweethearts, and orphans in THE LOYAL STATES." This appeal to broken hearts preceded a brief preface, in which the Count pointed out that he chronicled what he had seen and what he had heard from veracious friends. "I recorded impressions as immediately as I felt them," he said, explaining that the experiences of his tempestuous life taught him "the first impressions are the purest and

230; J. C. Derby, *Fifty Years Among Authors, Books and Publishers* (New York, 1884), 517–25; Gurowski to Lee and Shepard, November 28, [1862], in Lee and Shepard Papers.

8 Washington *National Intelligencer,* December 13, 15, 16, and 18, 1862; Washington *National Republican,* December 13, 15, 16, 17, 18, and 19, 1862; Washington *Chronicle,* December 13, 1862; Washington *Globe,* December 15, 16, 17, 18, and 20, 1862, January 2, 3, 5, and 6, 1863; New York *Tribune,* December 17, 18, and 19, 1862; Cincinnati *Commercial,* December 24, 1862.

the best." He warned that friends and acquaintances would find in the *Diary* their "confidential conversations and discussions, what in letters and by mouth was a subject of repeated foreboding and warnings."[9]

The book's analytical table of contents was cryptically written and designed to substitute for an index. Then followed the text, printed as monthly entries until July, 1862, after which daily entries appeared with increasing frequency. The author's faulty rhetoric, proofreading errors, and ambiguous statements dismayed the reader, who was amply rewarded for his patience, however, by morsels such as the concluding paragraph: *"Dictatorship with McClellan* seems to dawn upon the horizon; the smallest disaster—Burnside, ah!—will precipitate the catastrophe. I pray to God (and for the first time) that I may be mistaken."[10]

Press opinion on the new book came from both the pro- and the anti-Lincoln papers of New York, with the Radical-tinged *Times* and *Tribune* conspicuously silent. The Conservative *Herald* lashed at Gurowski and his *Diary* in a series of caustic editorials. The opening piece was titled "The Count Adonis Gurowski on the Rampage." Dubbed a dandy after Adonis, the handsome youth beloved by Aphrodite, the Count was described as "a sort of a semi-civilized savage . . . ill-bred, shrewd and ill-natured." What he wrote was "sometimes very silly, sometimes very witty, and sometimes very sarcastic." The editor conceded that in spite of the author's disposition and prejudice, the book contained much that seemed sensible and shrewd, written in a style always amusing and interesting.

The *Herald* reviewer contended that Gurowski wrote with authority, but predicted in cutting words that the exposé would doom him to ostracism: "his handsome face, his elegant figure and his refined manners will no longer be—if they have ever been—the brightest ornaments of the *salons* of our good society." Confidential conversations and secrets revealed by the Count were like turning state's evidence against friends, for although legally right, was morally and ethically reprehensible. But the *Herald* noted the Count's advice to Lincoln to muster courage and act for himself, and queried: "Will not the President take good advice

9 *Diary,* I, dedication and preface, dated Washington, November, 1862.
10 *Diary,* I, 315 (November 12, 1862).

even from Gurowski?" Pursuing the *Diary* in its entirety, the critic wrote: "One seems to be overhearing the gossip of a gang of Washington scandal mongers, standing in a dirty barroom and drinking bad whiskey as they chatter. Gurowski has noted down the gossip, but the odor of the bad whiskey clings round it still and makes the reader qualmish."

The *Herald* also found the Count's new book an indictment of all Radicals. The intention of the volume was to lay open Seward, said the paper, but instead Seward's enemies were unmasked. It exposed the methods of the Jacobins and divulged the sources of their inspiration, ideas, and information. The Pole ordered and warned Radical leaders, "and we have seen that his orders were obeyed and his warnings regarded. . . . Like all of his associates, Gurowski hates and despises his associates . . . and . . . spares few of them, great or small." The volume should have the "careful consideration" of Lincoln, who would "see in it such a portrait of the radicals, drawn by one of themselves, as may well make him shudder with disgust at the abolition harpies who cluster around him." The President was challenged to take this evidence against the Radicals and use it to force them from the cabinet. "This scathing exposure of the radical abolition intrigues by one of the radical agents," the *Herald* recommended, "should be universally read, remembered and inwardly digested."[11]

The New York *World*, anti-Lincoln and anti-Radical, carried a stinging editorial, titled "Asmodeus in Goggles," on Gurowski and his *Diary*. The epithet originated with Asmodeus, king of demons, and the Count's colored glasses. The *Diary*, the critic explained, had "something . . . of the interest of an hour spent with an Asmodeus in goggles upon half the housetops of official Washington." When Gurowski "tells us that all the gods of the radicals are idols of clay and brass we may believe him, for he has helped to set them up and has seen the interior arrangements by which they have been made to wink simulated wisdom upon a bewildered and excited nation. But when he tells us that he is himself the only real original Jacob of political divinity we must remember

[11] New York *Herald*, December 8, 10, 11, and 14, 1862.

166

how much harder it is for a man to know himself than to know all things else."

Never had the *World* known an individual who spoke with so few inhibitions: "Gurowski has absolutely no reticence. Nothing is sacred to him. The interests of party, the obligation of social relations, the force of personal favor, are to him as were the green withes of the Philistines to Sampson. He rends them all asunder." No person is mentioned, with few exceptions, the review continued, "in this strange farrago of sense and frenzy who does not undergo as many mutations in the author's mind as there are months in the year. . . . Children and madmen, we are told, speak the truth; and though Gurowski is certainly no child, he is evidently mad enough in one sense of that word to blurt out the most disagreeable facts about his friends. His opinions of individuals we need not say are for the same reason comparatively worthless." The *World* took comfort in the belief that the Count was too fat to be a military man: "Fearful as he is in goggles and with the pen, what a shape of dread would he not be in epaulettes and sword in hand!"[12]

Reactions of other Gurowski contemporaries, even those of fellow Radicals, contained a common air of dismay, if not disgust. The sensitive and cautious Edward Everett saw many an opinion and fact in its pages that he believed no respectable man could publish. A considerable amount of the data, he believed, the author obtained from his confidential position in the State Department. The *Diary* came from the mind of an "extremist," but there were "some plain truths in it." Everett, long a close acquaintance of the Pole, bought two copies, one for his library, the other to give to Mrs. Eames.[13]

Lawyer George Templeton Strong of New York, in whose home Gurowski had visited years before the war, was impressed, "due probably to the intensity of conviction with which he writes, for he records no new facts and no original thoughts. His English is obscure, and his temper, taste, and moral tone are bad . . . . He is, moreover, the Thersites of our camps and councils, denouncing and decrying every chief and

---

[12] New York (weekly) *World*, December 13, 1862.
[13] Diary of Everett, December 6, 1862, in Everett Papers.

every measure, but I fear his denunciations are justified, and that Lincoln, Stanton, Seward, McClellan, and all the rest are unequal to their work."[14]

Another lawyer, John C. Gray, Jr., Bostonian and a firm Lincoln supporter, believed the best account of the damage done by the Jacobins appeared in the Count's *Diary*. His correspondent, John C. Ropes, also a Boston attorney, thought otherwise. Ropes found more to endorse than to denounce. The book's many commendable qualities, he said, redeemed it from charges of reckless denunciation, which otherwise could justifiably be brought against it. Although the work displayed "remarkable sagacity," he doubted whether it had actually been written at the time the events occurred. The publication, said Ropes, defined the fundamental differences in point of view between Radicals and Conservatives.[15]

Navy Secretary Welles did not read the *Diary*, but friends told him that it was "unsparing in its assaults upon almost all in authority" and that it exuded "scandal and hate in bad English." A Washington journalist, Benjamin Perley Poore, labeled the book "one prolonged growl from beginning to end." Even those persons praised by the Count in early pages were usually abused before the end. Those who read Gurowski were certain to find "the particular object of their individual dislike" thoroughly maligned. Another journalist described the publication as no "catalogue of blandishments."[16] Still another called it "piquant, combining some sharp hints at incompetency and no small amount of wit."[17]

An anonymous Bostonian, judging the *Diary* a mixed blessing, considered it "amusing from its foreign idioms, its peppery peevishness, its personalities, and, above all, from its inordinate—I may almost say in-

[14] Allan Nevins and Milton Halsey Thomas (eds.), *The Diary of George Templeton Strong: The Civil War, 1860–1865* (New York, 1952), 279 (December 13, 1862).

[15] John C. Gray, Jr., to John C. Ropes, January 5, 1863, in Worthington C. Ford (ed.), *War Letters, 1862–1865, of John Chipman Gray and John Codman Ropes* (Boston, 1927), 62–63; Ropes to Gray, January 1, 1863, in *ibid.*, 49.

[16] Beale (ed.), *Diary of Gideon Welles*, I, 187–88 (December 4, 1862); Poore, *Perley's Reminiscences of Sixty Years in the National Metropolis*, II, 137–39; unidentified newspaper clipping, in author's possession.

[17] New York *Times*, May 6, 1866; see also unidentified newspaper clipping [May, 1863] in volume titled "Scraps," in John Hay Papers.

sane—conceit and self-importance . . . . The predictions it contains as to the inevitable results of certain measures which have now attained their fruition, would convince one that the writer had been imbued with the spirit of prophecy, were it not that they are evidently interpolations inserted since the results have been made known. The book is not instructive, but it is amusing. Ridiculous on some accounts, it nevertheless contains some . . . pungent sayings and sagacious observations." Charles A. Dana, Gurowski's old friend of the New York *Tribune* staff, thought the book entertaining. An Irish Democrat from Chicago, Colonel James A. Mulligan, called it a blundering volume of "perfidious stabs," one that "puffs and screams and abuses . . . in the manner of a fishwoman," and predicted that the public would forgive the author by forgetting him.[18]

Whatever the criticisms, the *Diary* sold rapidly, and within several weeks after its appearance the publisher had on hand only a few copies. Sales neared the three thousand mark and more than repaid costs of publication. Royalties did not reach Gurowski regularly, and it is doubtful that he received monies justly his, but Stearns evidently recovered his investment.[19]

3

When the Count's *Diary* had been off the press for several weeks, William Hunter, chief clerk of the Department of State, appeared in the Criminal Court of the District of Columbia and began a libel suit. Hunter alleged that the book contained damaging material concerning his competence. A grand jury served Gurowski formal notice of indictment on January 2, 1863, and waived imprisonment until the case should come to trial.[20]

[18] Letters signed "T.A.N.," January 26, 1863, in Springfield *Illinois State Journal,* February 3, 1863; Dana to Pike, March 13, 1863, in Pike Papers; Colonel James A. Mulligan Diary, January 14, 1863, in Chicago Historical Society.

[19] New York *Herald*, December 10, 11, and 14, 1862; Washington *Star,* October 9, 1863; Washington *Chronicle,* October 10, 1863; Gurowski to Gerrit Smith, November 16, 1865, in Archives and Museum, Polish Roman Catholic Union of America; Gurowski to Woodman, April 25, 1863, and May 9, [1863], in Massachusetts Historical Society, *Proceedings,* Vol. LVI, 236.

[20] Presentment 156, December, 1862, in Records of the Criminal Court of the Dis-

The Count was charged with publishing "false, scandalous, malicious and defamatory libel . . . contriving and wickedly . . . and unlawfully intending to aggrieve and vilify . . . William Hunter . . . and to bring him into public scandal and disgrace with all his fellow citizens and neighbors and to injure and disgrace him in his . . . office and to cause him to be considered and esteemed a person unfit to be employed therein, and to cause him to [be] thought a person accustomed to act in betrayal of his official trust." The Pole acted, the indictment concluded, not only to the "great scandal infamy and disgrace of . . . Hunter [but] to the evil example of all others in like case offending and against the peace and Government of the United States."[21]

Officially designated *United States* versus *Adam Gurowski,* the case took the form of a criminal action. The Count interpreted the indictment broadly, believing Hunter only the medium of attack. Undeniably this was a move against him by the Lincoln Conservatives, the European mused, when he challenged his adversaries: "Well, great masters, if you swallow me, you may not digest me. Let us try."[22] He reveled in his predicament because in suing him, the government had publicized his book and added to his Radical martyrdom.

Hunter, in bringing suit, introduced two separate passages from the *Diary* considered by him damaging to his professional reputation. In both the Count maintained that Hunter had revealed prematurely Lincoln's first blockade proclamation to the British ambassador, Lord Richard B. P. Lyons.

> Yesterday N—— dined with Lord Lyons, and during the dinner an anonymous note announced to the Lord that the proclamation of the

---

trict of Columbia, National Archives; Indictment, *United States* versus *Adam Gurowski,* and Bench Warrant for Gurowski, in Criminal Case File 594, Records of the Supreme Court of the District of Columbia, *ibid.* The New York *Tribune,* December 18, 1862, carried the following note, a special dispatch from Washington on the preceding day: "It is reported that Chief Clerk Hunter of the State Department has sued Count Gurowski for libel."

[21] Docket 37, in Criminal Docket Book, Volume I, 1863 Term of the Criminal Court, Records of the Supreme Court of the District of Columbia; Indictment, *United States* versus *Adam Gurowski,* in Criminal Case File 594, Records of the Supreme Court of the District of Columbia.

[22] *Diary,* II, 134 (February 9, 1863).

blockade is to be issued on to-morrow. N——, who has a romantic turn, or rather who seeks *midi a' 14¾ heures,* speculated what lady would have thus violated a *secret d'Etat.*

I rather think it comes from the Ministry, or as they call it here, from the Department. About two years ago, when the Central Americans were so teased and maltreated by the fillibusters and Democratic administration, a Minister of one of these Central American States told me in New York that in a Chief of the Departments, or something the like, the Central Americans have a valuable friend, who, every time that trouble is brewing against them in the Department, give them a secret and anonymous notice of it. The friend may have transferred his kindness to England.[23]

Later in the *Diary,* Gurowski returned to Hunter and elaborated on this incident. When the blockade was about to be declared, Hunter assisted Seward at an interview with Lord Lyons. Because of Seward's ignorance in foreign affairs, Hunter, "a man not even mastering the red-tape traditions of the department, without any genuine instruction, without ideas," was relied on to furnish the technical knowledge needed at the interview. All the Chief Clerk did was to state that a blockade had been in use during the Mexican War and that they were nearly annual occurrences in South America. The British ambassador asked for definite precedents or acts of the United States government concerning blockades, but both Seward and Hunter brushed the inquiry aside. Lyons then went to his Washington quarters, said the Count, and after a little inquiry sent the State Department the missing information. Then came another allegedly libelous passage in the indictment: "This chief clerk made Mr. Seward make *un pas de clerc,* and this at the start. As Lord Lyons took a great interest in the solution of the question of blockade, and as the chief clerk was the *oraculum* in this question, these combined facts may give some clue to the anonymous advice sent to Lord Lyons, and mentioned in the month of April."[24]

[23] *Diary,* I, 25 (April, 1861); Washington *Chronicle,* October 10, 1863; Washington *Star,* October 9, 1863; Indictment, *United States* versus *Adam Gurowski,* in Criminal Case File 594, Records of the Supreme Court of the District of Columbia.

[24] *Diary,* I, 52–53 (June, 1861); Washington *Chronicle,* October 10, 1863; Washington *Star,* October 9, 1863; Indictment, *United States* versus *Adam Gurowski,* in Criminal File 594, Records of the Supreme Court of the District of Columbia.

The Chief Clerk must have fumed again when he read a few pages farther about the State Department's sending a circular to foreign ministers, announcing that armed vessels of neutrals would be allowed to enter unmolested blockaded ports of the Confederacy, a step Gurowski thought highly inadvisable. The Pole recorded in his *Diary* that he called the attention of Seward to the possible complications and dangers of this move, but "the chief clerk adviser of the Department found out that President Polk's administration during the Mexican war granted a similar permission, and, glad to have a precedent, his powerful brains could not find out the difference between *then* and *now*." Also, Gurowski said, Hunter humiliated our representatives abroad by keeping them uninformed. No foreign office in Europe would treat its agents so flippantly. These errors in diplomatic procedure were to be credited in the main to the Chief Clerk.[25] Strangely, this aspersion did not appear in the libel indictment.

The Count's views of Hunter were not altogether unjustified. Concerning the blockade at Galveston, Texas, the Chief Clerk himself thought he possessed "very little knowledge and no practical experience of these matters except what took place during the Mexican blockade."[26] Some weeks later Lincoln called on Hunter, after receiving inadequate suggestions from Seward, for advice on the prize ship *Peterhoff,* but the Chief Clerk did not understand the case or what the President desired.[27] When the Secretary of State could not attend cabinet meetings while recovering from an assassin's attack, and on other occasions, he was represented by Hunter, conspicuous by his silence. Even Seward thought his chief clerk intellectually and emotionally dry, a good example of fossilization from long tenure in office.[28]

Before taking a position with the State Department in 1829, Hunter had studied law and practiced briefly in New Orleans, Louisiana, and

[25] *Diary,* I, 68–69 (July, 1861).

[26] Beale (ed.), *Diary of Gideon Welles,* I, 233 (February 6, 1863).

[27] *Ibid.,* 286 (April 27, 1863); see also *Diary,* II, 212 (April 28, 1863).

[28] Theodore Calvin Pease and James G. Randall (eds.), *The Diary of Orville Hickman Browning* (2 vols., Springfield, Illinois, 1927–33), II, 105, 152, 202, 210, 212, 222; Dennett (ed.), *Lincoln and the Civil War in the Diaries and Letters of John Hay,* 260 (February 2, 1867).

Providence, Rhode Island. He had served as translator from 1829 to 1833, as clerk in the diplomatic bureau from 1833 to 1852, as chief clerk of the State Department from 1852 to 1866, and would act as second assistant secretary of state for the twenty years of life that remained from 1866 to 1886.[29]

4

The case of *United States* versus *Adam Gurowski* dragged on through the spring and summer of 1863 without coming to trial. The Pole's counsel during a part of this time was James M. Carlisle, a prominent Washington attorney of Conservative bent, who in spite of disagreeing with his client's political and social views, "behaved," said the Count, "in this affair, as a thorough man of honor." Carlisle, a former Democrat and close friend of President James Buchanan, refused to take the recent "ironclad" oath of loyalty required for practice in the court system of the District under the congressional act of 1863.[30] For this reason Joseph H. Bradley, Sr., a Washington lawyer who had agreed to take the oath, replaced Carlisle as Gurowski's counsel. He opposed Lincoln and had a sarcastic tongue and the distressing habit of bullying and insulting witnesses. Thus Bradley, well known as one of the capital city's most experienced and successful pleaders before a jury, argued the Gurowski case when it came to trial in October, 1863.[31]

While the Count awaited the proceedings, the court system of the

[29] James Grant Wilson and John Fiske (eds.), *Appletons' Cyclopaedia of American Biography* (6 vols., New York, 1887–89), III, 323–24; Howard K. Beale (ed.), *The Diary of Edward Bates, 1859–1866* (Washington, 1933), 262n. In a statement of doubtful accuracy, a biographical dictionary eulogized Hunter's services: "His thorough familiarity with all branches of our foreign relations rendered him one of the most efficient servants of the government either at home or abroad. His memory was prodigious, and he was always able to set forth clearly the thread of a protracted by-gone negotiation or the history of a half-forgotten claim." Wilson and Fiske (eds.), *Appletons' Cyclopaedia of American Biography*, III, 324.

[30] *Diary*, II, 134 (note, February 9, 1863); H. W. Howard Knott, "James Mandeville Carlisle," *Dictionary of American Biography*, II, 394; *Eminent and Representative Men of Virginia and the District of Columbia of the Nineteenth Century* (Madison, 1893), 290.

[31] "Minutes of the Criminal Court," I, 423, and "Rule of Defendant to employ new Counsel," in Criminal Case File 594, Records of the Supreme Court of the District of Columbia; Eisenschiml, *In the Shadow of Lincoln's Death*, 269.

District of Columbia underwent complete reorganization. On March 3, 1863, by act of Congress, the Circuit Court, the District Court, and the Criminal Court were replaced by the newly organized Supreme Court of the District. During the decade of the fifties, the courts of the District had lost much of their prestige on account of the sluggishness with which they worked. With the advent to power of the purely sectional Republican Party in 1861 and the abolition of slavery in the District in 1862, politics entered the reorganization picture with unabated fury. Judges of the Circuit Court had for years returned fugitive slaves apprehended in the District. This angered both Conservative and Radical Republicans and brought the accusation that the court sympathized with the Confederacy. Thus Radicals considered their reorganization measure as one that would place the administration of justice in the District "upon anti-slavery, instead of pro-slavery principles."[32]

Gurowski came to trial before this new District Supreme Court. Lincoln's selection for chief justice was David Kellogg Cartter, a rude, blunt, arrogant, but brilliant Ohioan, who had been instrumental in nominating the President in 1860. Politically indebted, Lincoln had appointed him minister to Bolivia, a position in which he neglected his duties in favor of touring the Andes. After two years Cartter returned to the United States, anxiously awaiting the President's favor a second time. His appointment as chief justice opened opportunities to promote the extremist tendencies of Radicals. Long an abolitionist, he had been appealed to for legal counsel by his friend John Brown, following the Harpers Ferry raid. Cartter was also a close confidant and admirer of General Butler and did much to promote his political and military fortunes.[33]

Throughout most of the war the new Chief Justice largely confined his circle of friends to Radicals. Hardly a day passed without a meeting

[32] New York *Tribune*, March 5, 1864; F. Lauriston Bullard, "Lincoln and the Courts of the District of Columbia," *American Bar Association Journal*, Vol. XXIV (February, 1938), 117–20.

[33] Albert Gallatin Riddle, *Recollections of War Times: Reminiscences of Men and Events in Washington, 1860–1865* (New York, 1895), 3n.; Marshall (ed.), *Private and Official Correspondence of Gen. Benjamin F. Butler*, III, 65, 78, 115–17; Dennett (ed.), *Lincoln and the Civil War in the Diaries and Letters of John Hay*, 115–16 (November 3, 1863).

with Senator Benjamin F. Wade, Senator Zachariah Chandler, and Congressman Thaddeus Stevens. Chandler's attractive brownstone house was the gathering place for Cartter and his companions, often joined by Secretary Chase and Secretary Stanton. New York *Tribune* editor Greeley frequently gathered with these men in railing at Lincoln and the Conservatives. "Well, let's go up and swear at Lincoln a while," Cartter or another crony would exclaim to assemble the group.[34]

The reaction of two of the President's cabinet secretaries, both known Conservatives, represents the thinking of administration supporters concerning Cartter. Edward Bates, the attorney general, termed him "a fierce partizan, an inbred vulgarian and a truculent ignoramus." Secretary Welles thought him "a coarse, vulgar, strong-minded man" with a vigorous intellect capable of making himself felt. Later, during the Radical effort to unhorse President Andrew Johnson, Welles would pronounce the Chief Justice "a creature of Stanton."[35] There can be little doubt of the Radical tendencies of the judge under whom Gurowski was tried.

Cartter had a huge frame and bulky head. Smallpox roughly marked his impressive leonine face. When he spoke, his hearers seemed not to be aware of a slight impediment used effectively for humor and invective. "W-w-hy," he falteringly criticized a meticulous legal associate, "he-he is a-a-always p-picking up p-pins w-w-where there's crowbars lying r-round." Cartter delivered what he said with a voice and manner so vivid and unique that he invariably enlivened or created interest. His vigorous, epigrammatic speaking technique usually impressed the jury and always crowded the courtroom when he addressed the jurors. Radicals anticipated a peak performance in the Count's trial.[36]

[34] Ruth Gertrude Curran, "David Kellogg Cartter," *Ohio Archaeological and Historical Publications,* Vol. XLII (January, 1933), 112–13; Job Barnard, "Early Days of the Supreme Court of the District of Columbia," *Records of the Columbia Historical Society,* Vol. XXII (1918), 22; Marshall (ed.), *Private and Official Correspondence of Gen. Benjamin F. Butler,* III, 115–17, 133.

[35] Beale (ed.), *The Diary of Edward Bates, 1859–1866,* 310 (October 17, 1863); Beale (ed.), *Diary of Gideon Welles,* II, 259 (August 12, 1865), III, 157 (August 5, 1867).

[36] Barnard, "Early Days of the Supreme Court of the District of Columbia," *Records of the Columbia Historical Society,* Vol. XXII, 20–21, 25, 34–35; Curran, "David Kellogg Cartter," *Ohio Archaeological and Historical Publications,* Vol. XLII, 110–12.

The prosecuting lawyer for the United States in the Gurowski case was Edward C. Carrington, a Virginian serving as Washington district attorney. A man of unusual oratorical ability, he was a good friend of Attorney General Bates, and Bates's choice for public prosecutor. The other contender for the District post had been Edwin M. Stanton, who was not appointed because Bates maintained that he could not work with Stanton. Two abolitionist senators, Henry Wilson of Massachusetts and Kinsley S. Scott of Michigan, momentarily held up Carrington's appointment by spreading talk that several years earlier he had accepted a purse raised by popular contribution to assist a kidnapped Negro. The story alleged that Carrington then refused to help the Negro and permitted him to be sold as a slave in New Orleans. Carrington, like Cartter, had been well cast for his role in the Gurowski trial.[37]

[37] Beale (ed.), *The Diary of Edward Bates, 1859–1866,* 318, 376, 382, 420 (November 26, 1863, June 12, July 1, and October 18, 1864); Beale (ed.), *Diary of Gideon Welles,* I, 56–57 (no date); Pease and Randall (eds.), *The Diary of Orville Hickman Browning,* I, 487 (July 27, 1861).

CHAPTER IX

RADICAL JUSTICE

I

ON THE MORNING OF FRIDAY, October 9, 1863, the Gurowski case finally came to trial, nearly ten months after Hunter had filed charges. The Count was placed at the bar of the District Supreme Court, then sitting as a criminal court, and treated to a reading of the indictment. He answered "not guilty," whereupon a jury of twelve was empaneled.[1] District Attorney Carrington opened by explaining the indictment and the law on the subject. His purpose, he said, would be to prove that Gurowski's *Diary* containing the libel had been widely circulated, and that in it Hunter was charged not only with inefficiency but also with betraying government secrets. He would "teach the Count, and through him the world, that the character of a public officer was not to be lightly impugned."

Gurowski's counsel Bradley then pointed out to the jury that it must first decide whether the *Diary* had been written and published by the alleged author and then, if necessary, must determine whether the content was libelous. In any case, Bradley argued, Hunter was evidently not injured by the *Diary*, for he had continued in his position. Moreover, an American citizen could rightfully criticize the acts of government officials on the basis of freedom of speech and press. In the *Diary* Hunter was mostly "charged with error," Bradley continued, and that could not

[1] "Minutes of the Criminal Court," I, 423, in Records of the Supreme Court of the District of Columbia. The jurors were John B. Blake, Henry N. Johnson, John E. Neale, Charles Cumberland, Henry Burch, John C. Lievel, James L. Davis, James Manken, Frederick A. Klopfer, Samuel R. Sylvester, William H. Fanning, and John B. Davidson, and are listed in *ibid.*; Washington *Star*, October 9, 1863; Washington *Chronicle*, October 10, 1863; Washington *National Republican*, October 9, 1863.

be termed libelous, for he was not "charged with maliciously commit-
ting an error."

The District Attorney now produced his first witness, O. H. Morrison, Washington bookdealer, who testified he had sold many copies of
Gurowski's *Diary*. Bradley objected on the ground that the federal government must prove a particular copy of the *Diary* as the work of Gurowski. Next Henry Chase, the State Department bookbinder who had
reported the proof-sheet diary to Seward, took the stand and stated
that the Count had brought the printed but unarranged pages of his
diary to him for assembly, with the entreaty to show them to no one.
Carrington hoped to prove by Chase that the proof-sheet diary "contained
language similar to that in the printed book," and handed the witness
a copy of the *Diary*. Bradley objected to such evidence, unless Chase
could recall the "exact language." Without hesitation Judge Cartter ruled
that such evidence was not competent, whereupon Carrington maintained that Chase could legally look into the *Diary* "at the matter charged
as libelous, and thus refresh his memory."

Carrington asked Chase to read from the *Diary*, and to "say whether
the matter there was not the same as that on the paper brought to him
by Mr. Gurowski." Again Bradley objected, arguing that Chase could
either have the indictment read or read it for himself in order to revive
his memory. "But then," Gurowski's counsel continued, "he must be
able to give the identical language, for, to say that the language in the
indictment is similar to what [the] witness saw, is not evidence." Cartter
sustained Bradley's opinion that the testimony could not be accepted as
competent evidence. Carrington then obtained permission to give written notice to the Count requiring him to provide the proof-sheet diary,
whereupon the defendant looked astonished and the audience laughed.
Bradley cross-examined Chase by inquiring whether Gurowski had
told him that the proof sheets were for his own use, but the bookbinder
did not recollect such a statement by the Pole.[2]

2 The official stenographic court proceedings of the first day of the Gurowski libel
trial are in the Washington *Star*, October 9, 1863, and the Washington *Chronicle*, October
10,1863. An unofficial newspaper-reporter version, somewhat abbreviated but substantially
like the official proceedings, is in the Washington *National Republican*, October 9, 1863.

2

The District Attorney opened the second day by indicating his intent to prove that the Count had brought the proof-sheet diary to Chase, the State Department bookbinder. Through Chase, said Carrington, he could prove that Gurowski was the author of the libel. But first he would serve notice on Gurowski, as authorized yesterday by Judge Cartter, "to produce certain manuscripts or proof-sheets presented by you to Henry Chase, on the 17th of September, 1862, to be arranged and covered . . . for the purpose of being read in the case of the United States against Adam Gurowski."

Bradley argued that the alleged libel was in a specific form and must be so proved. Yesterday, he said, Carrington had stated that the proof-sheet diary contained a title page indicating that it included material to November, 1862. This could not be, Bradley explained triumphantly, for the proof sheets as stated in the testimony, had been presented by Gurowski in September of that year. Moreover, Bradley continued, the fact that the defendant had taken proof sheets to Chase did not prove that he had composed the printed material. Asking Gurowski to produce the alleged proof-sheet diary at once, said Bradley, was not reasonable notice. Judge Cartter encouraged the defense, suggesting doubt that the notice to the Count could be deemed reasonable as required by law. Bradley jumped to the helm by reading from two studies on evidence, showing that notice during a trial could not be considered reasonable and that it should have been presented well before the case came up. Furthermore, Gurowski's counsel continued, the defendant did not have the proof sheets at his Washington residence, but with his papers in New York.

Carrington now called for a decision by Judge Cartter on the adequacy of the notice. After pointing out that the question must be settled on "some general principles," the Judge concluded that Gurowski could not be expected to "carry around these proof sheets in his pocket, or in

A short notice is in the New York *Times,* October 10, 1863. From 1840 to 1875 the opinions of the courts of the District of Columbia were not published in book form, but were ordinarily released to the newspapers of the District. The manuscript stenographic record of the Gurowski libel trial is not known to be extant.

his trunk, as he would a greenback or a railroad ticket," and that therefore the notice was unreasonable.

George Randall, a printer apprentice in the shop of William H. Moore, where type had been set for the proof-sheet diary, came next to the witness stand. He related the Count's visits in August, 1862. Randall was handed the indictment and requested to read the alleged libel. "Have you seen the libel charged in the indictment," Carrington questioned, "in any published book?" "I saw the matter in the book published as a 'Diary,'" Randall answered, adding that he had not read the entire book, but had recognized a portion of it in a Washington bookstore. Bradley objected to further testimony by Randall, a request Judge Cartter sustained without question.

Moore, the print shop proprietor, was the next witness for the government. He said that the Count turned over to him the longhand diary to be set in type, then printed on letter paper with wide margins. The author, according to Moore, said he "intended to rewrite it and publish it in the form of a book." Moore concluded by remarking that he knew no other Adam Gurowski.

A clerk in the Washington bookstore of Frank Taylor, a man named Bestor, briefly took the stand and testified to selling the Count's *Diary*. Then Chief Clerk Hunter was called. "I do not know Adam Gurowski," said Hunter in disdain, "and don't wish to know him. I know him by sight. Have seen him frequently in the State Department, but always avoided him on account of his previous character . . . . What his business exactly was I cannot say. The only thing I ever saw him do was . . . read the foreign papers, from a presumption that no one else in the United States could do it. There is no one else of that name in the city."

At this point Bradley boldly stated his intention to ask Judge Cartter to instruct the jury that there was no evidence that the Count had written the alleged libel in the *Diary*. The trial now hung solely on this technical question of authorship. The District Attorney offered as evidence the *Diary* itself. Bradley objected, insisting that Carrington had not connected Gurowski with the book. In fact, said Bradley, Gurowski had no more to do with the publication of the book than had Bradley himself.

The District Attorney then argued that ample circumstantial evidence identified the writer. "The book," said Carrington, "is offered as a fact in connection with the other facts already in evidence, tending to show that the defendant is the author." But the prosecution, the District Attorney maintained, had labored under extraordinary handicaps in locating witnesses. "Strange to say," Carrington complained, "I cannot find a witness in Washington city or elsewhere, who is willing to appear in court and testify that the defendant admitted that he was the author of this libellous book. It is a remarkable fact . . . . Perhaps he is exceedingly exclusive, and has no friends or acquaintances to whom, in an unguarded moment, he divulged his secret. Perhaps, in consequence of his position, his friends are above the reach of judicial process. Perhaps he is so good a man that his friends are unwilling to appear and testify against him."

Continuing his argument, Carrington related that "unusual efforts" had been made by the prosecution to cajole Gurowski into admitting authorship of the book, but the reluctant Count had refused to comment. However, circumstantial evidence already submitted clearly and conclusively pointed to the Pole as author of the *Diary*. This evidence, said Carrington, fell into three categories: (1) Gurowski's action and statements relating to the *Diary* before its publication, (2) Gurowski's declaration and acts relating to the volume following its appearance from the press, (3) the evidence in the book itself considered in relation to the Count's activities and comments.

Carrington now pleaded with Cartter to consider the evidence:

Perhaps your Honor will say no single item of this testimony, considered apart and by itself, proves any thing. But the whole evidence considered together cannot fail to produce the conviction that . . . Gurowski is the author of the book containing this libel. One thing is very clear. When I remind your Honor of the facts, to which the witnesses have testified, you cannot say that there is *no evidence* to be weighed by the jury. You must admit . . . there is *some evidence*—that is all I ask the court to admit—for then you are bound to let me at the jury, and I will have no difficulty . . . in satisfying them from the evidence who published this libellous book. . . .

The chain of evidence is complete, it cannot fail to produce conviction . . . . Yet, your Honor is called upon to say that there is no evidence from which the jury may infer that the defendant is the author of this book, and to take the whole case away from them . . . . You cannot exclude this testimony . . . . I invoke you not to do it; I protest against it. You cannot do it without, in my judgment, violating that great fundamental principle that it is the exclusive province of the jury to determine questions of fact . . . . This, I repeat, you cannot consistently do.

With Carrington's argument concluded, Gurowski's counsel rose and bellowed that he never before had heard a "proposition so monstrous." A person's name, exclaimed Bradley, upon the title page of a publication alleged to contain libelous passages could not be evidence of authorship. It was the duty of Carrington, Bradley said, to prove that Gurowski had written the *Diary;* in fact, no evidence whatever had been presented to fix authorship on the Count. It would, therefore, be out of order to give the *Diary* to the jury.

The question of Gurowski's authorship of the *Diary* was now before Chief Justice Cartter. To keep the jury from considering the adequacy of the evidence, Cartter had to hold that no evidence had been presented by the government pointing to Gurowski as the writer. In a series of successive blows, Cartter audaciously crushed the testimony and arguments of the United States. The evidence submitted, said Cartter, proved Gurowski neither author nor publisher of the *Diary*. The fact that Gurowski's name appeared on the title page could not be considered evidence, for it was printed rather than in his handwriting. "Now," stuttered Cartter, "what kind of principle would it be to establish that these Roman characters were peculiarly the characters of Count Gurowski [laughter], or any other Count [renewed laughter]; and still you have got to do it to give any significance whatever to that fact. It not only does not constitute perfect proof, but it constitutes no proof at all—not an item of proof . . . . If this is internal evidence, it is internal evidence of nothing—simply and absolutely nothing in connection with the identity of the party."

Cartter found the remaining evidence equally worthless. The title did not identify the book with the Count, since it was common to that class of literary production. Gurowski's residence in Washington for the period of the *Diary* also meant nothing to Cartter. The Count's employment in the Department of State was likewise brushed aside. Any clerk in that department, Cartter reasoned, except Hunter himself, could have written the *Diary*. After all, it could have been composed "outside or inside with the same precision." The testimony that the Count had a manuscript or proof sheet diary before publication and that he had admitted to witnesses that he intended to publish it Cartter dismissed in these words: "What that diary was we do not know." The book could therefore not "be read to the jury for want of proof of authorship and publication on the part of the defendant."

The District Attorney retaliated by requesting a *nolle prosequi* for the discontinuance of proceedings and reopening of the case at a later date. He explained that he desired time to summon the publisher from Boston and had not earlier arranged for this because he did not wish to put the government to unnecessary expense. If the Count were not the author, Carrington said, a great injustice had been done him; Hunter and the public were entitled to know the identity of the writer. But Gurowski's counsel objected to the District Attorney's request on the grounds that a jury could not be carried over after testimony had been given. Chief Justice Cartter sustained the objection. Since no evidence concerning authorship of the *Diary* had been submitted to the jury, the verdict "not guilty" was returned immediately.[3]

---

[3] An abbreviated version of the official stenographic court proceedings of the second day of the Gurowski libel trial is in the Washington *National Republican*, October 10, 1863, and the Washington *National Intelligencer*, October 12, 1863. What evidently is a newspaper reporter's version of the second day of the trial, an account apparently containing the complete argument of Chief Justice Cartter, is in the Washington *Star*, October 10, 1863; an identical clipping is in the Edward C. Carrington Papers, possession of the Otto Eisenschiml estate, Chicago. Carrington's argument, evidently in full, appears in the Washington *National Intelligencer*, October 13, 1863; an identical clipping is in the Carrington Papers. Copies of the summons of the witnesses of the United States in the Gurowski case are in Criminal Case File 594, Records of the Supreme Court of the District of Columbia. The "not guilty" verdict is recorded in Criminal Docket Book, I, Criminal Trial 37, Presentment 156, Records of the Supreme Court of the District of Columbia.

3

Few comments on the case were made by the press. Noah Brooks, Lincoln's friend and Washington correspondent for the Sacramento *Union,* maintained at the close of the first day of the trial that Gurowski felt confident he would be vindicated. The Conservative-minded New York *Herald* commented at the close of the first day: "Some rich developments were expected, but have not yet come to light." When sensations failed to materialize, the *Herald* simply recorded the verdict, as did the New York *Times.*[4]

Gurowski, too, said little. On the day he emerged victorious from Cartter's court, he wrote in his *Diary:* "And the power-holders let loose their mastiffs. And the mastiffs ran at my heels and tried to tear my inexpressibles and all. And they did not, because they could not. Because my friends (J. H. Bradley,) stood by me. And the people's justice stepped in between the mastiffs and me, and I exclaim with the miller of Potsdam, 'There are judges in Washington.' "[5]

Gurowski and the Radicals prevailed, thanks to Chief Justice Cartter. From the beginning of the trial, the prosecution had labored under difficulties. Never had the presiding justice ruled favorably for the United States. Although the government's evidence was circumstantial, a reasonable view suggests that enough evidence had been presented to cause an impartial justice to permit the jury to pass on its adequacy. The partisan conduct and attitude of Cartter throughout the trial substantiates his known attitude toward the Radical Republicans, and Gurowski himself admitted the Chief Justice's Jacobin position in his *Diary.*

In fact, the trial had been a travesty on justice. By refusing to permit the jury to consider the evidence presented by the United States, Cartter had kept the nonpartisan element from evaluating the adequacy of the evidence. The Chief Justice then killed the last hope of the Lincoln Conservatives to overcome his Jacobin stand by refusing to permit District

[4] Letter from "Castine" [Noah Brooks], October 9, 1863, in the Sacramento *Union,* November 4, 1863; New York *Herald,* October 10 and 11, 1863; New York *Times,* October 11, 1863.

[5] *Diary,* II, 342 (October 10, 1863).

Attorney Carrington to summon the Boston publisher of the *Diary* and to continue the trial. Carrington clearly indicated in his argument for the United States the unreasonable nature of the Radical forces he had attempted to conquer. To Edward Everett of Boston the fact that Gurowski had written the *Diary* was "as notorious as the rising of the Sun . . . . Common sense ought not be wholly banished from our courts."[6]

The libel indictment, strictly speaking, originated with Secretary Seward, although action had been brought against the Count by Chief Clerk Hunter. Seward could not have proceeded openly against the Pole in his position as secretary of state, and Hunter was a convenient and inconspicuous channel through which to get at the troublesome Count. If the jury had found Gurowski guilty of libel as charged by Hunter, the effect would have been the same as if the jury had found the defendant guilty of libel against Seward. Gurowski would then have been thwarted in his efforts to denounce and expose Seward and other Lincoln Conservatives on the printed page.

4

The jury had no sooner declared Gurowski "not guilty," than he was ready to publish the second volume of his *Diary*. The verdict virtually sanctioned publication of additional volumes, but a prompting factor, in addition to the Count's desire to criticize Conservative Republicans, caused him to act. He was financially destitute. The book, he believed, would relieve this condition, and he expedited publication. In less than a month after his trial he announced that Volume Two would soon be out, predicting that he would probably be sent to Fort Lafayette "for saying the truth." Despite the revelations of the first volume, a newspaper correspondent maintained that Gurowski still had access to "the best sources of information." Not until early in the following February, however, did the book finally appear, and in the meantime, Governor Andrew came to the Count's rescue by a secret business loan of three hundred dollars, made through an intermediary in Washington and based on a six-month personal note. Gurowski's pride pre-

6 Diary of Everett, February 20, 1864, in Everett Papers.

vented a direct loan from Andrew, whom he believed had no money to spare.[7]

The publisher was the New York firm of G. W. Carleton, one of the city's smaller book businesses active in the low-price field. A Carleton success had been a translation of Victor Hugo's *Les Miserables,* which sold hundreds of thousands. American humor of the period appeared in quantity under the Carleton imprint, and particularly the books of Artemus Ward, Lincoln's favorite humorist, and Josh Billings. Sensationalism, the forte and the taste of Carleton, undoubtedly was in great part responsible for his production of the second volume of the *Diary.* Gurowski's experience in bringing out the book was made unpleasant by duplication of proofs, insufficient typesetters, and delays in the mail. He feared that these circumstances may have left their unwanted impact in his new book.[8]

Volume Two in appearance, general design, grammatical errors, and nature of content differed little from its predecessor. This time, however, the cover was in black, entries were by exact date throughout, and the dedication was to the Count's countrymen. Comment was more detailed than previously. The period covered was November 18, 1862, to October 18, 1863, a span of eleven months, whereas Volume One had surveyed in fewer pages more than the twenty months following Lincoln's inauguration.

On February 4, 1864, the New York *Times* carried Carleton's blurb announcing the publication of Gurowski's new book, and predicted that it would "stir up the dry bones of incompetent and incapable officials throughout the land, and make a sensation generally." The publisher represented the new *Diary* as containing "sharp criticism, alternating with epigrammatic, trenchant, caustic praise and castigation," and claimed that the book would "bear away the palm from all others ever

[7]Gurowski to Andrew, October 27 and November 5, 1863, in Andrew Papers; unidentified newspaper clipping [May, 1863] in volume titled "Scraps," John Hay Papers; Andrew to Major W. L. Burt, November 18, 1863, copy, in Andrew Papers. Said Andrew: "I am sorry to trouble you, but this must be confidential strictly, understood only by us two, least of all by the Count."

[8] Derby, *Fifty Years Among Authors, Books and Publishers,* 235–44; Lehmann-Haupt and others, *The Book in America,* 226–27; Madeleine B. Stern, "G. W. Carleton: His Mark," *Publisher's Weekly,* Vol. CL (August 17, 1946), 711–13; *Diary,* II, 348n.

printed in this country." The New York *Tribune's* advertisement touted it as the "sharpest, raciest, most brilliant and readable book ever published on Military and Political matters." Carleton ran the same sales notice in the *National Intelligencer* and the *National Republican,* both Washington newspapers. The West also was treated to more of Gurowski, for Rickey and Carroll of Cincinnati, book distributors for that area, announced the new volume.[9]

The New York *Herald* again used its editorial page to lash and praise Gurowski's *Diary,* in a column titled "Vitriol on the Administration." This "curious and wonderful" book, said the *Herald,* has an "extremely brilliant opening." In fact, this volume seemed more "bitter and pungent" than the first: "Gurowski was very sour, severe, sarcastic, and satirical before, but his dismissal by Seward, the increasing imbecility of the administration, and various other circumstances . . . have so intensified his acidity that he throws vitriol right and left, and his words burn whomsoever they touch." While disagreeing with the Count on his undivided support of Stanton, the review maintained that the Pole had "a very clear idea of the disease which now afflicts us. 'The official brains of the nation,' says he, 'are in a morbid condition.' " The *Herald* explained that it had no objections to Gurowski's crying for blood instead of ink, but it did object to his self-termed Cassandra gift of foreseeing. "Why, without this gift," the editorialist chided, "the illustrious Count would be a mere ordinary mortal while now he is an ornament to the age and the author of the most readable 'Diary' ever printed in this country."[10]

The New York *World,* detested by Gurowski, greeted the second volume of the *Diary* by lamenting that "the 'accursed thirst of gold' should have led to the spoiling of so much nice white paper." The book and its author, as if to reciprocate the Count's biting criticism of the *World* in his new volume, were attacked as equally disagreeable and displeasing: "the flesh and the devil receive the dregs of his ill-nature in

[9] New York *Times,* February 4, 5, and 6, 1864; New York *Tribune,* February 6, 1864; Washington *National Intelligencer,* February 13, 16, and 18, 1864; Washington *National Republican,* February 10, 13, 17, and 18, 1864; Cincinnati *Commercial,* February 12, 1864.

[10] New York *Herald,* February 5, 1864.

an odorous shower." To Gurowski's comment that General Halleck would not go to hell, because imbeciles were not admitted there, the *World* replied that "the Count evidently regards [hell] as his own destined home and place of rest, 'where alone his fireworks can be surpassed.'" In this book, the *World* commented, Gurowski "went at his war dance, tomahawk in hand and scalps at his belt, more riotously than ever."[11]

Bostonian John C. Gray, Jr., serving with federal military forces in South Carolina, asked his family to send him the Count's second volume, "which will be a treat." Edward Everett likewise sent for the book, described by him as "a little more abusive than the first." George Templeton Strong went away impressed by the fury of Gurowski's patriotism in the new volume but noted that the author also "scolds more viciously and in worse language than any Russian count.... Many of the points are strong, but his style and temper are those of an enraged Tartar Khan, full of raw horse and bad liquor. This book will exert little influence."[12]

5

The third and final volume of the *Diary* appeared in early April, 1866, sixteen months after Gurowski had made his last daily entry. This time the Count had considerable difficulty arranging for publication. The shift of interest brought about by the close of the war and the insistence of the author that the book be brought out in Washington, which had no commercial publishing firm, compounded the problem. In November, 1865, Gurowski solicited Gerrit Smith, the wealthy abolitionist of up-state New York, for a loan of eleven hundred dollars to publish the book as a private venture.

Gurowski had reason to expect help, since Smith customarily supported antislavery activity, having backed John Brown's Virginia plot. The book, said its author, must be published in Washington to permit

---

[11] New York (weekly) *World*, February 11, 1864.

[12] Gray to Ropes, received February 19, 1864, in Ford (ed.), *War Letters, 1862–1865, of John Chipman Gray and John Codman Ropes*, 295; Diary of Everett, February 20, 1864, in Everett Papers; Nevins and Thomas (eds.), *The Diary of George Templeton Strong: The Civil War, 1860–1865*, 405 (February 11, 1864).

him to superintend the process, for the two other volumes had been "filled with errors [and] misconstructions sufficient to disgust the reader and the author himself." The loan should be an outright business matter, with the money returned to Smith soon after publication. "I give you my word of honor," said the pledge, "that I shall not toutch a cent from the sale, until you be repaid." The Count assured Smith that the third volume, as well as the first and the second, would be published in England under the supervision of John Stuart Mill, economist and reformer. He also dangled before Smith an appeal to his abolitionism: "This 3d volume points to several phisiological results of scientific investigation concerning the *fallacy* of an inferiority of Africo-Americans [,] results hitherto mostly overlooked by the friends of right and of justice." Gurowski appealed to Smith for an early reply: "Suspense is worse than blasted hope."[13] But Smith did not oblige.

Soon after the Count had scrawled the last nearly undecipherable longhand entry in the third volume of the *Diary*, in November, 1864, he took the sheaf to a Washington printer to be set in type. The plan was to provide a preliminary copy or two, as with the first volume, for author's corrections.

A copy of this proof, along with the two published volumes, would soon be on its way to England. Gurowski addressed the package to Mill, a friend of more than thirty years' standing, dating back to their mutual interest in St. Simonianism while in Paris. The Count requested Mill's advice as he would that of "a physician for a disease." He contacted Mill because he had been confused by the invective and disdain showered upon him for the first two volumes of his *Diary*, and "by the seemingly impossibility with which no one could find out that behind the thus called abuse, there was a comprehension of the great events." Then came Mill's reply: "I have read your three volumes through . . . and the result is that on their own account as well as on yours, I am desirous that they should be published. You have fully established the claim to your view of the last years of American history, to be heard and considered. Your Diary will be an important part of the evidence which future his-

13 Gurowski to Gerrit Smith, November 16, 1865, in Archives and Museum, Polish Roman Catholic Union of America.

torians of these great events will have to study. It will be very instructive even in this country."[14]

Perhaps this was in part reciprocal flattery, for Mill must have been pleased when he read this statement in the proof of the third volume: "I wish every American would read and learn J. S. Mill's book on *Liberty,* in the same way as most of them learn the Scriptures. Many, very many verses of Mill's gospel are more full of life than some of the worshipped Hebrew hallucinations." Elsewhere in the proof and in Volume Three, Mill found other glowing compliments. Moreover, a mutual intellectual radicalism and reform spirit tied the two men. Mill even had a bust of Gurowski in his home.[15]

A Washington book and stationery store, located on Pennsylvania Avenue and operated by Obadiah H. and William H. Morrison, agreed to act as publisher for the third volume. Presumably the Morrisons financed the book. Since the firm did not have its own presses, arrangements were made to print as well as to bind the volume elsewhere in the city. This was not the first such publication venture of the Morrison bookshop, for *Morrison's Strangers Guide to the City of Washington and its Vicinity,* revised and reissued periodically since 1842, had been the standard guide book of the capital. The Morrisons also published law books from time to time. At last, during the first week of April, 1866, the concluding volume of the *Diary* appeared, the edition limited to a thousand copies, perhaps fewer.[16]

Bound in ornamented black cloth, the new book looked in most respects like its two predecessors. But the grammar seemed more pol-

[14] Quoted in Gurowski to Woodman, April 9, 1866, in Massachusetts Historical Society, *Proceedings,* Vol. LVI, 239. Gurowski's quoted statements in this paragraph are also from the letter to Woodman. Mill's letter to Gurowski is also quoted identically in Gurowski to Gerrit Smith, November 16, 1865, in Archives and Museum, Polish Roman Catholic Union of America.

[15] *Diary,* I, 215–16 (May, 1862), III, 96 (February 8, 1864), 273 (July 5, 1864), 389 (November 5, 1864); John Stuart Mill to Truebner and Company, January 9, 1866, in John Stuart Mill Papers, London School of Economics, London.

[16] Mrs. Paul Davis Morrison, February 12, 1954, to the author; Gurowski to Gerrit Smith, November 16, 1865, in Archives and Museum, Polish Roman Catholic Union of America. Volume III is now a choice collector's item. Copies of volumes one and two are often available on the second-hand book market.

Mathew B. Brady Collection, Library of Congress

WILLIAM H. SEWARD, Lincoln's Secretary of State, said by Gurowski to control international relations and military affairs to a greater degree than the President. The Count served in the State Department as a clerk and said his task was to "keep Seward from making a fool of himself."

Mathew B. Brady Collection, National Archives

EDWIN M. STANTON, Lincoln's Secretary of War and the leading Radical Republican in the Cabinet. "He is the *statesman*," said Gurowski, "so long searched for by me." "I am Stanton's Man."

Mathew B. Brady Collection, Library of Congress

SENATOR CHARLES SUMNER of Massachusetts, although a Radical Republican and friend of Gurowski for more than a decade, ordered the Count to get out and stay out of his Washington apartment in October, 1862.

War Department General Staff Collection, National Archives

COLORED VOLUNTEERS of the Twenty-Sixth United States Infantry Regiment. Gurowski considered Negro military service a step toward racial equality and citizenship. In June, 1862, he petitioned Secretary of War Stanton to commission him colonel of a colored regiment.

Mathew B. Brady Collection, Library of Congress

PRESIDENT ABRAHAM LINCOLN was pronounced by Gurowski as spiritless, exhausted, and careworn, as if his nights were sleepless and his days without comfort. "I do not deny to Abe," said the Count, "all kind of good qualities, but they are *all negative,* and therefore unproductive and worthless."

Mathew B. Brady Collection, Library of Congress

DAVID KELLOGG CARTTER, a rude, blunt, arrogant, but brilliant abolitionist partisan, was Chief Justice of the Supreme Court of the District of Columbia and presided at the Gurowski libel trial.

Mathew B. Brady Collection, National Archives

WALT WHITMAN was considered by Gurowski the "incarnation of a genuine American original genius." The Count circulated in Whitman's literary coterie in both New York and Washington and recognized the poet's ability and contribution decades before the American public.

Frederick H. Meserve Collection

THOMAS NAST'S CARICATURE of Adam Gurowski. A New York *World* editorial called the Count "Asmodeus in Goggles," after the king of demons and Gurowski's blue side-blind goggles.

ished, the entries were by exact days throughout, as in the second volume, and an appendix filled the last pages. Footnotes had been added and dated by the Count during the months between completion of the text and publication. The most unusual feature was the list of names of people mentioned in the volume, in three categories, "praise," "half and half," and "blame."

The "praise" column totaled 101 names, replete with Radicals. The "half and half" list numbered 22 and contained the names of Lincoln, Welles, Bates, and discredited Radicals such as Burnside, Greeley, Hooker, Rosecrans, and Sumner. In the "blame" column, 40 names included Buell, Franklin, Halleck, McClellan, Scott, Weed, Seward, Lincoln's secretaries Nicolay and Hay, the editor of the New York *World,* Manton Marble, and other leading Democrats and Conservatives. "The two former volumes," Gurowski explained, "contain the same proportions of blame and praise as prevail in this volume."[17] In this way he answered critics who maintained that the volumes of his *Diary* scolded and scoffed at most public figures.

The new book was dedicated to the late General James S. Wadsworth, the Count's hero, who had fallen in the Wilderness. The period covered was from October 19, 1863, to November 10, 1864, nearly thirteen months, compared to eleven of the second volume, and was the longest of the three books by sixty-five pages. Footnotes and appendix, moreover, served to bring the Count's comments up to date.

Press notices diminished, for the newspaper world had little interest in Gurowski's new book. Under the disguised heading of a book review, the New York *Herald* carried only a short notice of the third volume on the editor's page. This time the *Herald* had nothing but praise: "In the shrewd sentences of Gurowski there is much good sense and some history. The thoughtful reader . . . will find abundant food for reflection on the practical and philosophical peculiarities of life in the capital." The Count's list of persons the *Herald* considered "a sufficient refutation of all possible declarations" that Gurowski was "ill-natured, cross, sore-headed and quarrelsome." Of the Count's praise list, the reviewer concluded, perhaps sarcastically, that "the world will see

17 *Diary,* III, 7. The lists are on pages 5–7.

that a man must be the very acme of amiability if he can find it in his soul to praise one hundred and one men."[18]

Gurowski tried to stir up the silent newspapers. He urged Horatio Woodman, journalist with the Boston *Transcript,* to plug his new book. "I hope you will [be] a truer friend to me and to my third child," the Count wrote, "as you showed yourself to have been to the second Volume. I hope you will not snubb me . . . as you did three years ago. I still believe in you." The plea was to a fellow Radical. Woodman had defended Stanton in a series of articles for the press, when Democrats charged the Jacobins with mutilating McClellan's army during the Peninsula campaign, and had continued to support the Secretary for the rest of the war.[19] Gurowski now vainly hoped to win the same support.

6

The Count's first reaction to the criticism of his *Diary* volumes was resentment and scorn. He considered unjust the charge that he abused all people and seemed displeased with most things around him. His record praised the masses and the army, he claimed, whereas he censured but some thirty or forty public officials and thereby brought the indignation of "every dirty souled lickspittle . . . . The blame of such people is far preferable to their praise!"[20] Resentment soon gave way to a desire to be understood. Many, no doubt, he contended, thought he found pleasure in being critical.[21] "But day after day passes by, page heaps on page, and I must criticize," he mourned, "when I would be so happy to prize."[22] For this reason he even regretted having started his chronicle. With the concluding volume, his desire to overcome impressions of a hypercritical attitude manifested itself in the unique "praise," "half and half," and "blame" lists.[23]

Of the three volumes, the first is the most valuable as a source of

18 New York *Herald,* April 19, 1866.

19 Gurowski to Woodman, April 9, 1866, in Massachusetts Historical Society, *Proceedings,* Vol. LVI, 238; Williams, *Lincoln and the Radicals,* 233.

20 *Diary,* II, 48–49 (December 24, 1862).

21 *Diary,* II, 224 (May 11, 1863); see also 118 (January 31, 1863).

22 *Diary,* II, 234 (May 21, 1863); see also I, 157 (February, 1862).

23 *Diary,* III, 5–7.

confidential and secret data, considering the author's employment in the State Department, and it is consequently one of the more significant printed sources on the diplomatic history of the war.[24] The Count also gained from officials and prominent men of all parties greater quantities of important information before the first volume appeared. Even close friends were dismayed and disgusted when they found their confidential statements in print. Thus the second volume contains less intimate material, but still enough to make the book a valuable historical source. In the last volume Gurowski ceased to record quantities of secrets. While it comments on events and men of political and military significance, the sharp and often brilliant criticism of the first and the second books is absent. The third volume is distinguished by detached, reflective thinking on the war and on the destiny of the United States' political, economic, and social systems.

In addition to Gurowski's long habit of writing for publication as a livelihood, he had other motives for his *Diary*. Regarding his background as matchless, he believed he could make a definite contribution to the interpretation and understanding of a great drama "equal to any one known in history." In his own way the Count was searching for the truth. "Conscientiously I make all possible effort to record what I believe to be true," he explained, "and then truth will take care of herself." He pledged himself to preserve at any cost "the true reflection of events, of times, and of the actors." To his adopted country he believed he owed not only his fortune and his life, but above all, truth.[25]

When a lady asked why he had written the *Diary,* Gurowski explained that he hoped "to give conscientious evidence before the jury appointed by history." The historical record was of no small importance in his mind: "I wish to throw an independent and unadulterated light on men and events which work out the destinies of this noble people."[26] He was sure of the value of his contribution: "Often I am ashamed to find that the bit of study and experience acquired by me goes so far

[24] Samuel Flagg Bemis and Grace Gardner Griffin, *Guide to the Diplomatic History of the United States, 1775–1921* (Washington, 1935), 320.

[25] *Diary,* I, ii, preface, 13–14 (March, 1861), 270 (September 11, 1862), II, 225 (May 11, 1863).

[26] *Diary,* II, 302 (August 18, 1863), III, 255 (June 11, 1864).

when compared with many around me, and in action. I foresee, because I have no earthly personal views, no cares, nothing in the world to think of or to aim at, no charms, no ties—only my heart, my ideas, my convictions, and civilization is my worship. Nothing prevents me day and night, from concentrating whatever powers and reading I can have in one single focus. This cause, this people, this war, its conduct, are the events amidst which I breathe. Uninterruptedly I turn and return all that is in my mind—that is all."[27] Gurowski's estimate of his ability to prognosticate should be discounted, but not dismissed. He forecast, for example, in a volume of his *Diary* printed months before Emperor Maximilian came to Mexico, that he would be overthrown and shot, as happened in 1867.[28]

In writing for the historical record, the Count left little to the imagination. He intended to glorify the masses of the North, including the armed forces, and to praise or criticize, as he considered appropriate, civil and military leadership. "O! could I from every word," Gurowski wailed when the Union cause moved slowly, "from every page of this Diary, for eternities, make coruscate the nobleness, the simple faith with which the people sacrifices all to the cause. To be biblical, the sacrifice of the people is as pure as was that made by Abel; that made by the people's captains, leaders, pilots is Cain-like." History, he maintained, would substantiate the keynotes of his *Diary*, "that not Lincoln, not the administration, (Stanton excepted,) saved the country, that not the press directed and enlightened it; but all was done by the people; by the nameless in the villages, in the army, in the navy, and then by the Congress, whose majority [Radical Republican] was and is the incarnation of the people's spirit."[29] The salty European hoped also to throw light on the issue "between the perennial vitality of the principle of self-government in the people, and the transient and accidental result of the self-government as manifested in Mr. Lincoln, in Mr. Seward, and their followers."[30]

27 *Diary*, II, 78–79 (January 9, 1863). A similar point of view is expressed in Gurowski to Woodman, April 9, 1866, in Massachusetts Historical Society, *Proceedings*, Vol. LVI, 239.

28 *Diary*, II, 285 (July 31, 1863); see also *Diary*, III, 184 (April 16, 1864).

29 *Diary*, II, 154 (February 27, 1863), III, 51–52 (December 22, 1863).

Another purpose of the *Diary* was to bring to public attention, through critical observation, conditions and people the Count considered hazardous to winning the war. Then, he hoped, pressures or ballots would bring about reform. Perhaps his pages would make clear to his contemporaries how the relatively small population of the South kept "so long at bay" the larger population of the North. Perhaps his *Diary* would also help his countrymen recall their yesterdays, for in the United States the past receded more rapidly than elsewhere, he believed.[31] Frustrations were many in his efforts at civil and military reform: "As a watchdog faithful to the people's cause, I try to stir up the shepherds— but alas! alas."[32] The *Diary* must be brought out at intervals despite its limitations and his disappointments: "I am *sure* in my conscience, in my soul and in my heart that a speady publication may do good, open [a] great many eyes, undeceive [a] great many honest and patriotic minds, as I am sure that the country is already gliding down a precipice."[33]

No restraint can be found in the Count's *Diary*. Regardless of consequences, he dared to write his innermost convictions. "I attempt to dismantle," he explained, "the strongholds of shams, and disrobe false gods. I dare to say that blue is blue; pinchbeck not gold; politicians and shifters not oracles; a rhetor not an inspired orator, nor a statesman. I speak out what many think but dare not publicly assert. I offer no incense to idols. I point out those great criminals whose imbecility or cowardice cost the people the lives of scores of thousands of its best children. I dare to shake to the foundations the clay pillars of the sham temples. I am a bad man, but I cannot help it—and I shall continue to record doings and to call things by their right names."[34]

Gurowski's chronicle is an accurate record of his thinking at the time, although indications are that he polished his rhetoric throughout, perhaps with the assistance of editors. The original meanings and points

[30] *Diary,* I, 280 (September 23, 1862); see also III, 395 (note, December 29, 1865).
[31] *Diary,* I, ii (November, 1862), II, 5 (October, 1863).
[32] *Diary,* II, 234 (May 21, 1863); see also Gurowski to Andrew, August 28, 1862, in Andrew Papers, and *Diary,* II, 53–54 (December 25, 1862).
[33] Gurowski to Andrew, November 1, 1862, in Andrew Papers.
[34] *Diary,* III, 164 (April 7, 1864).

of view were probably never changed, a conclusion drawn from the Count's numerous, lengthy, and frank letters to Governor Andrew. This view is supported by the footnotes in the concluding volume, added by the Count at later times and dated. Moreover, he was intellectually honest, incapable of distorting or violating his convictions. A critic of the initial volume accused Gurowski of writing his entries later than the purported dates. To defend himself, the Pole showed a friend a portion of his manuscript, "which squared with the printed book."[35] He did not claim that his printed diary was a word-for-word copy of the manuscript. On the other hand, he stoutly maintained that the published chronicle "squared" with the original in meaning, as all evidence indicates. Unfortunately, the manuscripts are not known to have survived, so that today no comparisons can be made.

Gurowski faithfully mirrored the Radical point of view throughout his *Diary*. But he considered himself much too discriminating to accept Jacobins, or their ideas and actions, without careful scrutiny and adequate reason. He believed he must continue candid evaluation. "I am Stanton's man . . . ," he explained, "but only as long as I find him to be *a man*."[36] Never, he conscientiously believed, could he uncritically follow any political party or faction. For this reason, his *Diary* has even greater merit. In the opinion of George Fort Milton, it "reflects the plans, aims, passions, ambitions and hatreds of the Radicals better than almost any other printed source."[37] After a century, it remains the Jacobin bible.

[35] *Diary*, II, 78 (January 9, 1863).

[36] *Diary*, II, 304 (August 23, 1863).

[37] George Fort Milton, *The Age of Hate: Andrew Johnson and the Radicals* (New York, 1930), 687.

CHAPTER X

INTERNATIONAL IMPACT

I

In view of the Count's background, it is not surprising that his reach sometimes exceeded his grasp in his chosen role as interpreter of a democracy at war. In foreign affairs, on the other hand, he was more knowledgeable. His keen mind, education, study, and experience equipped him to view and criticize men, measures, and opinions from abroad concerning the American struggle. In the Department of State his major task had been limited to reading and interpreting to Secretary Seward foreign newspaper editorials and opinions. But by self-appointment he also mingled freely with the diplomatic representatives of other governments in and out of the State Department. Foreign diplomats considered him an equal and confided to him many a diplomatic secret. "I am the only Northerner on a footing of intimacy with the diplomats," claimed Gurowski in a characteristic egotistical flurry. "They consider me an *exalté*."[1]

The Count contended that Europe's support, both official and unofficial, overwhelmingly favored the North throughout the war. The noisy exceptions were few, not fundamentally influential, and therefore of little danger. But the support from Europe remained dormant, in part due to lack of energetic military activity and victories. He feared that McClellan's strategy would cause Europe to become impatient and turn away from the United States, like *The Times* of London, which poured forth "the most malicious, poisonous, and lacerating derisions" at each Union defeat. When news of McClellan's failure to take Richmond reached Europe along with word of other Union disasters, the Count believed that Old World sympathy for the North became "un-

[1] *Diary,* I, 57 (June, 1861).

settled, unsteady," and he feared for a time that the masses would demand open assistance for the Confederacy. Halleck's ineptness contributed significantly to this reaction abroad, because he had no strategic plan, so dear to European commanders, for overwhelming the South, but rather a "groping and shy general policy . . . full of contradictions."[2]

United States civil authorities at home and abroad also did little to win European sympathies, Gurowski's argument continued, since European statesmen judged a country and its people by its leaders. Proof of able leadership and heroism seemed necessary, rather than oratory, doubtful legal arguments, diplomatic papers, and circulars. To use these makeshifts was the same as attempting "to eclipse bright sunlight with a burning candle." "Even I feel humiliated to continually ascertain," he complained, ". . . in what little estimation—if not worse—is held our administration by the principal statesmen and governments of the old world." Until the Radicals forced the Emancipation Proclamation, he believed that Europeans considered Lincoln's slavery policy vacillating and inhuman, but with the edict came Europe's wholehearted support of the North.[3]

2

The Count's observations concerning English attitudes and policies toward the American war were distorted by an Anglophobia which grew primarily from his useless London mission of 1832 in behalf of Polish independence. The English declaration of neutrality of May, 1861, recognizing the belligerency of the Confederate States he considered hasty and a demonstration of enmity to the United States by the English aristocracy and government. "Every steamer brings fresh proofs of the . . . official hostility of England," he said a month later, "hostility covered by the word 'neutrality.' . . . the English government gladly would see the breaking up of the Union."[4]

[2] *Diary*, I, 175 (March, 1862), 211, 215 (May, 1862), 254 (August, 1862), 260 (September 3, 1862), II, 206 (April 22, 1863).

[3] *Diary*, I, 254 (August, 1862), 306, 310 (October 26 and 30, 1862), II, 187 (April 4, 1863), III, 65 (January 7, 1864).

[4] *Diary*, I, 44–45 (May, 1861); Gurowski to William H. Seward, [June, 1861], in Seward Papers.

Gurowski followed closely the events and developments in the *Trent* incident, sensing fully their impact and significance. Before James M. Mason and John Slidell, Confederate envoys to London and Paris, had been arrested and removed from the British merchant ship *Trent* by Captain Charles Wilkes of the United States warship *San Jacinto,* he carefully followed the progress of the two Confederates. Their escape through the blockade to Havana, Cuba, enroute to Europe, produced the opinion that under international law the Union had the right to seize them, if carried in a neutral vessel, because they were "political contrabands of war going on a publicly avowed errand hostile to their true government." Secretary Seward, should he find it expedient, thought the Count, could legally permit the seizure of Mason and Slidell on leaving Havana.[5]

In a conversation with Lincoln's attorney general, the Count credited Captain Wilkes with "originality and boldness." Seward, however, Gurowski had heard, ordered the *San Jacinto* commander to remove the two Confederates from the *Trent*. This alleged order, at least in written form, was probably a myth.[6]

Although a number of foreign diplomats in Washington made "curious faces" upon news of the capture, Gurowski believed that Lord Richard Lyons, the British minister, "behaved with dignity." The representatives of the small powers, he told Seward's son Frederick, made out as if they were servile to Lyons, a customary and therefore meaningless pattern in diplomatic corps relations. Lyons gave no cause for concern at any time during the *Trent* incident, since his conduct throughout remained "discrete, delicate and generous." Also pleasing in the crisis, he added, had been the attitude and behavior of Henri Mercier, the French minister.[7]

Abroad the reaction to Wilkes's act was mixed, the Count said. The attitude of France, although serious and severe, could not draw complaint. Russia would certainly "behave well" and not send unwanted

[5] *Diary,* I, 109 (October, 1861).

[6] Beale (ed.), *The Diary of Edward Bates, 1859–1866,* 206 (November 27, 1861).

[7] *Diary,* I, 120–21 (November, 1861), 136 (December, 1861) 153 (February, 1862); Gurowski to Frederick William Seward, [December, 1861], in Seward Papers.

advice to the Lincoln government. Austria and Prussia, in submitting their opinions, used the occasion to take "the airs" of maritime powers along with England and France, but particularly with England. "The kick of asses," he explained, "at what they suppose to be the dying lion." In England there developed a "roar," as he had predicted, an uneasy and belligerent condition causing Charles Francis Adams, Lincoln's minister to London, to become "terribly unhorsed" and prepare to return to the United States.[8]

At home the people appeared to be "satisfied" over the capture of Mason and Slidell, Gurowski observed. Although "relative right" was on the side of the United States, the only acceptable way out would be to back down and surrender the two Confederates. He contended that Seward carried away the honors in settling the incident in his letter to Lord Lyons: "the argument is smart, but a little too long, and not in a genuine diplomatic style." "But Lincoln," he added, "ought to have a little credit for it, as from the start he was for giving the traitors up." To Seward himself he labeled the letter "statesmanlike" and "masterly."[9]

By spring of the second year of the war even Gurowski believed the attitude of the English government to be favorable. Queen Victoria sided with the North, as did Lord John Russell, English foreign minister, while in the House of Commons, barks of the pro-Southern William H. Gregory and John A. Roebuck availed but little. The armament of Confederate vessels in England and in the Caribbean appeared in keeping with the English "mercantile character," as was blockade-running. "The would-be English *noblesse,*" he railed, "the Tories, and all the genuine nobodies, or *would-be* somebodies, affect to side with the South. They are welcome to such an alliance, and even parentage."[10]

In the immediate wake of the Emancipation Proclamation, said the Count, the basic sympathy of the English people at last made itself evident. The working classes, through the voices of John Stuart Mill, Richard Cobden, John Bright, and other liberals of "like pure mind and

---

[8] *Diary,* I, 120 (November, 1861), 136 (December, 1861), 141 (January, 1862).

[9] *Diary,* I, 120 (November, 1861), 135 (December, 1861), 137 (January, 1862); Gurowski to William H. Seward, [January, 1862], in Seward Papers.

[10] *Diary,* I, 175 (March, 1862), 183–84 (April, 1862), 215 (May, 1862).

noble heart," unequivocally declared for the North. "The voice of the genuine English people," he continued, lashing at the aristocracy, "resounds altogether differently from the shrill *falsetto* with which turf hunters, rent-roll devourers, lord, lordlings, and all the like shams and whelps try to intimidate the patriotic North, and comfort the traitors, the rebels."[11]

During the spring of 1863 the Count sensed that "the treason of the English evil wishers" was making headway. So active did the English proslavery forces become in outfitting ships for the Confederacy that he gladly joined the leading Radicals in and out of Congress in advocating commercial nonintercourse. He likewise supported the Radical effort to urge the Lincoln Conservatives to declare as an act of war the departure from English ports of additional naval vessels intended for the Confederacy. "As long as England is ruled by her aristocracy, whether Tories or Whigs," he retorted, "a Hannibalian hate ought to be the creed of every American."[12]

Gurowski's wrath abated less than a week later, when he learned that English Foreign Minister Russell had prevented the commerce raider *Alexandra,* intended for the Confederacy, from going to sea. "The English Cabinet takes in sails," he observed, "and begins to show less impudence in the violation of neutral duties." Credit for this change of policy toward the people of the United States must go to their "bitter and exasperated" attitude, which had frightened the English government. But the problem of the Laird rams, under construction for the Richmond government, dragged on for five months after the seizure of the *Alexandra.* Then in July came Union victories at Gettysburg and Vicksburg, and the military tide of the South appeared contained if not in retreat. Perhaps as a result, the rams were placed in September under the close watch of the British government, to prevent their escape. "It seems that public opinion in England begins to turn in favor of right and justice," Gurowski noted, "that is, in favor of the North. The masses, honest and true, have been always in the right track. It is the

11 *Diary,* II, 89 (January 15, 1863); see also 186 (April 2, 1863), and 269 (July 16, 1863).
12 *Diary,* II, 191–92, 193, 200 (April 6, 8, and 18, 1863).

mean, snobbish, would-be enlightened or leading class in England that seems to wheel around."[13]

The Count dismissed the fears of the United States that the 1864 Tory denunciations of the Union in parliament would lead to a change in policy. If the Tories were in power, he reasoned, they would do no more for the South than was being done by the Whig Party in control. The government of England now definitely sympathized with the Union, but only because it appeared that the Confederacy would fall, it being to England's "better interest" to support and be friendly to the Union. In the meantime, he contended that the working classes and liberal leaders in England favorable to the North kept the government from openly siding with the Confederacy.[14]

3

At the beginning of the war Gurowski had been confident of the United States support by the people of France and their emperor, Louis Napoleon, because the interests and principles of that country called for a strong Union. The Count hoped the tariff on some categories of merchandise from France would be lowered for the purpose of alleviating the overproduction of French industry and thereby consolidating the spirit of fraternity between industrial laborers of France and the United States. He even made the suggestion to Senator Sumner, who some days later unsuccessfully moved in Congress that the tariff be lowered. "I have full confidence in Louis Napoleon," the approving comment followed, "and in the unsophisticated judgment of the genuine French people."[15]

A year after the opening of the war the Count still found no fault with the attitudes of France and Louis Napoleon, although Northern policies might, he thought, have soured the Emperor. French vessels were not running the blockade, and very little, if any, arms and ammunition were being purchased in France by Confederate agents. In spite

[13] *Diary*, II, 207 (April 22, 1863), 322, 335 (September 15 and 30, 1863), III, 45 (December 13, 1863).

[14] *Diary*, III, 131, 146 (March 6 and 22, 1864), 273 (July 5, 1864).

[15] *Diary*, I, 25 (April, 1861), 64 (July, 1861). For Sumner's motion, see *Congressional Globe*, 37 Cong., 1 sess., 316–17.

of all this, rumors persisted concerning "treacherous schemes" of Napoleon to take Mexico, to use it as a base for co-operation with the Confederates, and then to take the United States. Gurowski insisted that up to the day he wrote, *"not the slightest complaint can be made against Louis Napoleon."* He feared that the United States would commit a hostile demonstration, a "spread-eagleism" toward France concerning Mexican intervention and incur the Emperor's enmity. As late as early August, 1862, the attitudes of Napoleon toward the United States seemed completely friendly and trustworthy to Gurowski.[16]

But with Napoleon's offer to mediate the American crisis in late 1862 and the occupation of Mexico City by French troops in the summer of 1863, the Emperor became a "crowned conspirator," "full of treachery towards the North." The people of France, however, would not permit a rupture with the United States, the Count felt assured, even though Napoleon began "a war of treason" against the North. Before this would happen, the French people would do away with the Emperor. From the moment Napoleon offered mediation, Gurowski dubbed him the "Decembriseur," derived from "Septembriseur," the name given the men in the French Revolution who carried out a wholesale massacre in September, 1792. Louis Napoleon had come to power on December 2, 1852, followed by a massacre of barricade defenders.[17]

The Pole considered the other nations of Europe loyal to the North. At the outbreak of the conflict, he declared Russia "safe, very safe," and at the time of the proposed mediation by Napoleon, he believed the Czar's cabinet held "friendly views on the condition of our affairs." The visit of Russian fleet units to New York produced "unparalleled enthusiasm," as Gurowski observed the event, and proved anew that the loyalty of Czar Alexander II, Foreign Minister Alexander M. Gorchakov, and the whole Russian people "held steadfast and nobly" to the North. The governments and peoples of the German states remained true to the Union, because they hated slavery, were honest, and under-

---

[16] *Diary,* I, 173–74 (March, 1862), 191–92 (April, 1862), 227, 228 (June, 1862), 255 (August, 1862).

[17] *Diary,* II, 17 (November 25, 1862), 300 (August 13, 1863), 335 (September 30, 1863), 19–20 (October 20, 1863).

stood the nature of the conflict, and of all the continental states of Western Europe, "behaved the best" towards the United States. Perhaps Spain would "play double" because of the nearness of Cuba to the Confederacy, but after a year and a half of war, Spanish relations with the North were pronounced "most loyal."[18]

4

At the outbreak of the struggle, Gurowski believed the South would not be recognized as a full and independent nation in Europe, unless she should militarily win the war. "Before a struggle decides a question a recognition is bosh," he prompted, "and I laugh at it." The fact that England and France, in declaring their neutrality, had recognized the Confederacy as a belligerent did not imply future recognition of independence. Moreover, Lincoln's blockade proclamations, he believed, had agreed in international law to the belligerency of the Confederacy even before the English and the French neutrality proclamations, and therefore the United States was not justified in complaining. When certain distinguished Americans considered Britain's postponement of recognizing Confederate independence a diplomatic success, he concluded that the cabinet took this action for its own good: "A postponement spares the necessity to Russells, Palmerstons [and] Gladstones . . . to show their hands."[19]

In October of 1862, when Confederate hopes for victory appeared promising, even the Count believed that England and France might recognize the South as a nation, but that Russia, Prussia, Spain, and Austria would not follow. Anyway, this recognition would not materially assist the Confederacy or do away with the blockade. His opinion changed, however, when the North scored notable military successes. With Union victory apparent, *"whatever be its liberticide appetites or hatred of America, no European power will dare to interfere or to recognize the rebels."* He reasoned also that the European masses

---

[18] *Diary*, I, 26–27 (April, 1861), 269–70 (September 11, 1862), 305 (October 25, 1862), II, 293 (August 5, 1863), 337 (October 4, 1863).

[19] *Diary*, I, 18 (March, 1861), 24 (April, 1861), 55 (June, 1861), 182–83, 193 (April, 1862), II, 319 (September 10, 1863).

solidly favored the North and that a nation, to command foreign recognition, must have definite boundaries, unlike the Confederacy. Nineteenth-century Poland, like the Confederate states, excited vigorous sympathy, but did not exist on the political map because it lacked fixed geographical borders.[20]

At no time during the war did Gurowski consider foreign armed intervention a serious threat. The North nervously spoke of it, with the press "as silly as the public at large." Even if England and France should want to intervene, they did not have the means. But the "intermittent . . . fever" of intervention was talked of again and again, particularly by Union statesmen and diplomats, who desired to convince the public that their skill had prevented it. This "silly talk" seemed to be totally unfounded, since no foreign nation would dare to risk a move requiring at the outset a minimum of a hundred thousand men, which no foreign power had.[21]

5

The Count spurned the idea of foreign mediation for purposes of compromise. When European presses spoke of mediation in the autumn of 1861, he maintained that the North recognized the "utter impossibility" of the idea. He believed that a negotiated peace would but establish the military superiority of the Confederacy and open the way for piratical raids on the North by marauding Southern bands.[22]

A year later, when Lee invaded Maryland, Gurowski still affirmed that European governments would not then offer mediation, since "no possible terms and basis exist for any mediation." Persistent rumors of foreign mediation offers in the wake of Union disappointment over Antietam brought *"positive* information" that England and France would be glad to act, provided the Lincoln administration requested their good offices. The Count asked his Radical friend Andrew to warn Senator Sumner, chairman of the Senate committee on foreign relations, that Secretary Seward had despaired and desired "to commit . . . poor Lin-

---

20 *Diary,* I, 304 (October, 1862), III, 300–302 (July 29, 1864).
21 *Diary,* I, 82 (August, 1861), 117 (November, 1861), 233–34, 241, 243 (July, 1862).
22 *Diary,* I, 112 (October, 1861).

coln before the meeting of the Congress." He also suggested that Andrew immediately contact the distinguished Edward Everett, who in turn would admonish Lincoln. He reserved to himself the task of cautioning Secretary of War Stanton concerning the threatened mediation. If England and France were to recognize the South at this time, he believed that President Davis would probably ask these nations to mediate, but other European powers would not concur.[23]

Napoleon's initial mediation offer of November 10, 1862, the Pole interpreted as French moral support for the Confederacy, and he believed it came because of Union military "slowness," "administrative and governmental helplessness," and Seward's "lying and all-confusing foreign policy." The Emperor proposed that France and England join in suggesting a six-months armistice along with a discontinuance of the blockade, but his proposition failed when England did not support the plan. The Count believed that the French document offering mediation bore no marks of "Parisian origin" and had been written in Washington by Mercier, the French minister. In his opinion, the document dated from McClellan's inactivity following Antietam.[24]

December, 1862, brought the grim carnage at Fredericksburg and an avalanche of talk concerning foreign mediation. Not even then would Gurowski sanction such a movement. "Any, even the most favorable friendly mediation," he exclaimed, "is infamy. Any one entertaining a shadow of such an idea is traitor and deserves to be hung. A foreign minister bringing to the White House an offer of mediation ought to be torn to pieces; and I for one shall not hesitate to shoot him." He felt particularly vehement on this question, because similar "friendly" mediation had proved the undoing of his native Poland and had split his family. "My grandfather opposed," he explained, "my grand uncle favored foreign mediation—and I am here."[25]

When European governments asserted they must mediate because their financial interests were suffering, the Count suggested that they

[23] *Diary,* I, 270 (September 11, 1862), 301–302, 304 (October 20 and 23, 1862); Gurowski to Andrew, October 19, 1862, in Andrew Papers.

[24] *Diary,* II, 17–18, 19, 20 (November 25, 28, and 30, 1862).

[25] *Diary,* II, 24, 56–57 (December 7 and 28, 1862), 104 (January 24, 1863); Gurowski to Sumner, marked "warning," January 14, [1863], in Sumner Papers.

turn to Australia for future economic development, so as not to depend on the United States. "Keep aloof with your good wishes, and with your advices, and with your interference," the challenge resounded, reminiscent of a theme of the Monroe Doctrine. "You may burn your noses, and even lose your little scalps. You robbers, murderers, hypocrites . . . you presumptuous, arrogant curses of the human race, stand off, and let these people . . . work out its destinies, be it for good or for evil." He rejoiced, however, at what he believed to be a rising tide of sentiment in the United States against the meddling tendencies of the aristocratic governing group of Europe, except those in Russia.[26]

In late January of 1863, news from the Old World indicated to Gurowski that Napoleon "with his corrosive breath still intends to pollute the virginity" of the United States. "Never, never, any great nation or any self-respecting government," he exclaimed, "accepted or submitted to any similar foreign interference." When Napoleon's second offer to mediate reached the Lincoln government on February 3, 1863, Seward replied that the United States had no intention of giving up the war. Congress reinforced this action on March 3 with a joint resolution. "Catch it, foreign meddlers," Gurowski jubilantly retorted. Although the "soap" used by the French had been of the "finest and most aromatic quality, the democratic nerves of the American people resisted the . . . cunningly mixed aroma." Overjoyed, he hurled defiance: "Tigers, hyenas, jackels! clatter your teeth, smack your lips! but you shall not get at the prey."[27]

6

Gurowski's evaluation of Seward as a diplomat must be considered against the backdrop of his Radical Republican ideas and the Conservative Republican thinking of the Secretary of State. Moreover, the Count appraised American diplomatic practice by European standards, to him the ultimate in quality. By comparison, United States approaches, especially Seward's unconventional procedures, seemed to him elementary,

---

[26] *Diary*, II, 70–71, 76 (January 5 and 8, 1863).

[27] *Diary*, II, 104 (January 24, 1863), 136, 157 (February 13 and 28, 1863), 191 (April 6, 1863).

unrefined, and lacking in tact. The Count's European background and experience, notwithstanding his obvious prejudice, made him a competent critic of the sometimes blunt and always informal methods of Secretary Seward. His task in the State Department office of reading and interpreting European reactions to the American crisis kept him unusually well informed, and he did not hesitate to provide a deluge of oral and written advice designed to prompt the Secretary.

The Count believed Seward's diplomatic ability limited and warped. His first self-imposed task, after taking employment in Seward's office, was to suggest that the Secretary "elevate the American question to a higher region, to represent it to Europe in its true, holy character, as a question of right, freedom, and humanity." One of Seward's difficulties, he believed, was an imagination that caused him to minimize the future. Seward's prophecies that the war would be over in from sixty to ninety days and that minor Union victories presaged the Confederacy's collapse Gurowski considered damaging to the Secretary's standing abroad: "Mr. Seward's conversations and words have an official meaning for the diplomats, . . . and they continually find that when Mr. Seward says yes the events say no." The Count noted a continuation of this pattern. In the wake of ill-fated Union military efforts at Second Manassas and Antietam he observed Lord Lyons being assured by Seward that the war would soon be won by the North. The next month, as Burnside advanced to Fredericksburg and defeat, Seward again predicted a smashing victory to the governments of Europe. Gurowski, now at the end of his patience, said: "I suggested to some of the senators that a resolution be passed prohibiting Mr. Seward from playing either the prophet or the fool."[28]

In some instances the Count found Seward a capable foreign secretary in pursuit of the "right" foreign policies. Hard work, an elastic mind, and ability to argue were virtues in the man. He also had an aptitude for taking care of daily diplomatic complications. Although

---

[28] *Diary,* I, 31 (April, 1861), 53, 57 (June, 1861), 63 (July, 1861), 110–11 (October, 1861), 176 (March, 1862), and 193 (April, 1862), II, 13 (November 18, 1862), 32 (December 17, 1862), III, 44 (December 12, 1863).

possessing the "germs for an eminent statesman," the Secretary's "acquired information by study, by instruction, and by reading, is quite the reverse of what in Europe is regarded as necessary for a statesman." To develop Seward's potential, as well as to shape his thinking, Gurowski made many oral and written promptings. The *Trent* incident elicited the advice that Seward ignore the diplomatic representatives of the small powers when they catered to Lord Lyons. "This is the result," he explained, in justifying his advice, "of 40 years of contact with those social muskitoes." The settlement of the *Trent* problem caused him to extend "hearty congratulations" on Seward's message to the British government.[29]

But Gurowski's usual attitude toward the Seward foreign policy was highly critical. He considered the Secretary weak and unnecessarily willing to give in when dealing with other nations. This he believed especially true of problems arising from the blockade. "Mr. Seward has not at all given up his firm decision to violate the national statutes and the international rules," he said sarcastically in complaining of the restoration to England of the *Peterhoff's* unopened mail pouches and that same country's blockade-runner, the *Lauban*. Seward's instructions to the navy seemed to him so "obviously favorable" to blockade violations that ships' officers would perhaps give up their vigilance: "Mr. Seward's instructions concede more to England than was ever asked by England, or by any neutral from a belligerent of a third class power."[30]

Seward's attitude on captured neutral blockade-runners seemed weak and supine compared with the view of Navy Secretary Welles. When Napoleon Collins, commanding the U.S.S. *Octorara,* captured the British schooner *Mont Blanc* en route to a Confederate port, England at once protested. The State Department Secretary, with Lincoln's approval, offered an apology and damages and reproved Collins. Welles held the

---

[29] *Diary,* I, 62–63 (July, 1861), 81, 88 (August, 1861), 124 (November, 1861), 135 (December, 1861), 164–65 (February, 1862); Gurowski to Frederick William Seward, [December, 1861], in Seward Papers; Gurowski to William H. Seward, [December, 1861], in *ibid.*

[30] *Diary,* II, 196, 201 (April 12 and 18, 1863), 215 (May 2, 1863), III, 169–70 (April 11, 1864), 213–14, 234–35 (May 2 and 21, 1864).

censure unjustifiable, and later a prize court considered the capture lawful. "I hope Collins will be consoled," said the Count, "and light his segar with the reprimand."[31]

Gurowski considered Seward afraid of his own shadow in other aspects of foreign relations. His refusal in 1864 to recognize the revolutionary forces in Santo Domingo as belligerents in their fight for independence from Spain astonished the Count. He maintained that the Secretary did not wish to offend Spain, although Spain recognized the Confederacy as belligerent, and the Dominicans were actually not rebels at all. They were citizens fighting for the independence they had maintained for some years but had lost to Spain in 1861: "Seward almost forgets that the invasion took place since he mismanaged American affairs . . . and that he himself once protested against that invasion."[32]

Seward also did much to encourage Napoleon in establishing an empire in Mexico, according to Gurowski. The "feeble protest" of the Secretary's dispatches to France did not convey "a serious meaning, nor that the people was *decidedly* opposed to a Mexican empire." Unlike Seward, the Count did not consider Mexico at war with France after the establishment of Maximilian as Mexican emperor. He thought it a civil war between the legal government under President Benito Juárez and the usurper Maximilian: "I challenge Mr. Seward to find any authority whatever among writers on international law by which he can sustain his false position; or to show for it any precedent in the world's history."[33]

The Pole viewed Seward's diplomatic dispatches as generally unworthy performances, a judgment probably colored by his high esteem

31 *Diary*, II, 277–78 (July 20, 1863); Allan Westcott, "Napoleon Collins," *Dictionary of American Biography*, IV, 308–309; Beale (ed.), *Diary of Gideon Welles*, I, 394, 416–27 (August 4 and 24, 1863).

32 *Diary*, III, 95 (February 7, 1864), 144–45 (March 22, 1864). When Spain took over the Dominican Republic in 1861, Gurowski was similarly distressed with Seward: "I regret the untimely taking of high ground by Seward in the question of the Dominican Republic. We never recognized her, undermined her existence, what wonder that the Dominicans seek shelter under a Spanish protectorate. The Union (ours) considered and treated them hitherto as beyond the pale of nations." Gurowski to Sumner, May 10, 1861, in Sumner Papers.

33 *Diary*, III, 169 (April 11, 1864), 175–76 (note, October 2, 1865).

for the directives written by the foreign secretaries of European governments. Seward's first significant letter to William L. Dayton, United
States minister to France, Gurowski labeled as "bold, high toned, and
[one which] . . . shows an inexperienced hand in diplomacy and in
dealing with events." This opinion was but a foretaste. In December,
1861, Seward's dispatches appeared in *Papers Relating to the Foreign
Relations of the United States*. Why write special instructions to each
minister, asked the Count, in skimming the volume. In Europe the cus-
tom was to write circular explanatory letters and thereby save much
labor. Seward's productions were labeled "a curious agglomeration of
good patriotism and confusion" marked with "insincerity, and double-
dealing." They betrayed a beginner in diplomacy and exposed to Europeans the Secretary's ignorance of the nature of Old World diplomacy:
"It may be suspected that some of these instructions were written to
make capital at home, to astonish Mr. Lincoln with . . . knowledge
of . . . European affairs."[34]

Seward's dispatches, the Count continued, had little favorable influence on the governments of Europe. When the Secretary explained
to Europe the causes of Union reverses in the swamps of the Chicka-
hominy, Gurowski predicted that he could not "bamboozle the cold
clear-sighted European statesmen." He grew disgusted at a Washington
rumor circulated by Seward's Conservative Republican supporters that
the Secretary's dispatches to England would settle the Union's problems with that country. "How the wily Palmerston," he complained,
"must chuckle in Downing Street." But few people outside the United
States actually read Seward's dispatches, and of those abroad who did,
he cautioned that they would find their time wasted. The Secretary's
diplomatic notes, he said, "may throw dust in American eyes, but evoke
scorn and contempt among European statesmen and governments."[35]

On occasion, however, a Seward dispatch gratified Gurowski. "This
. . . haughty language pleases me exceedingly," he said to Senator Sum-

---

[34] *Diary*, I, 37–38 (May, 1861), 130–31 (December, 1861). For Seward to Dayton,
April 22, 1861, see *Sen. Exec. Doc. 1*, 37 Cong., 2 Sess., Vol. I, pp. 195–201.

[35] *Diary*, I, 240 (July, 1862), II, 13 (November 18, 1862), 162 (March 3, 1863), III,
93 (February 5, 1864); Gurowski to Andrew, April 10, 1863, in Andrew Papers.

ner early in the new administration. The Secretary's correspondence relating to the Paris Convention of 1856 also delighted him, as did the
Department's report on the Mexican situation.[36]

In the over-all pattern, the Count had little praise for Seward's dispatches. The second volume of the *Papers Relating to the Foreign Relations of the United States* appeared no better than the first: "O, what
an accumulation of ignorance! Almost every historical and chronological
fact misplaced, misunderstood, perverted, distorted, wrongly applied.
And how many, many contradictions!" Again Gurowski labeled the
papers as lacking in statesmanlike and diplomatic character. They were
full "of poor argument, of spread-eagleism, and of ignorant quotations
stolen from history," written with the idea of adding laurels to Seward's "goosequill crown." As he reflected on two full years of the Secretary's dispatches, the Count reminded dolefully: "*All* his dispatches
from 1861 are lies, prophecies unfilled, spreadeagleism, bosh, bad rhet-
orics and ignorance of facts, of history, of laws and of official customs."[37]

Seward ought to follow the example of Russia's foreign minister,
Gorchakov, Gurowski thought. "The Gortschakoff notes are master-
pieces for their clear, quiet, but bold and decided exposition and argument . . . . O, why cannot Mr. Seward learn from Gortschakoff how not
to put gas in such weighty documents?" A statesman, unlike Seward,
cautiously committed himself to writing: "Why could not Mr. Lincoln
choose for his Secretary of State some man who has a holy and whole-
some horror of pen, ink, and paper? Some man gifted with a sound
brain, who never is quick at writing a dispatch, and would demand
double salary as the price of writing one? Oh! Mr. Lincoln, had you
but done this, not only would all America, but all Europe also be truly
thankful for great immunity from the curse of morbid attempts at
diplomacy and statesmanship."[38]

[36] Gurowski to Sumner, May 6, [1861], in Sumner Papers; *Diary*, I, 131 (December,
1861), 212 (May, 1862); "The Present Condition of Mexico," dated April 14, 1862,
House Exec. Doc. 100, 37 Cong., 2 Sess.

[37] *Diary*, II, 162, 177 (March 3 and 25, 1863), III, 73 (January 13, 1864); Gurowski
to Andrew, April 10, 1863, in Andrew Papers.

[38] *Diary*, II, 13–14 (November 18, 1862), 45–46 (December 23, 1862), 320 (September 11, 1863).

The Count's observations concerning diplomatic opinions of Seward are revealing. Foreign representatives explained to him that the Secretary treated them rudely in interviews, never giving them opportunity to speak or explain, for Seward would interrupt with an "I know it all." Seward likewise used the "dictatorial I," said the diplomats, when speaking of the government. A Washington diplomat friend of Gurowski commented that in Europe a parliamentary government minister would be removed after regularly being contradicted by the facts, as Seward had been. "A diplomat calls Seward," reported the Count, "the evil eye of the Cabinet, and of the country." The Secretary's lengthy dispatches were also made light of by the Washington ministers. In Washington and abroad foreign offices held Seward in contempt and considered him a "humbug and liar," said the Pole, as did the lowly clerks in the Paris and London foreign offices.[39]

Gurowski believed Lincoln should be warned concerning Seward's unpopularity among the diplomats. Particularly problems with France and England had their origin in "personal contempt" for Seward, he thought. In addition to writing himself, he urged Governor Andrew to entreat Edward Everett to explain to Lincoln Seward's rating in diplomatic circles. Everett, he said, knew the temper of European statesmen, "of which Seward is as ignorant as any ass in a meadow."[40]

The manner in which Seward demonstrated his lack of tact and won the contempt of foreign representatives could be illustrated, the Count suggested, by an incident at a diplomatic dinner given by Gabriel García y Tassara, the Spanish minister to Washington, in July, 1862. The only Americans present were Seward and Senator John S. Carlile of Virginia. What occurred was reported to Gurowski by diplomats in attendance. Seward talked freely of his dislike of the second confiscation act, recently passed by the Radicals of Congress, because many foreign representatives with Confederate sympathies were present. Then

[39] *Diary,* I, 43, 46–47 (May, 1861), 110 (October, 1861), II, 32 (December 17, 1862), 237 (May 31, 1863); Carter, "Gurowski," *Atlantic Monthly,* Vol. XVIII, 633; Gurowski to Andrew, October 28, 1862, April 4, [1863], and April 10, 1863, in Andrew Papers; Gurowski to Lincoln, rough draft, not dated, in Gurowski Papers.

[40] Gurowski to Andrew, October 28, 1862, in Andrew Papers; Gurowski to Lincoln, rough draft, not dated, in Gurowski Papers.

he explained with the air of a braggart how he regretted the impossibility of making a Napoleonic *coup d'état* against Congress, and that he realized for the first time the necessity of a Cromwell. The diplomats were disgusted and horrified, and one "roughly" refuted Seward. Gurowski believed that this demonstration injured the Secretary and the administration and in effect invited foreign intervention. At once he wrote to Governor Andrew and early the next morning called on Secretary Chase and told him about it.[41]

Seward's lack of tact seemed matched only by his ignorance of international law, the Count said. He believed that the public would be "horror stricken could they suddenly be made acquainted with all the shameful ignorance which is corrosively fermenting in the State Department." Three years of international law practice had not caused the Secretary to master even the rudiments. At the end of the war it still appeared that Seward came out on the under side in "close, logical argument" and continued to display "a most astounding unfamiliarity with the bearing, the meaning, the reach and the use of expressions strictly technical in international laws and diplomacy." Gurowski explained to his own satisfaction why this condition existed. While working at the State Department, he observed that Sir Robert J. Phillimore's four-volume study of international law in the Department library had evidently not been used; its pages were uncut. The library had been well stocked, but no students opened its books.[42]

The fundamental danger was the Secretary's power in the conduct of foreign relations. "Perhaps Seward imagines himself to be a Cardinal Richelieu, with Lincoln for Louis XIII (provided he knows as much history)," the Count said, "or maybe he has the ambition to be considered a Talleyrand or Metternich of diplomacy." Cabinet differences over the military plight of the Union in the wake of the 1862 disasters caused him to declare Seward "more allpowerful than ever he was over the Kentucky mule [Lincoln]." Most of all, mediation reports from

---

[41] Gurowski to Andrew, July 20, 1862, in Andrew Papers; *Diary,* I, 243 (July, 1862); Donald (ed.), *Inside Lincoln's Cabinet,* 95 (July 21, 1862).

[42] *Diary,* II, 123 (February 1, 1863), III, 121 (March 2, 1864), 213–14, 234–35 (May 2 and 21, 1864), 214 (note, October, 1865). Phillimore's book was *Commentaries Upon International Law* (4 vols., Philadelphia, 1854–57).

Europe frightened the President, he said, and "this makes the strength of Seward, who lies to Lincoln and make him believe, that he, Seward, is the only man to avert dangers from Europe." So strong was the Secretary's hand in foreign relations, he concluded, "it is my *positive absolute creed* that the general mischief dates from Seward."[43]

7

Gurowski kept careful watch over foreign diplomats in Washington. While in the State Department he did this with every advantage. After Seward dismissed him, he relied on frequent visits to legations and hotels, where he conversed with diplomats and their office staffs. By this method and through other political chatter he collected quantities of confidential facts and opinions from foreign representatives.

The Count's quarrelsome personality and inquisitive nature, coupled with his ability to discover and expose the confidential, caused him to be disliked intensely by some of the diplomatic corps, a few of whom considered him a Russian spy. "Gurowski is the emanation of the Devil," exclaimed a member of a foreign legation to an associate. "The Devil, you say," was the response, "why, he is the Devil himself." The Danish minister, General Waldemar Rudolph de Raasloff, once refused to enter a box in a Washington opera house when he saw the Count there.[44]

Gurowski's opinions of foreign diplomats and their policies were sometimes warped by prejudice. This was undoubtedly accentuated by his personal unpopularity with some of the diplomatic corps and also their inherent conservatism and general disdain of Republican reform tendencies. Moreover, he delivered some opinions on the basis of rumors. But if anyone was capable of apprehending accurately the diplomatic gossip of the capital, of making his way among the foreign representatives, it was he. Viewed in this light, his observations should be but lightly discounted.

During the month preceding Fort Sumter's fall, Gurowski described Washington diplomats as "utterly upset, confused," apparently incap-

43 *Diary,* I, 111 (October, 1861); Gurowski to Andrew, October 27, 1862, and April 10, 1863, in Andrew Papers.

44 Gouverneur, *As I Remember,* 248–49.

able of adhering to North or South. They seemed unacquainted with the "genuine people" of the North, since all their associations had been with Southerners. "In the midst of this slave-driving, slave-worshipping, and slave-breeding society of Washington, the diplomats swallowed," he explained, "gulped all the Southern lies about the Constitution, state-rights, the necessity of slavery, and other like infamies."[45]

The rally of the North put the diplomats "altogether out of their senses," the Count thought, completely bewildering them, because of the energy, devotion, and sacrifices of the people of the North. But the Lincoln administration appeared not up to the emergency and in its vacillations caused the diplomats, accustomed to the vigorous action of unitary governments, to "laugh at the trepidation of ours."[46]

Gurowski saw none of the diplomats in Washington as fundamentally hostile to the Union or wishing its dissolution. All hoped for peace and the *status quo* because of thriving trade with Europe. Many of them desired to have slavery preserved and would have been happy to welcome John C. Breckenridge or Jefferson Davis to the White House. Some foreign representatives were Union men out of respect for a "lawful" government of any variety, but others were with the North in principle. The Pole considered the diplomats of the great powers more confused because of their multitude of interests and considerations, while representatives of the small nations, such as those of Central and South America, unquestioningly supported the Union.[47]

When the *Trent* affair caused heated discussion at home and abroad, the Count called one evening on Attorney General Edward Bates and informed him of the sensation in diplomatic circles over the incident. All the diplomats except Baron von Gerolt of Prussia and Gabriel García y Tassara of Spain, he said to Bates, were in a "furious flutter," sympathized with England, and thought she would be incited to the brink of war. Gerolt believed that England would not make war over the affair, whatever the circumstance. Then Gurowski related to Bates

[45] *Diary*, I, 17 (March, 1861), 36 (April, 1861).

[46] *Diary*, I, 35 (April, 1861), 41 (May, 1861), 56 (June, 1861); Gurowski to Sumner, May 1, 1861, and May 6, [1861], in Sumner Papers.

[47] *Diary*, I, 57–58 (June, 1861).

biographical sketches of a number of foreign ministers in Washington and amazed the Secretary with his knowledge of these men.[48]

Despite the Count's intense Anglophobia, Lord Lyons, the British representative (1858–65), was his ideal diplomat in the capital city. He liked Lyons' reserve, tact, discretion, and particularly his habit of listening more than he spoke. His dispatches to London Gurowski labeled "honorable," inspiring the "highest possible respect." Considering the difficulties of Lyons' position, he should be held in the highest respect, for even during the *Trent* affair his conduct seemed "discreet, delicate, and generous." But at times the British minister became confused in sounding public opinion, as when he visited Conservative Republicans in the Empire State. Although Lyons appeared to be defending British interests, the Pole considered this but the mark of a good diplomat. When significant principles were in question, Lyons came out inevitably on "the side of right and humanity." Though Gurowski considered most foreign diplomats in Washington misinformed and consequently quite useless to their governments, Lyons he thought objective, a vigilant observer, and enlightened.[49]

The Count also followed closely the opinions and activities of Mercier, the French minister (1860–63). His associations with him were even closer than with Lyons. Although Mercier at first appeared confused and did not expect the United States government to defend itself, Gurowski thought him "sagacious and good" and friendly to the Union by late summer, 1861. In his presence, Napoleon's representative told Sumner that he considered the United States too great a nation to receive reprimands from the French or English governments. In fact, Mercier continued so discreet that he never, while with Gurowski, spoke a word that could irritate "even the *thinnest-skinned* American." Gurowski attempted to influence him by warning him against associating with "politicians and busybodies."[50]

[48] Beale (ed.), *The Diary of Edward Bates, 1859–1866,* 205–206 (November 27, 1861).

[49] *Diary,* I, 36 (April, 1861), 152–53 (February, 1862), II, 182 (April 1, 1863), III, 11 (February 16, 1864), 231 (May 17, 1864), 361–62 (September 28, 1864).

[50] Gurowski to Sumner, May 10, 1861, in Sumner Papers; *Diary,* I, 100–101 (September, 1861), 174, 176 (March, 1862), 253 (August, 1862), II, 14 (November 18, 1862).

By autumn of 1862, with Union arms at ebb tide, the Count noted a change in Mercier's attitude. He seemed then to take the point of view of the Copperheads and Democrats, as demonstrated by his support of the French mediation scheme. He attributed Mercier's turnabout in part to contacts in New York during the summer with "low French adventurers" who caused him to be "taken with sickly diplomatic sentimentalism to conciliate, to mediate, to unite, to meddle, and to get a feather in his diplomatic cap." Moreover, he observed, Mercier had "germinated" Napoleon's mediation scheme.[51]

Throughout the war the foreign representatives seemed to Gurowski somewhat pro-Southern because they considered slaveholders aristocrats in their own image. With few exceptions, they "almost openly sympathize and side with secessionists, and patronize Copperheads, traitors, and spies," he explained. They swallowed proslavery speeches and snubbed and scorned Republican congressmen who did not play cards, drink socially, or dine elaborately. "Any other Government whatever," he said, "would long ago have sent home such enemies."[52]

Later, the Count pronounced the envoys opposed to Lincoln's policy on the Mexican imbroglio. When Grant hammered Lee back to Richmond in the spring of 1864, dissatisfaction appeared among many. "These diplomats have a great will to bite," Gurowski wrote, "but are toothless." The investigations of the Radical committee on the conduct of the war brought diplomatic sneers also. Never before had he observed such extensive dislike of any government by foreign representatives. With Union victory near in the autumn of 1864, he believed that most diplomats had not yet congratulated Lincoln on his successes, although in Europe this was absolutely necessary.[53]

A vast majority of the foreign representatives in Washington hoped not only to see the Republicans out of the White House, Gurowski said,

[51] *Diary*, II, 19, 20 (November 28 and 30, 1862), 57 (December 28, 1862), 126 (February 4, 1863).

[52] *Diary*, I, 216 (May, 1862), II, 20–21 (November 30, 1862), 62 (January 2, 1863), 124 (February 2, 1863) III, 111 (February 16, 1864).

[53] *Diary*, III, 184 (April 16, 1864), 226–27, 230 (May 14 and 17, 1864), 243 (June 1, 1864), 314 (August 9, 1864), 368 (October 8, 1864).

but to see the party undermined and broken up. The means to this end was to back General McClellan for the Presidency in 1864. Many European diplomats worked vigorously for his election, but their influence availed little, because they were mistrusted even by such groups as the Copperheads. As the election approached, a number of the envoys fell away from McClellan, the Pole observed, chiefly because they began to see the "treacherousness" of the Democratic platform and the impossibility of a party victory.[54]

8

The Count considered the diplomatic representatives of the United States in foreign capitals of limited ability and of little value in winning support. They failed to voice the sentiments and purposes of the people in the glowing, dynamic, and emotional terms envisioned by him, and their efforts tended to confuse rather than clarify and strengthen the position of the beleaguered Union abroad.

Charles Francis Adams, minister to England, Gurowski appraised as scholarly but narrow-minded, "cold, stiff, prickly, and dignified." He declared him subservient in every act and opinion to Seward. When Adams complained about being uninformed of the policies of the administration and consequently unable to answer questions asked in London, the Count attributed this circumstance to the minister's "deliberately degrading himself to the condition of a corporal under Mr. Seward's orders." An illustration of this subservience was the method by which Adams handled the slavery question. Seward, Gurowski said, had instructed him to exclude the problem from all official business. Finally sentiment in England forced its discussion in American diplomatic quarters in London. Adams coyly hinted, the Count believed, at this condition in a dispatch to Seward in which he labeled English public opinion "very sensitive" on the subject, with Confederate concessions to English antislavery sentiments likely to make an impression. Adams in addition worked untiringly to "assuage and soften the harsh odor" in which Englishmen held Seward, but without success. Adams excused

[54] *Diary*, III, 184 (April 16, 1864), 317 (August 16, 1864), 334 (September 8, 1864).

his failure by maintaining that always in the crisis of war "the most eminent of men . . . become selected for violent and vituperative attacks."[55]

William L. Dayton, minister to France, the Count admired for his "sound sense and discernment." Abroad he kept his thinking geared to events at home, unlike the other diplomats, and "maintained his ground" in dealing with Seward and Lincoln. Gurowski applauded when Dayton objected to Seward's intimations to France and England that they annul their recognition of Confederate belligerency because he considered the request "out of season." Although Dayton did not speak French, the Count contended that he had the respect of Napoleon and his foreign minister, Édouard A. Thouvenel. When rumors persisted in midsummer, 1862, that the United States representative would be replaced because he did not know the language, the Pole believed a change would not be agreeable "to the French court, to the French cabinet, and to the French good society."[56] He remained in Paris, however, his services being terminated only by sudden death in December, 1864. Most observers agreed with Gurowski's estimate of Dayton's mission.

No regularly accredited foreign representative of the United States disgusted the Count quite as much as Henry S. Sanford, minister to Belgium. Sanford would not favorably impress anyone in Europe, he said, and described his appearance and actions as those of an undistinguished traveling salesman. He questioned Sanford's high-priced purchases of war materials in Belgium to keep them from falling into Confederate hands. He threw up his hands in horror when he heard of Sanford as Dayton's probable replacement in Paris. But the greatest shock of all came when Congress debated a proposed increase in the scope and standing of the Brussels mission. Gurowski based his vigorous objections on the point of view that Sanford's elaborate dinners and parties had been useless and unnecessary, that he personally had made

[55] *Diary,* I, 31 (April, 1861), 59 (June, 1861), 161, 163 (February, 1862), 172–73, 178 (March, 1862), 306 (October 26, 1862).

[56] *Diary,* I, 147 (January, 1862), 176 (March, 1862), 204 (May, 1862), 253 (August, 1862), III, 64 (January 7, 1864).

enormous profits when purchasing war materials, and that he had not been effective enough as minister to keep the king of Belgium from encouraging his son-in-law Maximilian to become the future Mexican emperor. He urged his Radical Republican friend in the Senate, William Pitt Fessenden, to block promotion of Sanford and to spread the "truth" about him.[57] Sanford's responsibilities remained unchanged, nevertheless.

The Count believed Seward's unofficial diplomatic agents to be of slight or no value. Never would they reverse or even neutralize the low esteem of Europe's foreign offices for the Secretary, he said, or "deal offensive blows." Moreover, European governments distrusted special agents, so that the standing and influence of regular ministers were weakened. "And to think," he exclaimed, "that all these agents heavily phlebotomize Uncle Sam's pockets to obtain such contemptible results!" In labeling these special missions "petty expedients" and unworthy of the foreign ministers of a major government, Gurowski pointed to history as proof that "the times of personal diplomacy are almost gone." These "humbug missions" might be good to fog the eyes of the Lincoln administration, but in Europe they were sent to Coventry.[58]

When Seward dispatched Archbishop John Joseph Hughes of the Roman Catholic Church as special agent to Paris in the autumn of 1861, the Count expected Napoleon to "outwit a legion of Hughes." The governments of Europe, he added, a century or more ago had given up the use of clergy for political missions: "Mr. Seward stirs up old dust." Hughes's mission to France appeared "not over-successful," and was a failure in the opinion of the public, the press, and the Catholic clergy of that country: "I do not suppose that the whole diplomatic activity of his Eminence is worth the postage of his correspondence."[59]

Of Thurlow Weed, collateral agent to the Court of Saint James,

[57] *Diary*, I, 31 (April, 1861), 141 (January, 1862), 253 (August, 1862); Gurowski to William Pitt Fessenden, marked "confidential," March 14, 1864, in William P. Fessenden Papers, Duke University Library, Durham, North Carolina; Gurowski to Fessenden, Thursday Evening, no date, in *ibid.*; Gurowski to Fessenden, May 3, [1864], in *ibid.*

[58] *Diary*, I, 111 (October, 1861), 120 (November, 1861), 146–47 (January, 1862), 178–79 (March, 1862), 185–86 (April, 1862).

[59] *Diary*, I, 120 (November, 1861), 176–77 (March, 1862).

Gurowski thought little better. Weed would be considered pleasant, but would never be able to sway the English government or influence that nation's public. He later seemed somewhat surprised at the attention and courtesies showered on Weed in London. He doubted that the New Yorker increased the consideration of the English statesmen for Seward and thought the peerage "not yet softened" or deceived. Weed, like Sanford, he heard, finally turned up in Belgium to engage in speculative activity: "A schoolboy on a spree!"[60]

In the over-all pattern, the Count believed, Union diplomats abroad did little for their government. From his point of view, not one had succeeded in ending the construction and armament of vessels for the Confederacy or in doing away with the aid and comfort extended to that beleaguered government in Europe and its possessions. Likewise, American representatives had almost no influence on European public opinion. He found their dispatches "spiritless, monotonous, petty, and dragging" because of lack of contact with European public sentiment and fear to commit themselves beyond routine matters. All had become, degree by degree, alienated from the "scent, the perception, and the appreciation of domestic affairs" in the countries to which they were assigned.[61]

9

The Count closely observed foreign intervention in Mexico from the time of its inception. In January of 1862, France, Spain, and England sent a military force of ten thousand troops to Mexico to collect claims against Mexico. Gurowski recommended that Seward lay aside the Monroe Doctrine and remain neutral except to protest against "any eventual European interference in the internal condition of the political institutions of Mexico." There ought also to be a blockade of the Mexican shores of the Río Grande in addition to the blockade of the Gulf coast, the Count advised Seward and Chase, in order to keep English traders from carrying contraband to Texas and the Confederacy by way of Mexico. In May, 1862, when England and Spain withdrew their mili-

[60] *Diary*, I, 119 (November, 1861), 146 (January, 1862), 177 (March, 1862).
[61] *Diary*, III, 65–66 (January 7, 1864), 92 (February 5, 1864).

tary forces after obtaining satisfaction for debts, Napoleon not only retained the French troops but increased their number and made impossible demands on Mexico's President Juárez. "I am uneasy," Gurowski warned at this moment, "fearing we may commit some spread-eagleism toward France during this present Mexican imbroglio. I will do my utmost to explain to influential senators the truth concerning Louis Napoleon's political conduct towards the North, [and] the absurdity of any hostile demonstration against France."[62]

A year later the Count vigorously opposed Napoleon's plan to carve out a French-protected empire in Mexico. Napoleon, he wailed, "amuses himself in creating an imperial throne in Mexico for some European princely idiot or intriguer." The people of Mexico would never permit this to endure: "The future Emperor, even if established for some time on the cushion of treason propped by French bayonets, that manikin before short or long will be *Iturbidized."* Maximilian, the Austrian archduke, would perhaps not come to Mexico, he reasoned, if only the people of the United States assumed a stiff attitude toward Napoleon. Even if Maximilian did come, he would "pack his trunks and return to his Bourg as soon as the American people declare that his Hapsburg rags must no more pollute this continent."[63]

Gurowski predicted nearly two years before the close of the Civil War that when victory came the Monroe Doctrine would be applied vigorously, and Maximilian, along with similar European interests, would be removed from the Western Hemisphere. He again forecast with amazing accuracy when he reasoned that Maximilian's way to Mexico would not be difficult. His wish was also fulfilled in regard to the Emperor's fate: "I hope he will never be able to return with a whole skin to Europe."[64] Several months after Napoleon withdrew the last of the French troops from Mexico in February, 1867. Maximilian, who

[62] *Diary,* I, 102 (September, 1861), 227 (June, 1862), II, 323–24 (September 16, 1863); Gurowski to Salmon P. Chase, marked "strictly confidential," October 13, 1861, in Chase Papers.

[63] *Diary,* II, 285 (July 31, 1863), III, 85 (January 23, 1864). Augustín de Iturbide, Emperor of Mexico, 1822–23, abdicated and fled to Italy, but was shot summarily upon returning to Mexico in 1824 to regain his lost crown.

[64] *Diary,* II, 212–13 (April 28, 1863), III, 184 (April 16, 1864).

stayed behind, was executed by a firing squad.

The methods the Lincoln administration used in handling the Mexican problem disgusted Gurowski. Seward should be blamed primarily for a weak policy toward France, which encouraged the French Emperor in Mexico. "There is no doubt in my mind, that from the first day of the . . . intrigues and schemes in Mexico, Mr. Seward," he explained, "by his commonplace generalizations, by his confusing conversations and insinuations, made Louis Napoleon believe that neither the feeble protest made in Seward's dispatches had a serious meaning, nor that the people was *decidedly* opposed to a Mexican empire." Perhaps the Secretary even hoped French intervention would be permanently successful: "Mr. Seward may find it expedient to allow Napoleon to slaughter a sister republic." The Count believed and helped to spread a rumor contending that the Secretary supplied the French government with maps and charts of Mexico deposited in Washington by General Scott at the conclusion of the Mexican War.[65]

After Maximilian and Empress Charlotte had reached Mexico, Gurowski argued that never did "would-be statesmen" of any nation "give up a cause so shamefully" as Seward and Sumner. He considered Sumner a tool in the Secretary's hands. "The name of Sumner ought to be cursed by every Mexican patriot," he scolded, "and as for Seward, not only Mexicans, but mankind at large, cannot and never will bless him."[66]

Lincoln himself, Gurowski observed, paid special attention to the representative of the Mexican Republic at the 1864 White House New Year's reception. The President, acting in his "peculiar way," slyly, and in an undertone, told the Mexican that he wished they " 'may have the best of the invader.' All this was done in a manner as if Lincoln were afraid of the other diplomats, and above all, of Seward's ferule." The approaching Presidential election of 1864 carried overwhelming implications, the Count maintained, not only for the fate of the Union but also for Mexico and all Hispanic-America. A President "of energy,

[65] *Diary*, II, 285 (July 31, 1863), III, 169 (April 11, 1864), 247–48 (June 6, 1864), 176 (note, October 2, 1865); Beale (ed.), *The Diary of Edward Bates, 1859–1866*, 312 (October 26, 1863).

[66] *Diary*, III, 247–49 (June 6, 1864).

of farsightedness and of decision" would not only quickly crush the Confederacy, but also simultaneously cause the French to withdraw from Mexico and convince the monarchs of Europe to discard their ideas of Western Hemisphere empire. In addition to the pressure on the Mexican problem coming from Seward and Sumner, Gurowski thought that Lincoln had to contend with the pro-French attitude of the European diplomats in Washington toward the establishment of the proposed empire south of the border.[67]

The President, as well as the heads of the other American republics, the Count advised, should carefully scrutinize entry of all foreigners into their national borders to prevent future intervention. Adventurers had come to Mexico, made promises, exploited her people, and covered their thieving by invoking the protection of their native governments. Finally, they had entangled the country in war that resulted in loss of personal liberty and national independence. The present conflict in the United States, the Count continued, brought protests from similar foreign exploiters because of restricted business activities. For this reason, Gurowski wanted a law to prevent a foreigner in the United States from earning a wage or establishing a business until he took "the oath of allegiance to the American people." He believed this would be the only way to keep his adopted land from becoming "the prey of lawless adventurers."[68]

[67] *Diary,* III, 81, 85 (January 20 and 27, 1864), 184 (April 16, 1864).
[68] *Diary,* III, 313 (August 8, 1864).

CHAPTER XI

SLAVERY'S SCOURGE

I

TRUE TO THE RADICAL PATTERN, Gurowski hated slavery with bitter personal sentiment. Nor was this feeling recent in origin or at all superficial. When the Polish revolution of 1830–31 had no more than commenced, young Adam appeared before a notary for the purpose of freeing those of his serfs who were willing to fight with the insurrectionists. Unlike other Poles of his social and economic status, he had for some years believed in emancipation of serfs and at about the age of ten began to work for their freedom. The American slave question caught his attention at the time of the Compromise of 1850, just after he had reached the United States. At that time he denounced Senator Daniel Webster before Boston society for supporting the Fugitive Slave Law, and from then on, he gave the subject constant observation, study, and agitation.

Although the Count detested and fought slavery with the zeal of an abolitionist and ultimately became one, he did not neglect a purely intellectual and scholarly approach. Amazingly, he thereby attained a high degree of academic objectivity. Throughout the fifties he had been an avid student of the subject in the Astor Library of New York. His approach was mainly historical, because he believed that the record of the past would speak well for emancipation. He stoutly refused to give ear to abolitionist literature, but attempted to master writings favorable to slavery. He read everything within reach in the area of proslavery political speeches and discussions, laws, resolutions, governors' messages, sermons, orations, and statistical, philosophical, historical, and economic studies, even including John C. Calhoun's *Works,* published in six volumes between 1851–55. Heeding his scholarly desire to increase objectivity in his slavery studies, he did not attend abolition or antislavery lectures. For the same reason he avoided antislavery conversations with leading opponents of "the Peculiar Institution" such as Theodore Parker, Charles Sumner, and Wendell Phillips, whom he numbered among his friends. He was glad not to know William Lloyd Garrison, the leading immediate abolitionist; and even Gerrit Smith, a fellow antislavery gradualist, disgusted him with his "twaddle."[1]

Gurowski's first printed opinion on the slavery question appeared in a chapter of *America and Europe,* published in 1857. In sixty pages he struck not only at slavery but at much of Southern culture. After briefly explaining his attitude toward the problem, he treated point by point proslavery reasoning and shattered each premise through an array of skillful arguments based on history and ethnology. His appeal to learning and reason proved popular with the intellectuals. The well-known Boston abolitionist, Edmund Quincy, declared in an antislavery speech that Gurowski's chapter did more to condemn slavery than any other publication. But the publisher, D. Appleton and Company of New York, was so frightened by the vehement antislavery flavor of the book, that at first it was not distributed below the Mason and Dixon line for fear that their business with the South would suffer. William Henry Appleton, the firm's president, told Gurowski that, if he had known what the book had to say on slavery, he would never have published it, and Appleton's brother declared himself satisfied if the sale would cover the cost of printing. Financially, the book brought no more.[2]

With no royalties to show for years of work on *America and Europe,* the Count determined at once to produce a full-length book on the theme which had got him into this trouble. In 1860, he published *Slavery in History,* a 260-page volume, which was brought out by the small New York firm of A. B. Burdick, recent publisher of the scurrilous antislavery book, Hinton R. Helper's *The Impending Crisis of the*

---

[1] Gurowski, *America and Europe,* 171; Gurowski, *Slavery in History,* xiv; Norton, "Ten Years in a Public Library," *Galaxy,* Vol. VIII, 531; Gurowski to Pike, August 12, 1854, in Pike, *First Blows of the Civil War,* 257.

[2] Chapter V, "Slavery," 169–229; Gurowski to Sumner, May 25, 1854, in Sumner Papers; Gurowski to Pike, July 16, 1857, in Pike, *First Blows of the Civil War,* 375–76; Gurowski to Lowell, October 5, 1857, in Lowell Papers.

South: How to Meet It. Surprisingly little attention was given by Gurowski to slavery as it existed in the South. Only in introduction and conclusion did he actually write of the American slave problem. Although there were, at infrequent intervals, comparisons of the contemporary system with those of history, he sought rather to impress his readers with the scholarly soundness and authority of his investigations. In chapter after chapter, he treated the historical development of slavery in the principal races and nations, heading each unit with a list of authorities ranging in number from three to twelve.

Because of the intensity of the slave question at the time *Slavery in History* appeared, Gurowski had experienced considerable difficulty in finding a publisher. A friend suggested that he ask for the support of Horace Greeley and the New York *Tribune,* but the Pole's vanity prevented him from doing this. Rather, he would prefer not to publish the manuscript than request the aid of his former employer. "The world will not be a bit better if I . . . publish my book," he said in a rare moment of humility and depression. "After all, if it would be a Helper, help would have been found."[3]

To the pleasant surprise of publisher and author, they fared well financially with *Slavery in History,* for at the moment the book hit the market, antislavery literature was at peak demand. Yet similar publications must have outsold the volume, for its intellectual qualities limited its appeal. The Count himself considered his book a work of scholarship, with remote money-making possibilities. Written for the select few, it could never have circulated widely, although the list price was one dollar. While Senator Sumner believed the volume, written with "consummate ability," would "naturally take a place in libraries," he stoutly recommended that "all inquirers into the character of Slavery, and especially all practical Republicans, ought to welcome it as an ally." Greeley also found the Count's historical approach satisfying and useful in his own thinking on slavery.[4]

---

[3] Gurowski to Pike, May 12, 1860, in Pike, *First Blows of the Civil War,* 515; see also Gurowski to Pike, Friday, [1860], in Pike Papers, and Gurowski to Pike, July 13, 1860, in Pike, *First Blows of the Civil War,* 524.

[4] *Ibid.;* Charles Sumner to a Republican meeting at the dedication of the Republican

2

As Gurowski viewed the slave South in contrast to the free North, a strange anomaly seemed apparent:

It is the lot of the American Union to represent man in his highest . . . development, by the side of the most appalling degradation. It is the lot of American institutions to evince that the noblest realization of freedom . . . can be marred, distorted and prostituted. At the side of the highest solutions attainable by society in its present stage . . . stands Slavery with its degrading, agonizing contradictions. There it stands, bidding defiance to the moral sense of humanity, to religious conceptions, to civilization, to social progress . . . . There it stands, preventing and debasing all the cardinal notions of American social and political association . . . . There stands slavery, poisoning . . . seeds which have here been scattered broadcast by reason, conscience and freedom.[5]

The Count vigorously disagreed with mounting public opinion which voiced the idea of different and distinct civilizations north and south. Slavery could never produce a civilization; thus the term could not be applied to the South. "This so-called civilization of the slave holders," he said, "is the Devil's counterfeit of a genuine civilization." Gurowski chose, rather, to recognize the two sections as possessing different and diametric social conditions. Slavery tended to drag the South in the direction of total ignorance and barbarism, while teachers from the free states established schools and classes in the South and prevented the complete ruin and debasement of its whites.[6]

Proslavery arguments concerning the chattel himself drew thorough analysis from Gurowski. He did not believe slaves were better fed, clothed, and cared for than the free laborers of the North. Slave labor was itself expensive and scarcely covered its cost. It would follow naturally that the master would first care for himself and his family, with

Wigwam in New York, August 6, 1860, in Sumner, *The Works of Charles Sumner*, V, 235; Jeter Allen Isely, *Horace Greeley and the Republican Party, 1853–1861: A Study of the New York Tribune* (Princeton, 1947), 171–72.

[5] Gurowski, *America and Europe*, 169.

[6] *Diary*, I, 166 (March, 1862), III, 324 (August 25, 1864); Gurowski to Pike, Thursday, [December, 1860], in Pike, *First Blows of the Civil War*, 514; Gurowski, *America and Europe*, 297–98.

the barest minimum remaining for the bondmen, who even lived in "desolated huts." "For one working chattel, well-fed and tolerably dressed," he conjectured, "there are necessarily hundreds and hundreds covered with rags, fed on the scantiest and coarsest allowance." Admitting that the physical condition of the slaves was as favorable as represented, this was no more than would be done by every reasonable farmer for his cattle and domestic animals because of the labor expected of them. To the argument that the American slave loved the institution which enmeshed him, he fired a barrage of questions. Why an ever increasing number of state laws to defend and strengthen slavery? Why did masters fear that slaves would escape? Why the need of the Fugitive Slave Law of 1850? Why the newspaper advertisements for runaway slaves? Why did owners of bloodhounds advertise to hunt fugitives? "Strange evidences of the felicity and satisfaction of the oppressed," he quipped.[7]

The press of the South, according to the Count, had been completely depraved by slavery. Publishing had become "the most unrelenting apostle" of the chattel system, and in this role was perverting the mind of the masses in the South. Violence, lawlessness, and aggression received encouragement from that section's journalists, who also distorted science, politics, and economics in their support of slavery. The Pole pointed to the unauthorized military expeditions to Latin America during the 1850's as evidence of slaveholders made lawless by an uncontrollable martial spirit born in idleness and contempt of labor.[8]

If the Civil War were to conclude with an independent Confederacy, Gurowski predicted that the South would teem with thousands of men ready for piratical, filibustering raids into the free states of the North and the West. "The Cylician pirates, the Barbary robbers, nay, the Tartars," he exclaimed, ". . . were virtuous and civilized in comparison with what would be an independent, man-stealing, and man-whipping Southern agglomeration of lawless men." The entire Western Hemisphere would soon be under attack by these mobs, who eventually

---

[7] *Ibid.*, 196, 197, 198–99.
[8] *Ibid.*, 227–28, 253; Gurowski, *Slavery in History*, 256–57.

would take to the sea, and ultimately the European maritime nations would need to make costly expeditions to uproot the raiders. "The *slavery gentleman* is a scarcely varnished savage," he said, "for whom the highest law is his reckless passion and will."[9]

For the first time in the history of slavery, said the Count, the institution in the South had become a vital part of the religious, political, intellectual, and social creed of that area. Because of its many advocates, some fanatical, in all walks of Southern life, it was virtually an overshadowing "new faith." The South appeared aware of its "degradation, its backwardness," and its industrial and commercial dependence on the North, the explanation continued, but did not understand that its complete support and dependence on slavery was the cause, judging from its attempted solutions. Commercial conventions, resolutions to increase city population, expand trade, navigation, and industry were not answers, but liberty, free speech, free press, free labor, and educated people. "Not conventions and resolutions, but freedom has made New York, Boston, Philadelphia . . . while Charleston and Savannah, old already by centuries," the argument concluded, "backed by the cotton-growing and slave-whipping South, situated near the ocean, see the grass growing in their desolated streets."[10]

European nations carefully watched the self-government experiment in the United States in the years before Southern secession, Gurowski observed, and even sent agents to investigate the schools, manufacturing activity, and agricultural progress of the North. However, they never dispatched messengers South to study slavery, "for they know well that by the action of self-government and universal suffrage, qualitative and quantitative knowledge is more generally spread, and has reached a far higher grade in the American Free States than among all the militant oligarchs and knight-errants of slavery the world over." The claim of slavery protagonists that the South did not believe in popular sovereignty he answered by reasoning that it could exist only in intelligent, orderly and labor-centered communities as found in the North, for "an ignorant and degraded population of oligarchs, op-

---

[9] *Diary*, I, 112–13 (October, 1861), 143 (January, 1862), II, 179 (March 28, 1863).
[10] Gurowski, *Slavery in History*, vii; Gurowski, *America and Europe*, 211–12.

pressors and slave-breeders never were capable of exercising popular sovereignty, and consequently nowhere could they ever have faith in it: barbarians generally mistrust civilization."[11]

The year before the armed clash of the sections the Count noted that "oligarchic despotism" in the slave states had rapidly negotiated all the stages of individual tyranny outlined in history. Already free speech and free thought had been suppressed, censorship of periodicals accomplished, mail sanctity violated, and political control lodged in the hands of office-holding cliques. Four years later, with slavery a certain casualty of the war, he believed that few still understood that the larger issue of the conflict continued to be self-government in the South, impossible with the chattel system. "The victory won by the North," the explanation unfolded, "will mark a new era for those millions of brutish but good-natured whites, perverted, degraded, lowered by the slaveholding aristocracy . . . . Then only self-government in the South will cease to be a blatant lie."[12]

Before war came, the "withering breath" of slavery subtly affected in undesirable ways the population of the North, said Gurowski. Economic temptation sometimes could not be avoided by Northern businessmen in dealing with the South, a sting that the Count was to feel in the very book in which he made this statement, since the publisher refused to circulate it in slave territory. Political climbers in the North also on occasion sold out to the South to accomplish ambitions. "Sadness and even despair," the complaint continued, "fill the mind when witnessing the loftiest and best social structure ever erected by man sapped to its foundations by the sacrilegious champions of human bondage!"[13]

With secession in its beginning stages at the end of 1860, the Count voiced the extreme abolitionist viewpoint of elation. The country and its principles would not be ruined, and after a year or two of unavoidable confusion because of the transition, a new, brilliant start would be made by the free states. "A body, politic or animal, to be healthy," he explained, ". . . must throw out the deleterious poison from its vitals."

[11] Gurowski, *Slavery in History,* 254, 255–56.

[12] *Ibid.,* 256; *Diary, I,* 65 (July, 1861), III, 333 (September 7, 1864).

[13] Gurowski, *America and Europe,* 221–22; Gurowski, *Slavery in History,* 260.

Truth, liberty, man, and civilization would win as the result of secession by the South.[14]

Gurowski's disease theory of slavery provided curative measures in addition to diagnosis of the ailment. First, slavery policy must not prevail on the national level. Second, the expansion of slavery into the territories must be stopped, thus confining it as a physician confines a person with a contagious disease. Third, the slavery question must be forced back historically to the period when it was considered undesirable and deserving of eradication by leading Southerners, like Washington and Jefferson. Fourth, slavery in the long run must be done away with, completely destroyed, for the problems that it created would recur, like a blight, again and again, and would force their way into all political questions.[15]

When it appeared that the North would not permit the South to secede in peace, Gurowski concluded that slavery must be eliminated in the conflict, "even if the whole North, Lincoln and Seward at its head, should attempt to save it." Reflecting further on the desired impact of the war, he hoped it would also "uproot domestic oligarchy, based upon living on the labor of an enslaved man; it has to put a stop to the moral, intellectual, and physical servitude of both, of whites and of colored."[16]

At no time before secession had the Count favored immediate and absolute emancipation. "Such a violent passage . . . without preparatory measures, without a gradual transition," he believed, "would produce inexpressible evil, ruin and destruction." Steps toward emancipation, nevertheless, should be taken: "Even the transformation of the slaves into serfs . . . would be an alleviation, and a cheering sign of progress." With the coming of the war, he favored immediate emancipation and became irritated with those who would compromise the issue. Still the Garrisonian brand of abolitionist caused him to complain: "It is true that among those who ardently work to see slavery abolished, there is

[14] Gurowski to Pike, Thursday, [December, 1860], in Pike, *First Blows of the Civil War*, 514–15; see also *Diary*, I, 20–21 (March, 1861).

[15] Gurowski, *America and Europe*, 229; Gurowski, *Slavery in History*, 253–54, 258.

[16] *Diary*, I, 33 (April, 1861), 118 (November, 1861); Gurowski to Andrew, March 1, 1862, in Andrew Papers.

a certain number constituting the *small church,* whose mental horizon is neither much expanded or clear. But these constitute that very small minority, known under the party name of *abolitionists.*"[17]

3

The problem of emancipation suggested to Lincoln and a few Conservatives the possibility of Negro colonization outside the United States, an issue on which Gurowski joined the abolitionists, including Garrison, in vigorous opposition. When Lincoln, in his first annual message to Congress, recommended the colonization of slaves presumably freed under the confiscation act of 1861, the Count retorted that a comprehensive program of this nature would devastate the South and transform it into a wilderness. The President through all of 1862 considered colonization an active policy. In April, Congress passed the District of Columbia emancipation act, and in this legislation provided one hundred thousand dollars for foreign colonization of freed slaves. Gurowski commented that colonizers evidently forgot that, if as many as one hundred thousand slaves were exported annually, an equal number would be born. If the scheme were carried out on a small scale, it would be valueless, and on a broad pattern, "altogether impossible, besides being as stupid as it is recklessly cruel." "Look from whatever side you like," he chided, "a colonization schemer is a cruel deceiver, he is an enemy of emancipation, and if he claims to be an emancipator then he is an enemy of the planter and of the prosperity of the southern region."[18]

The Count was amazed at the President's additional plan to colonize Negroes in Chiriquí near present-day Panama, then a part of New Granada (Colombia). Lincoln's choice of location, he explained, had resulted from speculative influence and was intended to assist such an undertaking. Central America, he believed, was always in a state of revolution, a condition certain to cause the sacking of the colonists' homes. Being Protestant, moreover, the new settlers would be treated by "the stupid Catholic clergy as being heretics and miscreants." "It

[17] Gurowski, *America and Europe,* 171; Gurowski, *Slavery in History,* 258–59;*Diary,* II, 211 (April 27, 1863), 260 (July 2, 1863), III, 155–56 (April 2, 1864), 234 (May 20, 1864).

[18] *Diary,* I, 130 (December, 1861), 187–88 (April, 1862).

will be a new kind of apprenticeship," the criticism continued, "under cruel masters." In disgust he wrote Wendell Phillips concerning the Chiriquí scheme, and to his friend Andrew he related the Washington rumor that had government personnel backing Lincoln in his Chiriquí planning in order to permit him to *"play his hobby."* The Count questioned how the leader of a democracy could follow his avocation when European despots were no longer permitted to pursue theirs.[19]

Gurowski growled again at the Chief Executive for inviting a committee of colored men to the White House to confer on the Chiriquí colonization plan less than a month before the preliminary Emancipation Proclamation was announced. "Mr. Lincoln promised them an Eden—in Chiriqui," the lament commenced. "Mr. Lincoln promised them—what he ought to know is utterly impossible and beyond his power—that they will form an independent community in a country already governed by orderly and legally organized States . . . . Happily even for Mr. Lincoln's name, the logic of human events will save from exposure his ignorance of international laws, and his too light and too quick assertions."[20] The President probably had in preparation the day of the interview his preliminary proclamation of September 22, but even with it a finality, he continued to press for colonization.

4

The Count observed with little satisfaction the actions of the Lincoln administration leading to emancipation. The basic problem, as he viewed it, was lack of will to free the slaves, which suggested compromise with the South. With the coming of the war, he believed emancipation to be a sacred duty made imperative by the conflict itself, and a task to be carried out immediately, boldly, and broadly by Presidential edict, without the slightest hedging. Viewing emancipation as the highest social and economic duty of man, he clashed constantly with the attitude and action of the administration on the issue.

When General Benjamin F. Butler had dared to emancipate several

[19] Diary, I, 188 (April, 1862), 227 (June, 1862), 252 (August, 1862); Gurowski to Andrew, August 28, 1862, in Andrew Papers.
[20] *Diary*, I, 251–52 (August, 1862). For Lincoln's remarks before the group, see Basler (ed.), *The Collected Works of Abraham Lincoln*, V, 370–75.

fugitive slaves within his lines in Virginia in the first spring of the war, the Count considered this the beginning of nation-wide slave liberation. To the General, he said, must go the credit for "introducing" the Negro into the war and for causing the administration to become "almost frantic" over the new issue. Similarly, General John C. Frémont's proclamation (August, 1861) granting freedom to Missouri slaves, whose masters resisted the United States, was justified "by the slowness, nay, by the stagnancy of the administration." Lincoln's reversal of Frémont's edict brought the comment that the General was right in principal and legality, and although the administration hesitated "to give to the struggle a character of emancipation," the people meanwhile had taken the Missouri commander "to their heart." The General's snag on emancipation, the Count noted, had been that he was "ahead of the times."[21]

A third Union commander, General David Hunter, likewise tried to force the hand of Lincoln by proclaiming slaves free in the Military Department of the South (Georgia, Florida, and South Carolina) in May, 1862, only to have the Chief Executive revoke the declaration. Gurowski thought Hunter's decree "the greatest social act" of the war to date. "How pale and insignificant," came the criticism, "are Mr. Lincoln's disquisitions aside of that proclamation . . . . It is too human, too noble, too great, for the tall Kentuckian." "How can Lincoln look into General Hunter's eyes? Lincoln . . . disavowed Hunter," the Count complained a year after the Emancipation Proclamation, "and subsequently adopted Hunter's emancipation policy. And Lincoln struts now before the people, wrapped in Fremont's, Hunter's, and Butler's actions."[22]

Gurowski believed that the pressure of public opinion for emancipation relentlessly pushed Lincoln step by step toward abolition. The President's special message to Congress in March, 1862, announcing a plan of compensated emancipation by voluntary action of the slave states came for this reason, as in the following month did Lincoln's signature to the bill abolishing slavery in the District of Columbia. Month after

---

[21] *Diary*, I, 50 (June, 1861), 91 (August, 1861), 93, 98 (September, 1861), II, 314 (September 5, 1863).

[22] *Diary*, I, 210 (May, 1862), III, 118 (February 27, 1864), 124–25 (March 4, 1864).

month, however, exclaimed the Count, Lincoln continued "at heart" with slavery, considering emancipation a task so huge it would "smother" the free states.[23] The President's unwillingness and delay in signing the second confiscation act in July, 1862, Gurowski said, seemed additional evidence that he wished to avoid making a deadly blow at slavery. Lincoln's reported fear of antislavery riots in the North following a general proclamation of emancipation also pointed in the same direction.[24] When in midsummer, 1862, the President called for huge new levies of troops, the Count believed this action was designed to kill emancipation by conquering the South before the slave question could be settled. Even when the Chief Executive made concessions to the enemies of slavery, Gurowski thought it was "to mollify their urgent demands by throwing to them small crumbs, as one tries to mollify a boisterous and hungry dog." In calling for additional troops, he evinced the same purpose: "By such a trick Lincoln and Seward try to save what can be saved of the peculiar institution, to gratify, and eventually to conciliate, the South."[25]

5

The President's preliminary Emancipation Proclamation (September 22, 1862) announcing liberation on the following January 1 in those areas of the Confederacy still in rebellion Gurowski viewed as the administration's "last desperate effort" to save slavery. This conditional proclamation came only because the "decided, authoritative will of the masses" could no longer be resisted; very little, if any, credit for the declaration should rest with the administration. Fortunately "for humanity and for national honor," the South would not turn loyal by the following January and thus cheat the people in the North. "The proclamation is written in the meanest and the most dry routine style," the complaint followed, "not a word to evoke a generous thrill, not a word reflecting the warm and lofty comprehension and feelings of the im-

23 *Diary*, I, 167 (March, 1862), 192–93 (April, 1862), 223 (June, 1862); Gurowski to Andrew, May 7 and June 16, 1862, in Andrew Papers.

24 *Diary*, I, 242 (July, 1862), 245 (August, 1862); Gurowski to Andrew, July 31, 1862, in Andrew Papers.

25 Gurowski to Andrew, July 31 and August 7, 1862, in *ibid.*; *Diary*, I, 159 (February, 1862), 248 (August, 1862).

mense majority of the people on this question of emancipation. Nothing for humanity, nothing for humanity. . . . it is clear that the writer was not in it either with his heart or with his soul; it is clear that it was done under moral duress, under the throttling pressure of events. How differently Stanton would have spoken!"[26]

While labeling the preliminary proclamation an "illogical, pusillanimous, confused half-measure," the Count believed that the document for the first time incorporated the concept of general emancipation into the Constitution, and for that reason should be considered a great event. He noted also a warm reception of the proclamation and considerable gratitude to Lincoln by a huge majority of the people of the North for issuing the edict. In Europe, however, the desirable effect would be considerably less than if it had been issued a year earlier and if it had appeared as "an act of justice and of self-conscientious force," reflecting "the lofty, pure, and ardent aspirations and will of a high-minded people," and not as "an action of despair made in the duress of events."[27]

As the day scheduled (January 1, 1863) for the final Emancipation Proclamation approached, Gurowski looked to its publication as "our only hope," reflecting undoubtedly his despair over the Union military disaster at Fredericksburg a fortnight earlier. Then he exulted over the proclamation's announcement. "The foulest relic of the past," he exclaimed, "will at length be destroyed." "Yes! The new era rises above darkness, selfishness, and imbecility." But to Lincoln he gave no credit, for he thought him to be but the legal recorder of what the people had "long demanded and now inexorably dictate." Specifically, the Radicals of Congress had whipped the President in line for the proclamation, Gurowski's explanation unfolded, and the "people's blood, the fallen heroes, tore the divine work of emancipation, from the hands of jelously watching demons. To the shadows of the fallen the glory, and not to your round, polished or unpolished phrases. Not the pen with which the proclamation was written is a trophy and a relic, but the blood steam-

---

[26] *Diary*, I, 277–78 (September, 23, 1862).
[27] *Diary*, I, 280, 282, 285–86 (September 24, 25, and 27, 1862), 292 (October 4, 1862).

ing to heaven, the corpses of the fallen, corpses mouldering scattered on all the fields of the Union."[28]

Viewing emancipation as man's highest social and economic solution, the Count took offense at Lincoln's use of the war power to issue the document. Early in the conflict he had warned that this approach would be "an offence to reason, logic, and humanity," since war power was by "its nature violent, transient, established for a day." He recognized, however, that by this approach emancipation was acceptable "to millions of small, narrow intellects" who otherwise would oppose it. In addition to degrading the high nature of emancipation, he thought the war-power approach would be effective only in those areas controlled by the army, "as long as bayonets back it." The civil authority of the President would have been far preferable, because it penetrated beyond the picket lines; and clothed with it, Lincoln should have said to the slaves: "Arise, you are free, you have no servitude, no duties towards a rebel and traitor to the Union. I, the president, dissolve your bonds in the name of the American people." When there were two choices, the Count asked, was it not the better part of wisdom to select the broader one? Instead, the proclamation had the smallest and narrowest basis that could have been selected.[29]

Gurowski believed enforcement of the declaration would be a continuing problem. Some days before the final document appeared, he felt certain that great confusion would prevail after its announcement. With its appearance he noted not the slightest sign of measures to carry out its broad meanings. The problem was that the President did not have his heart in the edict, for if he had, on the day after it appeared, he would have taken steps to work out "its expansion, realization, execution. I wish Lincoln may lift himself, or be lifted by angels to the grandeur of the work." "Any one but an idiot ought to have seen at the start," the castigation continued, "that as the rebels fight to maintain slavery, in striking slavery you strike at the rebels." Months after the

[28] Gurowski to Andrew, December 27, 1862, in Andrew Papers; *Diary,* II, 62, 63, 75–76, 99 (January 1, 2, 8, and 20, 1863).

[29] *Diary,* I, 67 (July, 1861), II, 64–66, 70 (January 3 and 5, 1863).

announcement of the final Emancipation Proclamation, he believed that Lincoln had not made a choice between immediate and piecemeal emancipation. Because of re-election hopes, the President moved a little in both directions in order to placate the two groups. However, the problem of emancipation would eventually be solved, Gurowski predicted, in spite of the inability of the administration to accomplish the task, by "the principle of self-government and by the self-governing People."[30]

6

Another problem of primary concern to the Count and most other Radical Republicans was the recruitment and use of Negro soldiers in the Union armies. Gurowski's thinking settled on the slaves who had escaped from Confederate lines or were freed by the advancing military forces of the North. These men seemed to him to fill a manpower need, and in addition, they would be able to prove their loyalty, ability, and courage. By this means they also would win their birthright of American freedom and move toward racial equality, as his serfs had done in the Polish revolution of 1830–31, when he had freed those willing to fight with the insurrectionists. Then he had stood almost alone, but during the American Civil War he was vigorously supported by a host of like-minded Jacobins.

No one was more deeply concerned with the Negro soldier question. Soon after the fall of Fort Sumter, Gurowski expressed the desire to have Negroes in the ranks, a hope so intense that he almost wished for a misfortune to force the issue. Seeing innumerable able-bodied blacks on the streets of Washington prompted him a year later to resolve to form a colored regiment. He proposed to use these troops for "whipping" the aristocratic slaveholding first families of Virginia and establishing "beyond doubt, the perfect equality of the thus called races." After considering the idea for several weeks while still employed in the State Department, he petitioned Secretary of War Stan-

[30] Gurowski to Andrew, December 12, 1862, in Andrew Papers; *Diary,* II, 97 (January 18, 1863), 119 (February 1, 1863), 211 (April 27, 1863), 343 (October 12, 1863).

ton to commission him colonel of a colored regiment, when the "current of events may render it necessary." He explained to Stanton that his military experience and knowledge was no better, but perhaps no worse, than that of many in the armed services. Twenty-six Radical Republican friends had "cordially" countersigned to recommend that his request be honored. With few exceptions, the signers were members of the House of Representatives, including Owen Lovejoy of Illinois, brother of the abolitionist martyr Elijah Lovejoy, and James M. Ashley of Ohio, later to introduce the bill to abolish slavery throughout the nation.[31]

Months passed with no action on the Count's premature request. Many Union leaders in the party's Conservative wing believed that colored men should be used only as laborers. In the meantime, Gurowski continued to ponder the problem, noting that Lincoln remained opposed to the use of Negro soldiers, and in so doing made necessary another large levy of white troops.[32] After the announcement of the preliminary Emancipation Proclamation in September, 1862, and especially following the final document on the following January 1, sentiment for the use of colored soldiers developed, and he again took up the cudgel for organizing the long-hoped-for Negro regiments.

For this purpose, he arranged a visit with Secretary Stanton. He talked of his personal ambitions and national policy concerning the use of Negro forces, and found the Secretary more understanding on the question than anyone else he knew. Stanton agreed that "the cursed land of Secessia ought to be surrounded by camps to enlist and organize the enslaved, as a scorpion surrounded with burning coals." These collecting and training posts, Gurowski explained, "introduced rapidly and simultaneously on all points, would shake Secessia to its foundations." The Secretary made no promises and skillfully evaded the issue of the Count's military commission by assuring him that they would "again

[31] Gurowski to Sumner, May 1, 1861, in Sumner Papers; *Diary*, I, 211–12 (May, 1862); Petition, Gurowski to Stanton, June 22, 1862, in Gurowski Papers.

[32] Gurowski to Andrew, August 5, 1862, in Andrew Papers; *Diary*, I, 246 (August, 1862).

think and talk it over." Although Gurowski did not tell Stanton, he at first intended to use contrabands and actual slaves, rather than free blacks, for his Negro-soldier project.[33]

With public and official sentiment now clearly favoring Negro soldiers, the Count continued to develop the plan. Earnest, bold, and large-scale action without loss of time would be necessary. Washington ought to serve as the focal point for arming the chattels "in the face of slave-breeding Virginia, this most intense focus of treason; . . . that the loyal freemen of Virginia's soil be enabled to fight and crush the F. F. V.'s, the progeny of hell." "What a splendid position for such a camp," he exclaimed, "is Harper's Ferry under the shadow of immortal John Brown!"[34] He envisioned a large organization of Negro soldiers, "a powerful social and military machine" for crushing slavery, secession, and rebellion "in a thrice." He would not permit the men of his own regiment to take prisoners in battle, nor would he allow them to be captured alive. "The Africo-Americans," he explained, "will sell their lives so dearly as to disgust the rebels with the task of attempting to capture them."[35]

Little more than a week after the interview with Stanton, Gurowski wrote to the Secretary detailed suggestions for organization of a large and effective Negro army. Because of prejudice and ignorance, he reasoned that a colored regiment would perhaps be left unsupported during a battle. To prevent this, he recommended that they be organized into larger units like brigades and divisions to withstand an overwhelming enemy onslaught until relief arrived. These new legions should be drilled and armed for service as light infantry, and better still, light cavalry, but, above all, for set fighting. The dress of the dark soldier ought to promote agile movement of the entire body, especially the feet and legs, not then possible with the equipment of Union army infantry.

Because of the longer range of weapons, the Count continued, rapid marching techniques should be emphasized to force the enemy from

---

[33] *Diary*, II, 97, 112 (January 18 and 27, 1863), 133 (February 9, 1863).

[34] *Diary*, II, 104–105, 113 (January 24 and 27, 1863), 133 (February 9, 1863).

[35] *Diary*, II, 105, 107, 113, 118 (January 24, 25, 27, and 31, 1863).

his positions at bayonet point. When firearms were not available to equip all Negro troops, the third line should be armed with scythes, "that really terrible weapon," he said, after the pattern of the Polish peasant militia of Kosciuszko in the insurrection of 1794. He would simplify drill for colored troops, and he recommended to Stanton that the soldier's handbook of tactics and regulations be revised or that a new book be written for their use. He suggested for the task General Silas Casey, a Radical then in command of a division of troops assigned to the defense of the capital city, and author of an army manual titled *Infantry Tactics,* adopted in 1862.[36]

Simultaneously Gurowski sent to Lincoln a letter with most of the same ideas concerning Negroes in military service. He assured the President, as if to convince himself, that he believed him "earnest in the question of arming the Africo-Americans free or emancipated." Black forces, he suggested, would be the only means of wiping out enemy guerrilla activity in the border states, and they should be armed with pikes to strike the greatest terror. He explained that "several foreign thoroughbread officers" had offered to join him the previous year when he applied for permission to form a colored regiment. Although many of these officers had disappeared, he still hoped that similar capable commissioned men from abroad would be available to command the units "free from any baneful prejudices." He implored that he and "such devoted men if used would be gladdened to see that the government itself gives a good tone to such formations." For the command supervision of all Negro troops he recommended his friend, General Casey. He offered his personal services in general to the President, but "above all in any relation with the Africo-Americans."[37]

Several days later the Count felt encouraged by news that Stanton had appointed General Casey to shorten and revise *Infantry Tactics* for the use of light-infantry colored regiments. He soon made it a point to discuss his ideas and suggestions with Casey and found him receptive

---

[36] *Diary,* II, 115–17 (January 30, 1863); see also Miecislaus Haiman, *Polish Past in America, 1608–1865* (Chicago, 1939), 112.

[37] Rough draft of a letter, Gurowski to Lincoln, no date, in Gurowski Papers; see also *Diary* II, 97 (January 18, 1863).

to the extent of adopting some of them. The General was then hard at work on the manual, he noted, and its publication appeared certain. Within a month after Gurowski's visit, the three volumes of the 1862 edition had been reduced to one, primarily through omissions. Strangely, Casey's name appeared nowhere in the volume, but Stanton's introduction, as well as the title page, designated the publication for "the use of colored troops of the United States Infantry."[38]

Then at last, in the spring of 1863, a reply came from Stanton's office. Assistant Secretary of War Peter H. Watson wrote that the Secretary intended to use the Count in the organization of Negro forces as soon as he could devote "the requisite time" to the problem. Gurowski was assured that his suggestion for a special manual of tactics for the use of Negro troops had been acted upon and was already in press. Watson spoke of the Secretary's "highest opinion of your ability," and he himself hoped to see him soon in "a field of duty commensurate to your abilities and capacity to serve the government."[39]

Gurowski never realized his ambition to lead a colored regiment or to work otherwise with the arming of Negro soldiers. Again his role was that of contributing ideas, promotion, and Radical propaganda. Although personally thwarted, even by his good friend Stanton, his hope for the extensive use of Negro soldiers continued undiminished. He thrilled to the successful use of Negroes in combat in 1863 and greeted their military future hopefully: "I see the freedmen, the Africo-American, take a stand among the defenders of right, and by his blood consecrate his accession to manhood. I see the Africo-American justify what I, and better than I, expected from him."[40]

The efforts toward Negro soldiers of two stalwart Jacobins, Stanton and Andrew, did much to keep up the Count's enthusiasm. A month after the final emancipation proclamation appeared, he believed that the War Secretary was "earnestly at work" preparing to organize colored forces "on a mighty scale" with the assistance of young men he ap-

38 *Diary*, II, 125, 133 (February 3 and 9, 1863). Casey titled his revised volume *U.S. Infantry Tactics . . . for the Use of the Colored Troops of the United States Infantry* (New York, 1863).

39 Peter H. Watson to Gurowski, March 22, 1863, in Gurowski Papers.

40 *Diary*, III, 58 (January 1, 1864).

pointed to his office to replace the "old fogies." But he could go only so far, he said, since his hands were tied by administrative and congressional Conservatives.[41] Governor Andrew's vigorous efforts in organizing Negro units from free blacks several weeks after the final proclamation pleased Gurowski even more. He thought Andrew intended "to give the start, to stir up the Government and other Governors and to drag them in his footsteps." While insisting that the Massachusetts Governor's units of free Negroes did not interfere with his own idea of organizing slave forces, he told him without hesitation that colored regiments in principle ought to be raised "all along the frontiers of the revolted States" and not only in the upper North, as in Boston.[42] Andrew's efforts to win pay equality for colored forces were also commended by his Washington admirer.[43]

Despite the active support of Stanton and Andrew in organizing Negro troops, the result was far from pleasing to Gurowski, the path to fulfillment a thwarted and tortuous route. With emancipation proclaimed, he noted no decisive steps by the Lincoln administration to enlist and equip Negro units and no "clear comprehension" of how to use this new reservoir of manpower. The weeks passed into months and still no action, he said, for Seward and Postmaster General Montgomery Blair had persuaded Lincoln not to push the arming of Negroes on the perimeters of the Confederacy. Disappointment over continuing delays prevented Gurowski from acclaiming the action taken in 1864 to organize military forces of former slaves in South Carolina, Georgia, and Alabama. "And why not sooner?" he questioned, "why not a year ago? If this measure is good to-day, it was even better a year ago."[44]

"The country ought to have had already about one hundred thousand Africo-Americans, either under arms, in the field, or drilling in camps," Gurowski said some months earlier in analyzing the problem.

[41] Diary, II, 128–29 (February 5, 1863); see also 293 (August 5, 1863), and III, 80 (January 20, 1864).
[42] Diary, II, 111–12 (January 27, 1863); Gurowski to Andrew, April 10, 1863, in Andrew Papers.
[43] Diary, II, 326 (September 19, 1863), III, 272 (July 3, 1864).
[44] Diary, II, 113 (January 27, 1863), 207 (April 23, 1863), III, 80 (January 20, 1864); Gurowski to Andrew, April 10, 1863, in Andrew Papers.

"But today Lincoln has not yet brought together more than ten to fifteen thousand in the field; and what is done, is done rather, so to speak, by private enterprise than by the Government. Mr. Lincoln hesitates, mediates, and shifts, instead of going to work manfully, boldly, and decidedly. . . . It seems as if Mr. Lincoln were ready to exhaust all the resources of the country before he boldly strikes the Africo-American vein." Constant talk of organizing Negro units for more than a year had resulted in the bringing of very, very few into the military service, the Count observed fretfully.[45]

7

Closely associated with Gurowski's championing of the Negro soldier was his belief in potential intellectual, psychological, and physiological equality of the races. Because the Negro in the South had been almost always a slave, he had been kept in ignorance and in a depraved condition, the Count reasoned, but provide him with freedom, education, and broad opportunity, and he would in time reach the status of Caucasians. "The African speaks, thinks, loves, hates, reasons, comprehends," he explained, "and therefore he is capable of being initiated into a higher life. However distant the hour of initiation may be, strike it will for the African race." In reading the proslavery literature, he noted that writers regularly classified Negroes as an "intermediate link" between man and beast, a point of view he did not find in any of the published studies by impartial students of science in the fields of psychology and physiology. He was particularly impressed by the "melodies of peculiar intonation and beauty" coming from blacks even "in their degradation by American slavery."[46]

The Count viewed with disgust the widespread idea of Negro inferiority, which was voiced in the North both in and out of Congress even after the Emancipation Proclamation. Except for Stanton, he believed, most officials of the Washington government as well as the important forces shaping public thought were at least a quarter of a century

---

[45] *Diary*, II, 186–87 (April 3, 1863), 293 (August 5, 1863), 326–27 (September 19, 1863), III, 218 (note, August, 1865).
[46] Gurowski, *America and Europe*, 179.

behind the published scientific findings of scholars. Even those who claimed psychological and physiological equality for the Negro were uninformed, he said, among them the learned Senator Sumner and other Radicals. Practically no one in positions of leadership had read the research literature on the subject. The Negro was truly the American Remus, murdered by both North and South because of "prejudice, sham science, sham religion, sham philanthropy."[47]

While Gurowski approved of immediate emancipation, he also believed, unlike many other Radicals, in government planning for the readjustment period. He preferred a comprehensive arrangement for organizing the freedmen and for handling related social, economic, and legal questions. Then and then only, he said, would emancipation benefit the former slave and his master.[48]

The Count's own proposal was to contribute "small" freeholds or homesteads to the former chattels, after the pattern of his decision in the Polish insurrection of 1830–31. Then he had given each of his serfs willing to fight with the revolutionaries not only freedom but also twenty-four acres of land. "Freedom without land is humbug," he exclaimed, and he proposed to provide the land by cutting up the plantations or by acquiring state-owned soil of the Confederacy. He believed the "immense majority" of the emancipated would make "orderly, laborious, intelligent" farmers, an "excellent peasantry." The freedmen would thus reinvigorate the agricultural economy of the South with small to middle-size farms, more productive than the "very large" farm or plantation, a point he maintained had been proved conclusively by the productivity of free labor on smaller farms in the North during the war years.[49]

In another plan for freedmen, Gurowski suggested, though probably with no high degree of conviction, that the owners of plantations would be forced to offer suitable terms to former slaves to have their

[47] *Diary,* III, 225 (May 12, 1864); see also II, 164 (March 6, 1863), 298–99 (August 13, 1863), III, 139–41, 152 (March 19 and 28, 1864), and 189–90 (April 19, 1864).

[48] Gurowski to Andrew, December 27, 1862, in Andrew Papers; *Diary,* II, 298 (August 13, 1863), III, 63–64 (January 6, 1864).

[49] *Diary,* I, 129–30 (December, 1861), 165–66 (March, 1862), II, 87 (January 11, 1863), III, 218 (note, August, 1865).

plantations cultivated. Without their labor the estates would go untilled, while the planters became "poor starving wretches." In this aspect of readjustment, he predicted mutually beneficial private relations between freedman and planter.[50]

The Count labeled as grossly ignorant those in the North who feared that former slaves would stream to the free states. He believed this uneasiness to be needless, since the emancipated would remain in the South because of the "congenial climate, and . . . favorable . . . conditions of labor and of existence." Moreover, the black population of the North, attracted by the elements holding the emancipated slaves in the South, would migrate southward "as small streamlets and rivulets run into a large current or river."[51]

8

Theorizing about the future of freedmen soon gave way in Gurowski to consideration of their actual status. The ideals of emancipation and racial equality, to be realized to any degree, he soon maintained, called for protection against the former slave owner.

From the time of Lincoln's reconstruction proclamation of December, 1863, specifying a 10 per cent nucleus of citizens loyal to the United States, Gurowski was actively concerned over the status of freedmen. He questioned, as did most Radicals, how the Southern Negro could actually hope to be free under the proclamation, for other than requiring the 10 per cent group to agree to the abolition of slavery, it contained no guarantees for the Negro's freedom. The President, in effect, had abandoned the freedman "to the *good-will* of the . . . incurable slaveholder."[52]

The published report of the Count's old friend and fellow Jacobin, General Wadsworth, on undesirable health conditions in refugee Negro settlements on the lower Mississippi in the autumn of 1863 appeared a portent of things to come. "Before the runaways started in search of freedom, of refuge, and of bread," Gurowski explained, "they had been

50 *Diary*, I, 187–88 (April, 1862).
51 *Diary*, I, 149–50 (January, 1862).
52 *Diary*, III, 53–54 (December 26, 1863); see also 41 (December 9, 1863).

already starved on the plantations, starved under the eyes of, and by their so-called patriarchal masters." Wadsworth's observation that the refugees had been deeply terrorized by slaveholders suggested that "without a strong watchfulness and protection, the slaveholding whip might easily drive the poor Africo-American back into chains." He agreed with Wadsworth that the government ought to educate refugee children and distribute arms among the older generation that they "may thus be self-sustaining and enabled to repulse any encroachments on its rights."[53]

Nearly two years later, with Presidential reconstruction in full swing, Gurowski continued to complain that the whites of the South were deciding on the social and political status of the former slaves. "Leave the fate of the lamb to the hyena!" he exclaimed. "Nine hundred and ninety-nine out of a thousand of the whites in the slave and rebel states are the deadly enemies of the Africo-Americans." The old prejudices, he believed, had intensified because of the freedman's loyalty to the Union, and were presently entrenched behind the argument of Negro intellectual inferiority as disqualifying him from enjoying political and social equality with the whites. He retorted that the slaves had intellect enough to recognize in loyalty to the Union, "a virtue as well as a benefit," but that the "rebellious white man recognized and bowed to treason, perjury and murder." Congress, Gurowski hoped, would inaugurate a "genuinely humane" reconstruction policy for "the salvation of the whites and of the Africo-Americans."[54]

For at least a year the Count had in mind the pattern he would like to see Congress apply in the South. The Republicans must reform that area "from the bottom to the top," and carry out a program that "must have as a basis the broadest recognition of *man* as an intelligent, self-governing being . . . . The loyal Africo-American ought to be the corner-stone of the reconstruction, and the disloyal white man should become an apprentice to loyalty, to human rights and to intelligent liberty. The time is past and gone to force the loyal Africo-American

[53] *Diary*, III, 42–43 (December 11, 1863).
[54] *Diary*, III, 54–55 (note, September 10, 1865); see also 404–405 (note, January 12, 1866).

to be tutored otherwise than by laws of equality with the whites, and whoever legislates differently is a traitor to humanity and to his country." To keep the whites of the South from controlling that area, to keep it from the "hands of the disloyal," he would give the vote to the "always loyal" Negro, so that the balance should be restored, and "the political and legislative power [thrown] into the hands of the honest and devoted white patriots."[55]

Gurowski viewed the extension of suffrage in the narrowest sense as the Negro's legal defense against all whites of the South, especially the former slaveholders. Broader meanings, he said, were the equity, humanity, and self-government involved.[56]

The Count's plan for the reorganization of the South seemed on all fundamental points the program of the Radical Republicans as actually carried out. If his focus differed, it was over the intense idealism with which he viewed the former slave, for Radical reconstruction techniques often used the freedman merely as means to other ends. Gurowski did not live long enough to say more on the issue. Nevertheless, he had firmly asserted himself on the problem of racial equality and the role of the Northern and Southern Negro in the war. First, he insisted, they had won their right to equal status on a heroic pattern unprecedented in history. Second, they had been "true and loyal" to the Union. Finally, though "exposed to the most goading and cruel persecutions," they had "remained loyal and devoted to the defenseless families of their deadly enemies."[57]

[55] *Diary*, III, 342 (September 13, 1864); see also 262–63 (notes, October 8 and 16, 1865), and 396.

[56] *Diary*, III, 42 (notes, September 10 and 26, 1865), 55, 262–63 (note, October 16, 1865).

[57] *Diary*, III, 54 (note, September 10, 1865).

CHAPTER XII

PEACE AT LAST

I

Even before Lee's surrender in April, 1865, the intensity of Gurowski's lobbying and propagandizing had diminished. In the previous November, soon after the Republican Presidential victory, he had concluded the *Diary,* and did not commence another volume. While the manuscript awaited publication, he leisurely brought his thinking up to date from time to time by commenting in footnotes, primarily for the historical record. The long view, the decades and the centuries ahead, he pondered, must subscribe also to his political and social faith.

The Count sensed that his major task had been completed with the 1864 Presidential election. By that time the Radicals prevailed to a degree satisfying to him. Consolidation was all that remained, a development that would largely take care of itself. The re-election of Lincoln seemed no real menace, for the Chief Executive would soon be controlled by the national legislature. This had been assured by the Congress just elected, a body which contained a Jacobin majority for the first time, sent there by voters now substantially underwriting the Radicals. Thus the Presidential plan of reconstruction, together with its basis of white control by the former slaveholders, he predicted, would be overcome by Congress. Had not the Radicals already tossed the gauntlet down to Lincoln in the form of the Wade-Davis Manifesto? And slavery would also be destroyed, despite the lack of executive enforcement of the Emancipation Proclamation. The Jacobin-fortified House, able now to join the Senate in mustering the vote to pass a constitutional amendment act prohibiting slavery, and the pressure of the Northern masses would be certain to bring about state ratification.

What of the military? Grant then was doing magnificently with the Army of the Potomac, wearing down the enemy with his ever mounting numbers and incomparable tenacity. Winter, to be sure, would slow operations. There was no question, no question at all, that next summer, perhaps even spring, would bring the victory which had been so long in coming. One could wait it out undisturbed, the Count concluded.

Never before had satisfaction been so complete or a cause so fully realized. In the Polish uprising three and one-half decades earlier the gamble had been lost, for there in resisting tyranny he had rebelled against established authority, had refused the evolutionary process in government. The turncoat years in Russia had also brought no lasting satisfaction, no continuing political faith. Perhaps there had been some benefits, though, since that experience did bring a complete break with authoritarian government. A homeless wanderer in search of liberty, he had roamed over Europe when democratic uprisings were ruthlessly crushed. Even the sanctuary of Switzerland, isolated from the revolutionary ferment of the Continent, had contained no lasting contentment and had proved deeply frustrating.

Truly, the American experiment had provided the answer and had caused life at forty-four to commence anew, Gurowski reflected. Disappointments and personal problems there had been, as in Europe, but in the United States the arena was right, the balance of liberty and authority in agreeable proportions. Yet there stood slavery, a blot on the American conscience, and so incompatible with the promise of American life. To Gurowski the fight against it could be only personal, and on this issue he had to be heard. War had come over the slavery problem, but at last the nation's record would be cleared. This time there must be no failure. With it the best hope of man would be lost and the dreams of his twilight years blasted. Twice he had witnessed the forces of liberty collapse, and twice the problem had been leadership, and not the motivating concept.

The situation seemed again the same, the Count concluded, for the Lincoln government had not vigorously crushed the rebellion, and consequently had invited slavery to prevail. To assist in correcting this faulty leadership, he had worked once more with public opinion and propaganda. Employment had been necessary for subsistence, and it had been with the government, as in the Russian experience. Above all, he had worked again for adequate leadership, a principle with which there would be no compromise, even at the loss of livelihood. To this principle he had remained true. He had lost his employment, but he had seen his leadership concept largely supported by the Radical Republicans, now in the dominant political position. The ever loyal masses had seen the problem also and had rallied to the cause even before their leaders. As always, his uncompromising and difficult personality had caused quarrels, even with Radicals, but that was unimportant, he reflected, since in his opinion the war had been won and slavery crushed. Truly, he—and all the other Radicals—had prevailed. What could be more satisfying?

2

Gurowski's personal associations had been another matter. With friends he thought himself pitifully helpless, hopelessly prostrate. He had long known that he was his own worst enemy in human relations and, prompted by his intense and hotspur temper, early had turned from flexibility and expediency to rigidity and conviction. "I am aware that my temper and character make me *impossible,*" he admitted. "It was so always during the last forty years of my existance, and it proaved itself to be the prominent fact of my life on the immense space between Washington and Snt Petersbourg. But what can I do; I can break but not bend; I never could." "Loyalty to principles and convictions is the highest what a man can do be he in a great or a small condition," and personal loyalty usually endangered or ruined causes. This had been the fundamental keynote of his life—loyalty to principles rather than to individuals—and with this attitude he had readily compromised the individual, but never the principle. "Acting under the dictates of conviction," he emphasized, "I never hesitated to secede from an idea, or change a route, when by following them the inward harmony of conscience could have become endangered."[1]

[1] Gurowski to Stuart, March 13, 1865, in Lincoln National Life Foundation; Gurowski to Andrew, June 20, 1862, in Andrew Papers; Gurowski, *Russia As It Is,* xiii.

The Count had spent a lifetime sacrificing his personal status to his convictions, often injuring and usually alienating his closest associates. And the journey had been arduous, filled with accusations and recriminations. In Europe his elevated social position and personal fortune had been sacrificed. To avoid living under institutions displeasing to him, he early found himself without personal ties, a stranger cast upon the world, a foreigner everywhere. Much of the disagreeable side of life had come his way because he followed his convictions, but only in so acting had he remained true to himself.[2]

Individuals of conviction, Gurowski thought, must be as stern and unyielding as the intense forces from within and without that impelled them. Without convictions, people were hopeless; and yet when possessing convictions of "light and truth," they were often flexible enough to be problems. This continued to be the deepest hurt of all, he pondered, since this had caused incidents and voids with other Radical Republicans. These worthies had usually brought understanding when the inevitable argument developed, and this he reciprocated a day or two later by sending a note of apology. But sometimes statements had come in return, and in these another side of the Radical approach to reform was explained, written in self-justification in part, but also with the hope that he could be made to understand himself.

The new Chief Justice of the United States, Salmon P. Chase, told Gurowski that he had long esteemed him as "an implacable hater of wrong and as a faithful friend of man," and then said that he believed the "very intensity of your devotion to justice has . . . made you unjust . . . . I have been I think a patient worker for the same ends. Certainly I have aimed to be:—thinking, however, I could do most good without assailing men who may change from worse to better, while bad prin-

[2] *Ibid.;* Gurowski to Lincoln, March 12, 1861, in Lincoln Papers; signed statement by Gurowski, March 6, 1861, in author's possession; Gurowski to Horatio Woodman, April 9, 1866, in Massachusetts Historical Society, *Proceedings,* Vol. LVI, 238; *Diary* I, 157 (February, 1862); Gurowski to Stuart, March 13, 1865, in Lincoln National Life Foundation; Gurowski, *Aus Meinem Gedankenbuche,* 5, 17–18.

[3] Salmon P. Chase to Gurowski, January 23, 1865, in Gurowski Papers; reproduced, although with corruptions, in Robert B. Warden, *An Account of the Private Life and Public Services of Salmon Portland Chase* (Cincinnati, 1874), 634.

ciples never amend."[3] Henry Wilson, editor of the Boston *Post* during the Count's sojourn in that city and now a leading Radical in the Senate, advised similarly: "I often think you are too severe in your judgments of men, but I do not forget your large experience and observation, and your vast acquisitions which authorize you to criticize freely the acts of public men. I remember too your faith in our Institutions and in our people, and your intense devotion to our cause, and I know that faith and devotion prompt you to speak with freedom of the acts of public men who fail to come up to your standard of action."[4]

From Governor Andrew the judgment was much the same: "I do not attempt to refute the very strong position in your letter concerning the views and the moral responsibility of the President . . . . But, still I do not denounce a man who is sincere, is looking in the right direction, as I hope, who may yet get to the right place . . . . You are stern and inflexible. I reverence the spirit so immovable. But, I hesitate to believe that you are wholly correct in not allowing something more for differences of mental constitution, which must always be taken into our account."[5] Most fellow Radicals had reached the same conclusion. This was the Count's disappointing realization. He was simply too severe in his judgment of men.

This made sense, thought the Count, of those war-year incidents that had shamed him. Perhaps he should not have carried a pocket pistol, for his quick temper and the weapon did not mix. Yet he had never pulled the trigger. When he waved the firearm at a group of firemen to make them move more quickly in their work, only Walt Whitman seemed to understand, for he said the incident appeared worse than it was. Even he missed the point, because he credited it to "a quite natural expression of . . . childlike resentments." No one seemed to comprehend the streetcar pistol-pulling, Gurowski thought, and to exploit the matter, a newspaper reporter had quipped cruelly that he would soon be in the army sharpshooters. For some time he had nursed anger arising from the times when he saw streetcar conductors deliber-

---

4 Henry Wilson to Gurowski, July 17, 1863, in Gurowski Papers; see also Gurowski to Henry Wilson, July 2, [1863], in Henry Wilson Papers, Library of Congress.

5 Andrew to Gurowski, June 25, 1862, in Pearson, *The Life of John A. Andrew*, II, 26.

ately passing Negroes desiring to ride, but even friends did not know this.[6]

The scorn and detestation of those who reacted to the Count's stings were often made evident through their arrogance in his presence and in barbs shot at him in the newspapers. Being avoided had been a pattern that went back to the years of the Warsaw plottings, a circumstance he met by reciprocating in masterly form. Typical of the journalistic snipes was a counterfeit letter, supposedly sent by the Count in reply to an invitation to attend a banquet at Delmonico's in New York. The honored guest was Miles O'Reilly, a recently acclaimed hero from the Union army. "Your invitation is received," the bogus letter read, "but to me it does not suit to be your guest invited. I, who have bearded a Russian Emperor, am not to bow in homage abject to any of the great asses who are in this country heroes made. The President (I have proved it) is a mountebank; Secretary Seward is a . . . traitor; General McClellan is a traitor and ass. Chase is an ass. I have no doubt Gillmore is an assish assinine ass; as indeed are all the men whose names we in the newspapers see, or in men's mouths hear, there being only one exception, who is with highest consideration, yours." Another enemy had fabricated an unpaid bill, published it, and further mortified him. Gurowski proposed to sue for libel, but William Curtis Noyes, a friend of the New York years, thought a court proceeding would only gratify the "combined malevolence" of his attackers and discreetly sent the proffered fee ($40.75) to the United States Sanitary Commission. The Count's *Diary* was ideal for striking back at the New York *Herald*, where the slander had appeared, as were other newspapers, and he used both channels to the maximum.[7]

Gurowski fully realized that he was considered universally critical and severe in his judgments. Fellow Radicals with friendly intent, had told him so. But Democrats and Republican Conservatives lashed at

[6] Chicago *Journal*, August 5, 1864; W. D. O'Connor to Walt Whitman, August 13, 1864, in Traubel, *With Walt Whitman in Camden*, III, 339–40; Boston *Post*, February 11, 1865.

[7] New York *Herald*, October 23, 1863; William Curtis Noyes to Gurowski, no date, in Gurowski Papers; Gurowski to Pike, July 16, 1857, in Pike, *First Blows of the Civil War*, 376.

him with unrelenting vehemence. Press editorials on his *Diary,* he noted, spoke again and again of his caustic criticism, and even his publishers' blurbs played up the idea. He would concede that he had been critical when he believed it justified, but never did he feel that he had abused most people and institutions. Was not his record, he questioned, one of praise for the masses and for the army? He had said he did not enjoy being critical, that he would much prefer to praise, but no one seemed to heed. He had created the wrong impression, and through the unique "praise," "half and half," and "blame" lists of his *Diary* hoped to correct the record. Then perhaps posterity, if not his contemporaries, would understand and agree.

3

No man was less intelligible. Those who knew the Count slightly were somewhat puzzled and disgusted, but those who knew him well were often increasingly disgusted and puzzled. Opinions never intended for his eyes and ears were naturally the most candid. What were these judgments by his generation?

Journalists had long eyed Gurowski, for apart from the fact that he inevitably attracted attention by his appearance, mannerisms, intellect, and personality, he was one of their own kind. Compositely they characterized him as strange, eccentric, omnipresent, abrupt, tender, wrathful, ardent, intellectual, erudite, childish, witty, impractical, serious, curious, honest, pointed, rough, relentless, true-hearted, troubled, cynical, appreciative, considerate, independent, instructive, entertaining, honorable, democratic, irascible, pugnacious, fierce, ugly, volcanic, unsparing, severe, and fiery. Undeniably, his temperament was truly variegated, many things to many people.

To these same men the Count seemed aflame with hatred of oppression and a dedication to humanity and justice. His feeling for any cause he supported was so intense that he could not believe that those who took opposite views were honest. As a conversationalist, he talked freely and impressively and inevitably contradicted his listeners. His denunciations were most bitter against injustice, intolerance, and snobbish pretension. He was fond of controversy and delighted in continuing a discussion from day to day, always with the same enthusiasm. He enjoyed talking to any individual who would listen, caring but little whether he was understood. He did not like joking with others, although he occasionally managed a little humor himself. His primary interest was serious discussion of problems of government, history, and theology, and in these areas he talked hour after hour in the best traditions of scholarship and broken English. He disliked natural sciences, an area of study that he considered unimportant, and he stayed away whenever possible from specialists in that field.[8]

Other evaluations of the Count varied widely. George Templeton Strong, who met and talked with him only a few weeks after he reached the United States, was initially much impressed and considered him "about the most entertaining man going." But his enthusiasm turned to disgust several years later, for in the meantime he had seen more of Gurowski both in New York and at a resort village in Vermont. He had become an "insufferable old hog . . . , ubiquitous, all-seeing, malignant, mischievous, and abominated." Nor did Strong's opinion change as he read the volumes of the Count's *Diary*. The Pole was then "an acclimated and naturalized wild boar from Slavonia," "a learned pig," "irritable," "merciless censor," "an enraged Tartar Khan." "The poor old savage Ishmaelitish count," said Strong at the time of Gurowski's death, "was a man of talent, experience, and culture, but universally abominated for his bearishness and his petty malignites." Nine years later Strong still thought of Gurowski as "that racy and high-flavored old boar."[9]

While in Boston, the Count got to know Edwin P. Whipple and

---

[8] Washington *National Republican*, May 5, 1866; New York *Times*, May 6, 1866; New York *Tribune*, May 5, 1866; unidentified newspaper clipping, in author's possession; "Nebulae," *Galaxy*, Vol. I, 269–71; Poore, *Perley's Reminiscences of Sixty Years in the National Metropolis*, II, 140; Waters, *Career and Conversation of John Swinton*, 15; Pike, *First Blows of the Civil War*, 252–53; Carter, "Gurowski," *Atlantic Monthly*, Vol. XVIII, 628–30.

[9] Nevins and Thomas (eds.), *The Diary of George Templeton Strong: The Turbulent Fifties, 1850–1859*, 2–3 (January 5, 1850), 289 (August 13, 1856); *The Diary of George Templeton Strong: The Civil War, 1860–1865*, 279 (December 13, 1862), 405 (February 11, 1864), 485 (September 12, 1864); *The Diary of George Templeton Strong: Post-War Years, 1865-1875* (New York, 1952), 83 (May 7, 1866), 553 (March 8, 1875).

usually attended the Sunday evening literary discussions in his home. Whipple was establishing his reputation as an author and lyceum lecturer, and became known for his keen and discriminating criticism, free from envy or censure, particularly in evaluations of personality. He characterized Gurowski as "a combination of cynic, gossip, philosopher and hero—intrepid, disinterested, with an eye for the weak points of character, enthusiastic in fault-finding, incapable of insincerity, with a mind which went to the heart of a question or a character; sagacious after his kind; furious at incompetency; wishing to hang all dunces in office; . . . insatiable in search of news—interior facts—intrigues— character of public men and generals." Whipple's best-remembered observation, however, is that Walt Whitman, author of *Leaves of Grass,* had every leaf but the fig leaf.[10]

Other Bostonians who also became well acquainted with Gurowski were Mrs. Julia Ward Howe and Theodore Parker. Mrs. Howe, author and reformer, attracted by Gurowski's abolitionism, viewed him as an individual of "remarkable contradictions, in which really noble and generous impulses contrasted with an undisciplined temper and an insatiable curiosity." He regularly snooped on friends and neighbors, she said, and if a family or individual on whom he called was said to be busy or not at home, he set about determining how they were occupied or whether they were really at home. Mrs. Howe considered the Count, although at times impolite, "a true hearted man, loyal to every good cause and devoted to his few friends." Parker, an abolitionist, but better known as a Unitarian minister, thought the Pole queer, but "more honest than men judge."[11]

Another prewar friend was James S. Pike. Like the Count himself, he was hotly antislavery, an ardent Republican, and a widower. The two men maintained a warm friendship over the years, but not without offense to Pike from time to time. "How can you be so tenderhearted," questioned his eccentric friend, "and take seriously my silly

10 Whipple's manuscript statement in Pearson, *The Life of John A. Andrew,* II, 25n.; Charles K. Bolton, "Edwin Percy Whipple," *Dictionary of American Biography,* XX, 67–68.

11 Howe, *Reminiscences, 1819–1899,* 221–22; Parker to Eduard Desor, August 9, 1852, in Frothingham, *Theodore Parker: A Biography,* 322.

abusing you? It was only to tease. Know it once for all, that you are among the few whom I never doubt." Gurowski could be severe with Pike, as when he called one of his newspaper feature articles "brilliant, superficial, and false." On other occasions merriment prevailed: "I am a big scamp for answering so late your kind letter. How it came I could not explain, but I call myself the worsest names, so you not need to do so." "I congratulate you on the general and special victory," read Pike. "But you do not know the reason. Nobody knows. It was because the elections in your State coincide with the birth day of the greates–t man or ass of all a–g–e–s."[12]

Pike concluded that Gurowski often demonstrated friendship "very much in the way in which the tenderness of a bear is sometimes manifested, by a hug which seems almost fatal to the subject of it." He thought the Pole's severe comments left no bite because they were always the result of sincere and usually fleeting condemnation. Pike maintained also that Gurowski did not curb his criticism even when he felt tender toward his targets, a trait he had inherited from his forefathers. Nevertheless, his "great genius, great learning, and great fertility of mind" made him "a welcome addition to all circles."[13]

Another journalist friend of New York and Washington was Whitman. Gurowski developed a profound appreciation for the poet's literary ability and for his attitudes on democracy and the Northern masses. "My Gott," exclaimed the Count less than a year after Whitman had reached Washington, "I did not know that [he] was such a poet, tell him so, I have been trying everywhere to find him to tell him myself." Whitman alone, the praise continued some months later, this "incarnation of a genuine American original genius," "in his heart and in his mind has a shrine for the nameless, for the heroic people." Whitman appreciated these sentiments, and they probably influenced his opinions of the Count.[14]

---

[12] Gurowski to Pike, August 31, 1860, Thursday, March, [1852], and July 16, 1857, in Pike, *First Blows of the Civil War,* 375, 411, 524; Gurowski to Pike, September 11, [1860], in Pike Papers.

[13] Pike, *First Blows of the Civil War,* 252–53.

[14] Gurowski in Ellen M. O'Connor to Walt Whitman, November 24, 1863, in Charles E. Feinberg Whitman Collection, Detroit; *Diary,* III, 128 (March 5, 1864); Walt Whit-

The poet considered Gurowski fascinating, a truly remarkable, "almost phenomenal" man of "great keenness" and "splendid intellect." Although at times easily angered, he would be at other periods "cordial, happy, as men rarely are." Also, "no doubt, very crazy but . . . very sane . . . noisy, violent . . . a man who rebelled against restraint—even when he would admit it was justifiable, . . . but underneath all he was a loving man: a curious mixture of the aristocrat and the nobody."[15]

Equally understanding was Governor Andrew, who believed some men would never apprehend Gurowski's temperament: "He went straight to the mark. He was so honest in his inner purpose, so sincere, so absolute in his decision . . . ." To the Governor he seemed also "so cordial in his affections," a man of "intense and original energy, to whom life was worth nothing—save as a theatre or an opportunity, for the play, or employment of the faculties." He was "in a certain sense impracticable," "carrying his individuality to the ultimate," yet a person of "so much capacity, knowledge and clearness of mind." Subtly, Andrew in part characterized himself in evaluating Gurowski, for in many ways he was a man of his own design. "He *drew me*," concluded the Massachusetts executive, "like a *magnet*."[16]

Lincoln's register of the treasury, Lucius E. Chittenden, had come to know Gurowski intimately at the time of the Washington Peace Convention in February of 1861, and discovered their mutual hatred, slavery. Observing the Count's lobbying activities designed to break up this compromise effort, Chittenden was impressed with his superior language and brilliant conversation, his unofficious attitude and ability to form the acquaintance of important people and ordinarily to win their favorable opinion. Everyone seemed accessible to him and accepted him as an equal. Chittenden also believed him to be extraordinary in obtaining reliable information, often of the secret variety, and in drawing accurate conclusions. Amusing, interesting, "thoroughly truth-

man to Thomas Jefferson Whitman, May 7, 1866, in Richard M. Bucke and others (eds.), *The Complete Writings of Walt Whitman* (10 vols., New York, 1902), V, 175–76.

15 Whitman in Traubel, *With Walt Whitman in Camden,* III, 78–79, 340, 381–82.

16 Andrew's evaluation of Gurowski, written at the request of Julius Bing and inserted in his "Life of Gurowski," 164–67; Andrew to Mrs. Eames, June 27, 1866, in Andrew Papers; Andrew to Stanton, November 12, 1863, in *ibid.*

ful," but prejudiced in judgment, were labels the treasury official used when speaking of the Count, whom he considered the most unusual among the extraordinary characters developed in Washington by the war.[17]

Senator James Harlan of Iowa, another delegate to the Washington Peace Convention, had first met the Count there. Himself a zealous partisan and a person of determined conviction, he admired the Pole for his open and direct speech and labeled him "an honest man—one who dares to know and tell the truth."[18]

The spectrum of Gurowski's character and range of personality shifted quickly in the minds of Conservative Republicans important in administration circles. Ward Hill Lamon, Lincoln's marshal of the District of Columbia, noted for his hatred of abolitionists, and consequently detested by the Radicals, described Gurowski as "a revolutionist by nature, restless, revengeful, and of a fiery and ungovernable temper." The President's attorney general, Edward Bates, who disliked the Radicals and all extremists, thought the Count an inveterate and free conversationalist, always "bitter and censorious."[19]

Another member of the cabinet who recorded his opinion of Gurowski was Navy Secretary Gideon Welles, stalwart opponent of partisan actions and viewpoints. His intense interest in people and his capacity for discerning character fixed his attention on the Pole as an appropriate subject for careful observation. The Secretary at first appeared interested in the man, but soon classified him as zealous, and therefore one with whom he could never associate. "He is," said Welles, "by nature a grumbler, ardent, earnest, rash, violent, unreasonable, impracticable, with no power of rightfully discriminating character; nor is he a correct judge of measures and results . . . . He wants, I think, to be frank and honest in his way, to be truthful, though given to scandal; brave he is without doubt, a rude, rough Polish bear . . . , a martyr to his opinions and his manners." Further, he was "splenetic and querul-

17 Chittenden, *Recollections of President Lincoln and his Administration*, 26–27; Chittenden, *Personal Reminiscences*, 320.

18 James Harlan to Gurowski, October 1, 1864, in Gurowski Papers.

19 Lamon, *Recollections of Abraham Lincoln, 1847–1865*, 274; Beale (ed.), *The Diary of Edward Bates, 1859–1866*, 205 (November 27, 1861).

ous, a strange mixture of good and evil, always growling and discontented, who loves to say harsh things and speak good of but few." The Count's memory Welles thought unusually retentive, and his mind strong but disconnected. His opinions on past problems were "sound and striking," although the reflection of the views of others rather than original thoughts. A man of no sense of honor, he could be as easily flattered as offended.[20]

4

While Gurowski's contemporaries were rounding out their judgments, life for him at the close of the war continued much as usual in the Eames home, still the gathering place of Washington's political, intellectual, and social leaders. The Count was more relaxed now; but when it came to conversation, he continued his offensive habit of contradicting everything, for he seemed to find it impossible to discuss any idea or event without disagreeing. Mrs. Eames and her husband kept on acting as arbitrators, and concluded that years of poverty and misfortune, with but few positive satisfactions, must have brought about his caustic and stinging attitude. They also wondered if his practice of contradicting may not have been an effort to overcome an inferiority complex. But the Count, in addition, had a happy side, periods of good humor not ordinarily known to the casual caller, and never tainted with an off-color word, which endeared him to the family. "Savage animals, and I am one by nature—," he should have said to his hosts and not to Seward, "when tamed by kindness, become the most devoted."[21]

Gurowski continued his customary propagandist activities, although not at the pace of the war years, for with the conflict won and the Radicals entrenched, the pressure was off. He demonstrated, nevertheless, that political rumor, scandal, and dissension were still his forte, when he took a leading role in the Jacobin whispering campaign to

20 Beale (ed.), *Diary of Gideon Welles,* I, 187–88 (December 4, 1862), 325–26 (June 8, 1863), II, 100–101 (August 9, 1864), 439 (February 23, 1866).

21 Gurowski to William H. Seward, June 7, [1861], in Seward Papers; statement on Gurowski by Laurence G. Hoes, December 26, 1950, in author's possession; Marian Gouverneur, *As I Remember,* 246–47, 249; unidentified newspaper clipping, in author's possession.

destroy the leadership of President Andrew Johnson. This movement would soon lead to an irreparable break between the President and the Radicals.

Johnson's veto of the Freedmen's Bureau bill on February 19, 1866, indicated his unwillingness to share Jacobin views. Gurowski immediately spread word that Secretary Stanton actually opposed the President's veto, but in a cabinet meeting had agreed with Johnson's proposed action. This apparent duplicity made Welles more distrustful than ever of Stanton, as it undoubtedly did other cabinet members, while it recommitted Stanton to the Radical fold and generally widened the chasm in the Republican Party. Several days later in an extemporaneous speech from the White House portico, the President insinuated that the Radicals hoped to remove him by assassination and named Phillips, Sumner, and Stevens as determined to demolish the basic principles of the government. Again the Count vigorously worked to undermine the President by alleging that he had "drunk too much bad whiskey to make a good speech."[22]

As Johnson stiffened and fought off Radical pressures, the Count became alarmed. He believed that the Chief Executive was unconsciously following the pattern of Emperor Napoleon III of France in 1849 and 1850, when he began to acquire absolute authority. Like Napoleon III, Johnson appeared to Gurowski as trying to concentrate Executive power and to subordinate Congress. Daily "bitter secessionists," observed the Count, were pouring into Washington and both "directly and indirectly" fanning the flames of Presidential usurpation. "There is rumor of *a coup d'état* against the patriots in Congress. The mob of Washington will abet Johnson and support him," warned the excited revolutionary.[23]

At this time the Count frequently visited in the home of William D. O'Connor, the meeting place of a group of intellectuals, much the same set that had visited Pfaff's New York restaurant in the late 1850's. As in the Eames home, the fellowship was at its best. Whitman, scented with cologne, could usually be found there sitting in a big armchair,

[22] Beale (ed.), *Diary of Gideon Wells,* II, 439 (February 23, 1866).
[23] Gurowski to Julius Bing, April 6, 1866, copy in Bing, "Life of Gurowski," 289.

dressed in the inevitable gray suit and fancy tailored shirt. He was then in the public eye because of his recent dismissal from a clerk's job in the Department of the Interior on account of his literary productions. He now held a similar post in the attorney general's office. Other New York friends who dropped in were John Swinton, chief of the editorial staff of the New York *Times,* and his brother William Swinton, a recent war correspondent for that paper, celebrated for his attacks on leading generals and his daring news-gathering. Also from the Empire City circle came Albert Brisbane, a social reformer who, like Gurowski, had studied under Hegel and Fourier.

New faces in the group were the robust Spencer F. Baird, the Smithsonian Institution's zoologist and authority on birds; John Burroughs, a youthful Treasury Department clerk doing a book on Whitman, but later a distinguished naturalist; George Wood, also an employee of the Treasury Department, author of satirical books and contributor to leading literary periodicals; Richard J. Hinton, a young journalist earlier attended by Whitman in a Washington military hospital; and Charles W. Eldridge, a Whitman intimate, his former publisher, now a War Department clerk. The coterie's genial Irish host, O'Connor, clerk of the government light house board, was an able journalist and vehement abolitionist, known for his personal magnetism, eloquence, and impetuosity. Together with his wife Ellen, he had befriended Whitman during the war, and in the cozy rooms of their apartment the poet whiled away many hours. With Whitman and O'Connor ordinarily leading the verbal whirlwind, Gurowski was at some disadvantage, although he managed to blast away at President Johnson and damn Secretary Seward.[24]

5

The Count was sixty years of age when the war concluded, but for some time had considered himself old, and in terms of the average life-

[24]Richard J. Hinton, "Walt Whitman at Home," New York *World,* April 14, 1889; Clara Barrus, *Whitman and Burroughs: Comrades* (Boston, 1931), 36. Gurowski's indignation over Whitman's removal from the Interior Department is recorded in his *Diary,* III, 372–73 (note, September 12, 1865).

time of his day he was undeniably in his decline. His contemporaries agreed with this view, although he still seemed robust and active. Actually, his delicate health had improved a little during the war. Except for the seizure of acute gastroenteritis in the Eames home during the summer of 1863, he managed well, buoyed always by his annual warm-weather visit to the seaside resort at Long Branch, New Jersey.

When another onslaught of gastroenteritis forced Gurowski to his bed in the Eames home in the second week of April, 1866, he was not deeply concerned, for similar attacks over the years had seemed no great hazard. Moreover, his present sickness came in the off-season, with a less severe condition usually resulting, since the illness occurred ordinarily during the summer months. The usual symptoms appeared: vomiting, diarrhea, spasmodic intestinal pain, cramps. This time, as in the 1863 illness, care and comfort were provided by Mr. and Mrs. Eames, with Dr. Thomas Miller again the attending physician. The only difference now was the assistance of a neighbor, called in by Mrs. Eames. What a change in attention and care from the time Senator Sumner had found him alone and stricken in his room in New York in the early 1850's.

The usual callers at the Eames home were told of the Count's illness, and often ushered to his bedroom. Among friends who came was the Spanish minister to the United States, Gabriel García y Tassara, who visited several times. Frequently the two men had talked of the problem of liberty within government and had agreed that, if the Confederacy won the war, humanity, broadly speaking, would be humiliated. García's thinking again invigorated Gurowski, who had for some time considered this former member and secretary of the Spanish Cortes a "great man," a "wonderful genius," who, like himself, had been a journalist.[25]

When the gastroenteritis symptoms were clearing, typhoid struck the Pole's weakened body, a common occurrence in his day. The inflammation of the intestines worsened, as did the diarrhea, while a

[25] Washington *Star*, May 5, 1866; Washington *National Republican*, May 5, 1866; New York *Tribune*, May 5, 1866; Beale (ed.), *The Diary of Edward Bates, 1859–1866,* 205 (November 27, 1861).

mounting fever developed. Then followed periods of helpless exhaustion and complete lethargy. Dr. Miller allowed no visitors. As the Count sensed his own physical decline, he asked the doctor if there was any hope. From the symptoms, came the reply, there seemed but little, with perhaps no more than twenty-four hours remaining. "Well," said Gurowski, "a brave man must not be afraid to die." Then he turned on his pillow, evidently resigned to the end.[26] But energy, temper, and defiance returned like a flash: "A New York doctor told me the same thing seventeen years ago, and then he wanted to send me a priest. I told my doctor, seventeen years ago, that if any d—d priest came to my room, he should be kicked out. I'll kick out any priest *now* if you send him here."[27]

In the agony of his illness, Gurowski could have reflected on the status of his religious faith. Reared a Roman Catholic, he had followed in the spiritual faith of his devout mother until his university years. Then, searching for truth in new liberal ideas, he had drifted away from his religious upbringing, never to return. The Church of Rome and its clergy were to him politically reactionary, a deterrent to social progress, and consequently undesirable. He had become a religious skeptic, a freethinker, doubting or perhaps disbelieving Christianity. The months he had spent in Cambridge, attempting to win a berth on Harvard's faculty, had brought him in frequent contact with the pace-setting Unitarian minister, Theodore Parker, and other members of this religious confession, to whom he took an immediate liking because of their liberalism and antislavery activity. This group, served by graduates of Harvard's then distinctly Unitarian divinity school, he concluded, possessed "the most elastic and all-embracing minds." He liked their increasing rationalism and found it much the same as he had experienced in his higher education in Germany.[28]

---

[26] Gurowski in Traubel, *With Walt Whitman in Camden*, III, 79; New York *Tribune*, May 5, 1866.

[27] Gurowski's purported statement as related in Nevins and Thomas (eds.), *The Diary of George Templeton Strong: Post-War Years, 1865–1875*, 83 (May 7, 1866).

[28] Gurowski, *America and Europe*, 328; Howe, *Reminiscences, 1819–1899*, 227; Nevins and Thomas (eds.), *The Diary of George Templeton Strong: The Civil War, 1860–1865*, 72 (December 7, 1860); Gurowski, *Slavery in History*, 253; *Diary*, I, 192 (April, 1862), 210 (May, 1862), 315 (November 12, 1862).

Several days before death appeared certain, a frequent visitor at the Eames home, Mrs. Julia Ward Howe of Boston, arrived in Washington for the purpose of winning the Greek mission for her husband. She registered at Willard's Hotel and picked up the news that Gurowski was sick. She went immediately to call. Eames met her at the door with word that the Count had become critically ill and could not have visitors. When he changed for the better, said Eames, he would send her word. Mrs. Howe returned downtown, purchased a basket of flowers for her sick friend, and personally delivered them.[29]

On the afternoon of Friday, May 4, a message came to her from Mrs. Eames that the Count was dying. She should come at once if she wanted to see him alive. When Mrs. Howe arrived, she learned that the patient was already unconscious. In a few minutes came the final writhings and contortions, "a hideous sight indeed," thought Mrs. Howe.[30]

Mrs. Eames, now completely exhausted, was put to bed with the assistance of Mrs. Howe, who stayed until early evening. On the next day at noon she returned to the Eames home and wrote invitations for the funeral to be held on the following day, Sunday, at 4:00 P.M., in the home. With his wife sitting nearby, Mr. Eames entered the room. "Mrs. Howe," said he, "my wife has always had a menagerie here in Washington, and now she has lost her faithful old grizzly."[31]

They discussed the problem of a clergyman for the funeral. Mrs. Eames suggested a Unitarian, a choice Gurowski himself would have made. Mrs. Howe was advised to look up an ancient Bostonian, aged eighty-one, the Reverend John Pierpont, long a Unitarian preacher,

[29] Diary of Julia Ward Howe, April 30, 1866, in Houghton Library; Howe, *Reminiscences, 1819–1899,* 225.

[30] Diary of Howe, May 4, 1866, in Houghton Library; Howe, *Reminiscences, 1819–1899,* 225–26; unidentified newspaper clipping, in author's possession; Washington *National Republican,* May 5, 1866; Washington *Chronicle,* May 5, 1866; Washington *Star,* May 5, 1866; New York *Times,* May 5, 1866; New York *Tribune,* May 5, 1866; New York *Herald,* May 5, 1866; Nevins and Thomas (eds.), *The Diary of George Templeton Strong: Post-War Years, 1865–1875,* 83 (May 7, 1866).

[31] Diary of Howe, May 4 and 5, 1866, in Houghton Library; Eames in Howe, *Reminiscences, 1819–1899,* 226.

but then a clerk in the Treasury Department in Washington. Too liberal even for his Boston congregation, he at last had resigned. Although known throughout the Eastern seaboard as a lecturer, those best acquainted considered him a genius. Gurowski undoubtedly would have approved the selection of Pierpont.[32]

Mrs. Howe and Mrs. Eames momentarily solved the burial problem by deciding to deposit the Count's body in a receiving vault in Georgetown Cemetery. Final interment could wait until Mr. and Mrs. Eames purchased, some days later, a family plot in Congressional Cemetery, the unofficial Arlington of the time.[33]

In the late afternoon, Mrs. Howe went off to search out the venerable Reverend Mr. Pierpont, finally located him, and found him willing to officiate. She then employed a messenger to deliver the funeral invitations and sent word to Georgetown Cemetery to receive Gurowski's remains the following afternoon. The arrangements complete, Mrs. Howe returned to Willard's only long enough to dine. She hurried to spend the evening with Mrs. Eames, now rapidly becoming more sad and depressed.[34]

In the meantime, the Count's body was returned to the Eames' drawing room. Mrs. Howe was much impressed with Gurowski's facial features, now a little sharpened, wholly distinctive, if not positively handsome, she thought. In death, the mutilated eye was no longer evident.[35]

Soon Senator Sumner was at the door, alone and solemn. He thought the body seemed strangely quiet, for Gurowski had long

[32] Diary of Howe, May 5, 1866, in Houghton Library; Howe *Reminiscences, 1819–1899*, 226; George Harvey Genzmer, "John Pierpont," *Dictionary of American Biography*, XIV, 586–87.

[33] Diary of Howe, May 5, 6, and 7, 1866, in Houghton Library. Gurowski is buried in the Congressional Cemetery, located at 1801 E Street, Southeast; his grave is in Range 53, Site 206. Eames himself, a man of but fifty-four, was interred beside the Count less than a year later.

[34] Diary of Howe, May 5, 1866, in Houghton Library; Howe, *Reminiscences, 1819–1899*, 226.

[35] Diary of Howe, May 5, 1866, in Houghton Library; Howe, *Reminiscences, 1819–1899*, 226–27.

reminded him of Barnum's whale that went round and round in its narrow tank and blew mightily whenever it hit the surface. Now at last this "perturbed spirit" rested. Then the tears came in a rush. The features, he said, were elegantly fine. Turning to the two ladies, the Senator concluded in a burst of oratory: "There is a beauty in life, and there is a beauty in death."[36]

Although she returned to Willard's for the night, Mrs. Howe spent the next day comforting Mrs. Eames. Eames also was much moved by his wife's grief over Gurowski and did all he could to buoy up her depressed mind and troubled emotions. Constantly she talked of the Count. Who would come to pay their final respects? Perhaps the day itself would bring additional people, since the government offices were closed on Sunday.[37]

Four o'clock, the funeral hour, held the answer. Now the impressive white of a large spray of calla lilies set apart the glistening black casket. When Sumner entered the crowded drawing room, he again looked long and solemnly on Gurowski's face and took a seat among the distinguished visitors. Assembled were a number who had received the Count's praise and blame. There sat Senator William P. Fessenden; nearby was Chief Justice Salmon P. Chase; the war secretary, Edwin M. Stanton; Senator Benjamin F. Wade; the Spanish minister, Gabriel García y Tassara; and the Russian minister, Edward de Stoeckl. Several legation attachés, heads of departmental bureaus, Mrs. J. Hubley Ashton, the wife of the assistant attorney general, and Mrs. Samuel Hooper, Washington hostess and wife of the wealthy Massachusetts congressman, were also among those present.[38]

The eloquent Reverend Mr. Pierpont arose to read a chapter from First Corinthians, concluding with an appropriate and impressive prayer. Meantime, Mrs. Eames wept bitterly, seated near the coffin, in the tender

[36] Diary of Howe, May 5, 1866, in Houghton Library; Carter, "Gurowski," *Atlantic Monthly*, Vol. XVIII, 633; Howe, *Reminiscences, 1819–1899*, 226.

[37] Diary of Howe, May 6, 1866, in Houghton Library.

[38] *Ibid.*; Bing, "Life of Gurowski," 291–92; Washington *National Intelligencer*, May 5 and 7, 1866; unidentified newspaper clipping, in author's possession.

care of her husband and Mrs. Howe. The prayer ended, Mrs. Eames kissed the Count's forehead. Nearby and unobserved, Walt Whitman decided that the funeral had been simple, impressive, but unusual— "all the big radicals were there."[39]

[39] Diary of Howe, May 6, 1866, in Houghton Library; Walt Whitman to Thomas Jefferson Whitman, May 7, 1866, in Bucke and others (eds.), *The Complete Writings of Walt Whitman,* V, 176; Frances Winwar, *American Giant: Walt Whitman and His Times* (New York, 1941), 277.

BIBLIOGRAPHY

Note on the Sources

GUROWSKI'S NUMEROUS LETTERS in the Governor John A. Andrew Papers (Massachusetts Historical Society) were by far the most important Civil War manuscript source used in the preparation of this book. Second in manuscript significance were the Count's letters of the war period in the Charles Sumner Papers (Harvard University Houghton Library). For the pre-Civil War decade, the James Shepherd Pike Papers (Calais Free Library) yielded Gurowski letters in quantity, as did the Henry Wadsworth Longfellow Papers (Craigie House). Other manuscript collections contained but small numbers of the Count's letters.

The Adam Gurowski Papers (Library of Congress) included only a few of the many letters received by the Pole. Andrew's replies were not there, and most of the other letters known to have been sent were also missing. Circumstances contemporary to Gurowski were largely responsible. Julius Bing, an obscure free-lance journalist and literary dilettante of New York and Washington, decided to write a biography of the Count at about the time of his death. Bing used Gurowski's personal papers, carelessly handled them, completed a rough book-length draft, and died in little more than a year after the Count. Gurowski's papers, together with Bing's manuscript biography, were returned to the Charles Eames family, with whom Gurowski had lived. Earlier, Bing sought permission of Andrew to include his letters in the biography, but the Governor hesitated and asked that they be sent to him to expurgate intemperate statements. Andrew delayed in censoring the letters and died the following year. The letters were apparently never returned, and are not known to exist. In addition to Bing's "Life of

Gurowski," the manuscripts of the Count's unpublished "History of the Elements of Roman Law" and his published *Slavery in History* and many research notes, not more than a dozen letters remained in the Gurowski Papers when they were given to the Library of Congress in 1914 by an Eames family descendant.

The Count's published books and pamphlets were also primary in the preparation of this study. Because he was basically a publicist throughout his life, more than skeletal information on his writings is included both in the text and bibliography. His books and pamphlets total 3,734 pages, while his unidentified newspaper and encyclopedia articles would probably more than double this figure, were it possible to calculate them in terms of book pages. For the war period, the three volumes of his *Diary* were of pivotal importance, and without them this book could not have been written. Until September 3, 1862, Gurowski regularly used the month alone to differentiate between his *Diary* entries. Thereafter, all entries were designated by the day of the month, except for the isolated passages of October 6, 1861, and July 4 and 10, 1862. Whether by day or month, the Count's *Diary* writings reflect the plans and actions of the Radical Republicans perhaps better than any other printed source contemporary to the Civil War. His three volumes, along with the diaries of Edward Bates, Orville Hickman Browning, Salmon Portland Chase, John Hay, George Templeton Strong, and Gideon Welles, are of the utmost importance for a thorough understanding of Northern wartime politics (Randall and Donald, *The Civil War and Reconstruction*, 762).

I. *Manuscripts*

American Antiquarian Society (Worcester, Massachusetts)
  Lee and Shepard Papers

Boston Athenaeum Library (Boston, Massachusetts)
  Miscellaneous Manuscripts

Boston Public Library (Boston, Massachusetts)
  Mellen Chamberlain Collection
  Henry Wadsworth Longfellow Papers

Brown University Library (Providence, Rhode Island)
Unclassified Manuscripts

Calais Free Library (Calais, Maine)
James Shepherd Pike Papers

Chicago Historical Society (Chicago, Illinois)
James A. Mulligan Diary

Craigie House (Cambridge, Massachusetts)
Henry Wadsworth Longfellow Journal
Henry Wadsworth Longfellow Papers

Duke University Library (Durham, North Carolina)
William Pitt Fessenden Papers

Otto Eisenschiml Estate (Chicago, Illinois)
Edward C. Carrington Papers

Charles E. Feinberg (Detroit, Michigan)
Walt Whitman Collection

Harvard University Houghton Library (Cambridge, Massachusetts)
Cornelius Conway Felton Papers
Julia Ward Howe Diary
James Russell Lowell Papers
Charles Sumner Papers
University Archives
Bequest of E. J. Wendell

Historical Society of Pennsylvania (Philadelphia, Pennsylvania)
Salmon P. Chase Papers
Edward Carey Gardiner Collection

Illinois State Historical Library (Springfield, Illinois)
John Hay Papers
John G. Nicolay and John Hay Collection
Lewis B. Parsons Papers

Jagiellonian Library (Kraków, Poland)
Jan N. Janowski Papers

Library of Congress (Washington, D.C.)
Adam Gurowski Papers
John Hay Papers
Robert Todd Lincoln Collection of the Papers of Abraham Lincoln
Edwin M. Stanton Papers

Henry Wilson Papers
Elizur Wright Papers

Lincoln National Life Foundation (Fort Wayne, Indiana)
Miscellaneous Manuscripts

London School of Economics (London, England)
John Stuart Mill Papers

Massachusetts Historical Society (Boston, Massachusetts)
John A. Andrew Papers
Edward Everett Diary
Edward Everett Papers
Miscellaneous Manuscripts
Horatio Woodman Papers

National Archives (Washington, D.C.)
Records of the Criminal Court of the District of Columbia
Records of the Supreme Court of the District of Columbia
Records of the State Department
Records of the War Department

New York Public Library (New York, New York)
Henry W. and Albert A. Berg Collection
Horace Greeley Papers
Miscellaneous Manuscripts

Polish Roman Catholic Union of America (Chicago, Illinois)
Miscellaneous Manuscripts
John Tyssowski Papers

University of Rochester Library (Rochester, New York)
William H. Seward Papers

State Archives (Turin, Italy)
Police Records

Author's Possession (Stillwater, Oklahoma)
Gurowski's Autobiographical Sketch
Miscellaneous Gurowski Letters
Statement by Mr. Laurence G. Hoes, Washington, D.C., December 26, 1950.
Statement by Mrs. Paul Davis Morrison, Washington, D.C., February 12, 1954.

II. *Gurowski's Published Books and Pamphlets*

La Cause Polonaise Sous son Véritable Point de Vue (*The Polish Cause from its True Point of View*). 35 pages, Paris, Levasseur, 1831.

Alexander Jagiellończyk (*Alexander Jagellon*). 4 pages, Paris, A. Pinard, 1833.

Przyszłość (*Future*). 32 pages, Paris, A. Pinard, 1834.

La Vérité sur la Russie et sur les Révoltes des Provinces Polonaises (*The Truth about Russia and the Revolts of the Polish Provinces*). 96 pages, Paris, Delaunay, 1834. Reprinted in 1835 and 1848.

La Civilisation et la Russie (*Civilization and Russia*). 232 pages, St. Petersburg, F. Bellizard, 1840. Translated into German and published under the title of *Russland und die Civilisation* (*Russia and Civilization*). 256 pages, Leipzig, Heinrich Hunger, 1841. Reprinted in 1848 and bound in paper.

Pensées sur l'Avenir des Polonais (*Thoughts on the Future of the Poles*). 50 pages, Berlin, A. Asher and Company, 1841. Translated into German by E. Herrmann and published under the title of *Der Polen Zukunft* (*The Future of the Poles*). 52 pages, Leipzig, Heinrich Hunger, 1842.

Aus Meinem Gedankenbuche (*From My Book of Thoughts*). 39 pages, Breslau, Carl Heinrich Storch and Company, 1843.

Eine Tour Durch Belgien im Jahre 1844: Aus dem Tagebuche (*An Excursion Through Belgium in the Year 1844: From my Diary*). 339 pages, Heidelberg, D. Pfisterer, 1845.

Impressions et Souvenirs: Promenade en Suisse en 1845 (*Impressions and Souvenirs: An Excursion in Switzerland in 1845*). 308 pages, Lausanne, F. Weber, 1846.

Die Letzten Ereignisse in den Drei Theilen des Alten Polens (*Recent Events in the Three Sections of Old Poland*). 42 pages, Munich, Franz Georg, 1846.

Le Panslavism, son Histoire, ses Véritables Éléments: Religieux, Sociaux, Philosophiques et Politiques (*Panslavism, its History, its True Elements: Religious, Social, Philosophical and Political*). Volume I, 313 pages, Florence, no publisher, 1848. No other volumes published.

Russia As It Is. 312 pages, New York, D. Appleton and Company, 1854. Three American editions were published, all in 1854. An English edition, titled *Russia and Its People,* was printed in Edinburgh and published in London by Nelson in 1854.

The Turkish Question. 43 pages, New York, W. Taylor and Company, 1854. The original manuscript is among the Miscellaneous Manuscripts in the Manuscript Division of the New York Public Library.

A Year of the War. 116 pages, New York, D. Appleton and Company, 1855.

America and Europe. 411 pages, New York, D. Appleton and Company, 1857.

Slavery in History. 260 pages, New York, A. B. Burdick, 1860.

Diary, from March 4, 1861, to November 12, 1862. 315 pages, Boston, Lee and Shepard, 1862.

Diary, from November 18, 1862 to October 18, 1863. 348 pages, New York, Carleton, 1864.

Diary: 1863–'64–'65. 413 pages, Washington, W. H. and O. H. Morrison, 1866.

III. *Newspapers*

Berlin *Neue-Oder Zeitung,* April, 1855.

Boston (weekly) *Museum,* April–June, 1851.

Boston *Post,* February, 1865.

Boston *Transcript,* January, 1851.

Chicago *Journal,* August, 1864.

Cincinnati *Commercial,* December, 1862, and February, 1864.

Newport *News,* July, 1854.

New York *Herald,* December, 1862, October, 1863, February, 1864, and April–May, 1866.

New York *Times,* December, 1862, October, 1863, February, 1864, and April–May, 1866.

New York *Tribune,* April, 1854, May, 1855, February and June, 1861, September and December, 1862, October, 1863, February–March, 1864, and May, 1866.

New York (weekly) *World,* December, 1862, and February, 1864.

Sacramento *Union,* November, 1863.

Springfield *Illinois State Journal,* February, 1863.

Washington *Chronicle,* December, 1862, October, 1863, February, 1864, and April–May, 1866.

Washington *Globe,* December, 1862, October, 1863, February, 1864, and April–May, 1866.

Washington *National Intelligencer,* December, 1862, October, 1863, February, 1864, and April–May, 1866.

Washington *National Republican,* December, 1862, October, 1863, February, 1864, and April–May, 1866.

Washington *Star,* December, 1862, October, 1863, February, 1864, and April–May, 1866.

IV. *Special Sources*

Athenaeum Association of New York. *Charter and Constitution of the Athenaeum Association, with a List of the Members.* New York, 1863.

———. *Constitution and By-Laws of the Athenaeum, with a List of the Members.* New York, 1859.

Bern University. *Verzeichnis der Vorlesungen vom 15. Oktober 1848 bis 1. April 1849 an der Hochschule Bern.* [Bern, 1848.]

———. *Verzeichnis der Vorlesungen vom 8. April 1849 bis 15. August 1849 an der Hochschule Bern.* [Bern, 1849.]

Black, Henry Campbell. *Black's Law Dictionary.* Third Edition. St. Paul, 1951.

Eminent and Representative Men of Virginia and the District of Columbia of the Nineteenth Century. Madison, 1893.

English Parliament. *Hansard's Parliamentary Debates.* 3rd Series. Vols. XII and XIII. London, 1832.

Harper's New Monthly Magazine, Vol. IX (June–November, 1854).

Harrison, James L., comp. *Biographical Directory of the American Congress, 1774–1949.* Washington, 1950.

Heidelberg University. *Verzeichnis der Sämmtlichen Studierenden auf der Universität Heidelberg im Sommersemester 1823.* [Heidelberg, 1823.]

———. *Verzeichnis der Sämmtlichen Studierenden auf der Universität Heidelberg im Wintersemester 1823-1824.* [Heidelberg, 1823.]

Lane, William Coolidge, and Nina E. Browne, eds. *A. L. A. Portrait Index.* Washington, 1906.

Lewak, Adam, comp. *Katalog Rękopisów Bibljoteki Narodowej, I: Zbiory Bibljoteki Rapperswilskiej.* Warszawa, 1929.

Living Age, Vol. LVII (April–June, 1858).

Massachusetts Historical Society. *Proceedings,* Vol. LVI (October, 1922–June, 1923). Boston, 1923.

Putnam's Monthly Magazine of American Literature, Science, and Art, Vol. IX (January–June, 1857).

Rodgers, Lois Eugenia. "Count Adam Gurowski: A Biography." Unpublished Master's thesis, University of Wisconsin, Madison, 1945.

Scribner's Magazine, Vol. XVII (January–June, 1895).

Unidentified newspaper clippings, author's possession.

United States Congress. *Congressional Globe,* 36 through 38 Congress, all sessions.

———. *House Exec. Doc. 100,* 37 Cong., 2 sess.

———. *Senate Exec. Doc. 1,* 37 Cong., 2 sess.

United States Interior Department. *Register of Officers and Agents, Civil, Military, and Naval, in the Service of the United States, on the Thirtieth September, 1861.* Washington, 1862.

———. *Register of Officers and Agents, Civil, Military, and Naval, in the Service of the United States, on the Thirtieth September, 1863.* Washington, 1864.

United States War Department. *The War of the Rebellion: A Compilation of the Official Records of the Union and Confederate Armies.* Four series, 128 vols. Washington, 1880–1901.

Wieckowska, Helena, comp. *Katalog Rękopisów Bibljoteki Narodowej, III: Zbiory Batignolskie i Towarzystwa Przyjaciół Polski w Londynie 2300-2666.* Warszawa, 1933.

V. *Articles*

Barnard, Job. "Early Days of the Supreme Court of the District of Columbia," *Records of the Columbia Historical Society,* Vol. XXII (1918), 1–35.

[Bowen, Francis.] "The War of Races in Hungary," *North American Review,* Vol. LXX (January, 1850), 78–136.

———. "The Rebellion of the Slavonic, Wallachian, and German Hungarians Against the Magyars," *North American Review,* Vol. LXXII (January, 1851), 205–49.

Bradley, Charles S. "The Bradley Family and the Times in Which They Lived," *Records of the Columbia Historical Society,* Vol. VI (1903), 123–42.

Bullard, F. Lauriston. "Lincoln and the Courts of the District of Columbia," *American Bar Association Journal,* Vol. XXIV (February, 1938), 117–20.

Carter, Robert. "Gurowski," *Atlantic Monthly,* Vol. XVIII (November, 1866), 625–33.

Curran, Ruth Gertrude. "David Kellogg Cartter," *Ohio Archaeological and Historical Publications,* Vol. XLII (January, 1933), 105–15.

Fischer, LeRoy H. "Adam Gurowski," *Dictionary of American Biography,* Vol. XXI, 366–67.

———. "Lincoln's Gadfly—Adam Gurowski," *Mississippi Valley Historical Review,* Vol. XXXVI (December, 1949), 415–34.

Francew, Włodzimierz A. "Adam hr. Gurowski w Polsce w Latach 1841–1844: Przyczynek do Jego Życiorysu," *Pamiętnik Literacki,* Vol. XXXIV (1937), 92–105.

Golder, Frank A. "Russian-American Relations During the Crimean War," *American Historical Review,* Vol. XXXI (April, 1926), 462–76.

Hinton, Richard J. "Walt Whitman at Home," *The* [New York] *World,* April 14, 1889, p. 28, cols. 1–3.

Janik, Michał. "Prądy Panslawistyczne i Rusofilskie w Okresie Wielkiej Emigracji," *Pamiętnik Literacki,* Vol. XXXI (1934), 58–88.

Liguori, M. "The Pole Who Wrote to Lincoln," *Polish American Studies,* Vol. X (January–June, 1953), 1–12.

McCormick, R. C. "Abraham Lincoln's Visit to New York in 1860," *Living Age,* Vol. LXXXV (May 20, 1865), 327–32.

Marx, Karl. "Oesterreichs Schwäche," *Die Zeit,* Vol. XIII (October 2, 1897), 1–2.

Mearns, David C. "The Lincoln Papers," *Abraham Lincoln Quarterly,* Vol. IV (December, 1947), 369–85.

"Nebulae," *Galaxy,* Vol. I (June, 1866), 268–76.

"Nebulae," *Galaxy,* Vol. VIII (July, 1869), 146–48.

Norton, Frank H. "Ten Years in a Public Library," *Galaxy,* Vol. VIII (October, 1869), 528–35.

Parry, Albert. "The Mad Pole of the Civil War," *American Mercury,* Vol. LXXI (September, 1950), 327–36.

Stern, Madeleine B. "G. W. Carleton: His Mark," *Publisher's Weekly,* Vol. CL (August 17, 1946), 710–15.

Stoddard, William O. "Face to Face with Lincoln," ed. by William O. Stoddard, Jr., *Atlantic Monthly,* Vol. CXXXV (March, 1925), 332–39.

Stone, Charles P. "Washington in March and April, 1861," *Magazine of American History,* Vol. XIV (July, 1885), 1–24.

VI. *Books*

Adams, Henry. *Letters of Henry Adams (1858–1891).* Ed. by Worthington Chauncey Ford. Boston, 1930.

Barrus, Clara. *Whitman and Burroughs: Comrades.* Boston, 1931.

Barzykowski, Stanisław. *Historya Powstania Listopadowego.* 5 vols. Poznán, 1883–84.

Bates, Edward. *The Diary of Edward Bates, 1859–1866.* Ed. by Howard K. Beale. Washington, 1933.

Bemis, Samuel Flagg, and Grace Gardner Griffin. *Guide to the Diplomatic History of the United States, 1775–1921.* Washington, 1935.

Berg, Nikolaĭ Vasil'yevich. *Zapiski N. V. Berg o Pol'skikh Zagovorakh i Vozstaniyakh 1831–1862 g.* Moskava, 1873.

Boehn, Hubert Oscar Friedrich von. *Generalstabsgeschäfte. Ein Handbuch für Offiziere Aller Waffen . . . Mit Vielen Figuren in Hochzinkguss.* Berlin, 1862.

Brooks, Van Wyck. *The Flowering of New England, 1815–1865.* New York, 1936.

Browning, Orville Hickman. *The Diary of Orville Hickman Browning.* Ed. by Theodore Calvin Pease and James G. Randall. 2 vols. Springfield, 1927–33.

Bryan, Wilhelmus Bogart. *A History of the National Capital from its Foundation Through the Period of the Adoption of the Organic Act.* 2 vols. New York, 1914–16.

Butler, Benjamin F. *Private and Official Correspondence of Gen. Benjamin F. Butler During the Period of the Civil War.* Ed. by Jessie Ames Marshall. 5 vols. Norwood, 1917.

[Casey, Silas.] *U. S. Infantry Tactics . . . for the Use of the Colored Troops of the United States Infantry.* New York, 1863.

Chase, Salmon P. *Inside Lincoln's Cabinet: The Civil War Diaries of Salmon P. Chase.* Ed. by David Donald. New York, 1954.

Chittenden, Lucius E. *Personal Reminiscences, Including Lincoln and Others, 1840–1890.* New York, 1893.

——. *Recollections of President Lincoln and His Administration.* New York, 1891.

——. *A Report of the Debates and Proceedings . . . of the Conference Convention . . . held at Washington, D.C., in February, A.D. 1861.* New York, 1864.

Cholodecki, Josef Bialynia. *Uczestnicy Powstania Listopadowego Wykluczeni z Amnestji Carskiej.* Lwow, 1930.

Clay, Cassius Marcellus. *The Life of Cassius Marcellus Clay: Memoirs, Writings, and Speeches.* Cincinnati, 1886. Title page indicates 2 vols, but only one appeared.

Congdon, Charles T. *Reminiscences of a Journalist.* Boston, 1880.

Cooper, James Fenimore. *Correspondence of James Fenimore-Cooper.* Ed. by James Fenimore Cooper. 2 vols. New Haven, 1922.

Cornish, Dudley Taylor. *The Sable Arm: Negro Troops in the Union Army, 1861–1865.* New York, 1956.

Derby, J. C. *Fifty Years Among Authors, Books and Publishers.* New York, 1884.

Dictionary of American Biography. Ed. by Allan Johnson and others. 22 vols. New York, 1928–58.

Donald, David. *Lincoln Reconsidered: Essays on the Civil War Era.* New York, 1956.

Durden, Robert Franklin. *James Shepherd Pike: Republicanism and the American Negro, 1850–1882.* Durham, 1957.

Dutkiewicz, Josef. *Francja a Polska w 1831 r.* Lodz, 1950.

Eisenschiml, Otto. *In the Shadow of Lincoln's Death.* New York, 1940.

Feller, Richard. *Die Universität Bern, 1834–1934: Dargestellt im Auftrag der Unterrichsdirektion des Kantons Bern und des Senats der Universität Bern.* Bern, 1935.

Frothingham, Octavius Brooks. *George Ripley.* Boston, 1882.

———. *Theodore Parker: A Biography.* Boston, 1874.

Gadon, Lubomir. *Emigracya Polska: Pierwsze Lata po Upadku Powstania Listopadowego.* 3 vols. Kraków, 1901–1902.

Gouverneur, Marian. *As I Remember: Recollections of American Society During the Nineteenth Century.* New York, 1911.

Gray, John Chipman, and John Codman Ropes. *War Letters, 1862–1865, of John Chipman Gray and John Codman Ropes.* Ed. by Worthington C. Ford. Boston, 1927.

Green, Constance McLaughlin. *Washington: Village and Capital, 1800–1878.* Princeton, 1962.

Gunderson, Robert Gray. *Old Gentlemen's Convention: The Washington Peace Conference of 1861.* Madison, 1961.

Haiman, Miecislaus. *Polish Past in America, 1608–1865.* Chicago, 1939.

Hale, William Harlan. *Horace Greeley: Voice of the People.* New York, 1950.

Halleck, Henry W. *Elements of Military Art and Science; or, Course of Instruction in Strategy, Fortification, Tactics of Battles, etc., Embracing the Duties of Staff, Infantry, Cavalry, Artillery, and Engineers; Adapted to the Use of Volunteers and Militia.* Third Edition. New York, 1862.

Harbut, Juljusz Stanisław. *Józef Chłopicki: w 100-letnią Rocznicę Powstania Listopadowego.* Warszawa, 1930.

Hay, John. *Lincoln and the Civil War in the Diaries and Letters of John Hay.* Ed. by Tyler Dennett. New York, 1939.

Hesseltine, William B. *Lincoln and the War Governors.* New York, 1948.

Holzman, Robert S. *Stormy Ben Butler.* New York, 1954.

Howe, Julia Ward. *Reminiscences, 1819–1899.* Boston, 1899.

Isely, Jeter Allen. *Horace Greeley and the Republican Party, 1853–1861: A Study of the New York Tribune.* Princeton, 1947.

Keene, Jesse L. *The Peace Convention of 1861.* Tuscaloosa, 1961.

Keyes, E. D. *Fifty Years' Observation of Men and Events: Civil and Military.* New York, 1884.

Kohn, Hans. *Pan-Slavism: Its History and Ideology.* Notre Dame, 1953.

Kucharzewski, Jan. *Epoka Paskiewiczowska: Losy Oświaty.* Warszawa, 1914.

LaFayette, Marie Joseph Paul Yves Roch Gilbert du Motier. *Generał M. R. LaFayette o Polsce: Listy, Mowy, Dokumenty.* Warszawa, 1934.

Lamon, Ward Hill. *Recollections of Abraham Lincoln, 1847–1865.* Ed. by Dorothy Lamon Teillard. Washington, 1911.

Leech, Margaret. *Reveille in Washington.* New York, 1941.

Lehmann-Haupt, Hellmut, and others. *The Book in America: A History of the Making and Selling of Books in the United States.* Second Edition. New York, 1951.

Lelewel, Joachim. *Pamiętnik z Roku 1830–31.* Warszawa, 1924.

Leslie, R. F. *Polish Politics and the Revolution of November 1830.* London, 1956.

Lincoln, Abraham. *The Collected Works of Abraham Lincoln.* Ed. by Roy P. Basler. 9 vols. New Brunswick, 1953–55.

Longfellow, Henry Wadsworth. *Life of Henry Wadsworth Longfellow: With Extracts from his Journals and Correspondence.* Ed. by Samuel Longfellow. 3 vols. Boston, 1891.

Lonn, Ella. *Foreigners in the Union Army and Navy.* Baton Rouge, 1951.

McKitrick, Eric L. *Andrew Johnson and Reconstruction.* Chicago, 1960.

Marx, Karl. *The Eastern Question: A Reprint of Letters [by Karl Marx] Written 1853-1856 Dealing with the Events of the Crimean War.* Ed. by Eleanor Marx Aveling and Edward Aveling, London, 1897.

———. *La Questione Orientale: Lettere di Carlo Marx (1853-56).* Ed. by Luigi Mongini. Roma, 1903.

Marx, Karl, and Friedrich Engels. *Briefwechsel.* 4 vols. Berlin, 1949-50.

———. *Gesammelte Schriften von Karl Marx und Friedrich Engels 1852 bis 1862.* Ed. by N. Rjasanoff. 2 vols. Stuttgart, 1920.

———. *The Russian Menace to Europe: A Collection of Articles, Speeches, Letters and News Dispatches by Karl Marx and Friedrich Engels.* Ed. by Paul W. Blackstock and Bert F. Hoselitz. Glencoe, 1952.

Meade, George Gordon. *The Life and Letters of George Gordon Meade, Major-General United States Army.* Ed. by George Gordon Meade. 2 vols. New York, 1913.

Michalski, Stanisław F., ed. *Encyklopedja Powszechna Ultima Thule.* 9 vols. Warszawa, 1930 to date.

Mickiewicz, Adam. *Korespondencja Adama Mickiewicza.* 2 vols. Paris, 1871-72.

Mickiewicz, Władysław. *Żywot Adama Mickiewicza.* 4 vols. Poznań, 1890-95.

Milton, George Fort. *The Age of Hate: Andrew Johnson and the Radicals.* New York, 1930.

Mochnacki, Maurycy. *Powstanie Narodu Polskiego, w r. 1830 i 1831.* 4 vols., Second Edition. Wrocław, 1850.

Morison, Samuel Eliot. *Three Centuries of Harvard.* Cambridge, 1936.

Nelson, Otto L., Jr. *National Security and the General Staff.* Washington, 1946.

Nicolay, John G., and John Hay. *Abraham Lincoln: A History.* 10 vols. New York, 1890.

Niesiecki, Kasper. *Herbarz Polski.* 10 vols. Lipsk, 1839-46.

Orgelbrand, Samuel. *Encyklopedja Powszechna Z Ilustracjami i Mapami.* 16 vols. Warszawa, 1898-1904.

Patelski, Jozef. *Wspomnienia Wojskowe Józefa Patelskiego z Lat 1823–1831*. Wilno, 1914.

Pearson, Henry Greenleaf. *James S. Wadsworth of Geneseo*. New York, 1913.

———. *The Life of John A. Andrew: Governor of Massachusetts, 1861–1865*. 2 vols. Boston, 1904.

Phillimore, Robert J. *Commentaries Upon International Law*. 4 vols. Philadelphia, 1854–57.

Pierce, Edward Lillie. *Memoir and Letters of Charles Sumner*. 4 vols. London, 1878–93.

Pike, James S. *First Blows of the Civil War: The Ten Years of Preliminary Conflict in the United States*. New York, 1879.

Poore, Benjamin Perley. *Perley's Reminiscences of Sixty Years in the National Metropolis*. 2 vols. Philadelphia, 1886.

Randall, J. G. *Lincoln the Liberal Statesman*. New York, 1947.

———. *Lincoln the President: Springfield to Gettysburg*. 2 vols. New York, 1945.

———. *Lincoln the President: Midstream*. New York, 1952.

Randall, J. G., and Richard N. Current. *Lincoln the President: Last Full Measure*. New York, 1955.

Randall, J. G., and David Donald. *The Civil War and Reconstruction*. Second Edition. Boston, 1961.

Reddaway, W. F., and others, eds. *The Cambridge History of Poland: From Augustus II to Pilsudski, 1697–1935*. Cambridge, 1951.

Riddle, Albert Gallatin. *Recollections of War Times: Reminiscences of Men and Events in Washington, 1860–1865*. New York, 1895.

Ripley, George, and Charles A. Dana, eds. *The New American Cyclopaedia: A Popular Dictionary of General Knowledge*. 16 vols. New York, 1858–63.

Schalk, Emil. *Summary of the Art of War: Written Expressly for and Dedicated to the U. S. Volunteer Army*. Philadelphia, 1862.

Śliwiński, Artur. *Maurycy Mochnacki: Żywot i Dzieła*. Lwów, 1910.

Stearns, Frank Preston. *The Life and Public Services of George Luther Stearns*. Philadelphia, 1907.

Strong, George Templeton. *The Diary of George Templeton Strong: The Turbulent Fifties, 1850–1859.* Ed. by Allan Nevins and Milton Halsey Thomas. New York, 1952.

———. *The Diary of George Templeton Strong: The Civil War, 1860–1865.* Ed. by Allan Nevins and Milton Halsey Thomas. New York, 1952.

———. *The Diary of George Templeton Strong: Post-War Years, 1865–1875.* Ed. by Allan Nevins and Milton Halsey Thomas. New York, 1952.

Sumner, Charles. *The Works of Charles Sumner.* 15 vols. Boston, 1870–83.

Toepke, Gustav, comp., and Paul Hintzelmann, ed. *Die Matrikel der Universität Heidelberg.* 7 vols. Heidelberg, 1886–1916.

Tokarz, Wacław. *Sprzysiężenie Wysockiego i Noc Listopadowa.* Kraków, 1925.

Traubel, Horace. *With Walt Whitman in Camden.* 3 vols. Boston, 1908–14.

Trefousse, Hans L. *Ben Butler: The South Called Him Beast!* New York, 1957.

Warden, Robert B. *An Account of the Private Life and Public Services of Salmon Portland Chase.* Cincinnati, 1874.

Waters, Robert. *Career and Conversation of John Swinton: Journalist, Orator, Economist.* Chicago, 1902.

Welles, Gideon. *Diary of Gideon Welles, Secretary of the Navy Under Lincoln and Johnson.* Ed. by Howard K. Beale. 3 vols. New York, 1960.

Whitman, Walt. *The Complete Writings of Walt Whitman.* Ed. by Richard M. Bucke and others. 10 vols. New York, 1902.

Williams, T. Harry. *Lincoln and the Radicals.* Madison, 1941.

Wilson, James Grant, and John Fiske, eds. *Appletons' Cyclopaedia of American Biography.* 6 vols. New York, 1887–89.

Wilson, James Harrison. *The Life of Charles A. Dana.* New York, 1907.

Wilson, Rufus Rockwell. *Washington the Capital City and Its Part in the History of the Nation.* 2 vols. Philadelphia, 1901.

Winwar, Frances. *American Giant: Walt Whitman and His Times.* New York, 1941.

Wittke, Carl. *Refugees of Revolution: The German Forty-Eighters in America.* Philadelphia, 1952.

Zornow, William Frank. *Lincoln and the Party Divided.* Norman, 1954.

INDEX

Lincoln's Gadfly, Adam Gurowski, printed on a paper having a life expectancy of three hundred years, has been set in various sizes of Linotype Granjon, designed in 1924 by George W. Jones. In the years since its creation, Granjon has become one of the most popular faces used in books, which is a tribute to the honest design and legibility distinguishing this type.

UNIVERSITY OF OKLAHOMA PRESS

NORMAN